FOUNDATION STONES
A Devotional

Building a Solid Foundation for
Your Relationship with Jesus

Volume 1

Jim Weaver

Copyright © 2025 Refuge City Church

All rights reserved. No part of this publication may be reproduced, stored or transmitted in any form or by any means, electronic, mechanical, photocopying, recording, scanning, or otherwise without written permission from the publisher. It is illegal to copy this book, post it to a website, or distribute it by any other means without permission.

Refuge City Church has no responsibility for the persistence or accuracy of URLs for external or third-party Websites referred to in this publication and does not guarantee that any content on such Websites is, or will remain, accurate or appropriate.

All scripture quotations are taken from the New King James Version, unless otherwise stated and cited in the text.

First edition

ISBN: 979-8-9924486-0-3

ACKNOWLEDGEMENTS

Foundation Stones didn't start out as the book you now hold in your hands. It started as a weekly small group and podcast. Soon, the dream was born to polish those teachings and publish them as a devotional book. This is no small feat and it has taken a talented team of people to make this book possible! Honoring them here with my gratitude seems like such a small gesture, but without each one of them, Foundation Stones would not be the resource it is today. Each one below has my deepest respect and honor.

- Jaime, your unwavering love throughout our marriage has been God's greatest gift to me. Thank you for understanding all the extra hours over the years. Many of those hours are represented in these pages, and hopefully results in many changed and empowered lives in God's Kingdom. I love you more than words can express.

- Lynnae, Josh and Grace, you are my inspiration! You bring me life and joy beyond expression and I am proud of who you are becoming in Jesus. Keep building your own foundations! Great days are ahead! I'm honored to be your dad.

- Dad and Mom, thank you for raising me in the fear of the Lord! You built a foundation in me that will never waiver.

- Eric and Tawnya, you inspire me everyday as you serve God's vision in Mozambique! I'm so proud of you. Your life always ignites more passion to serve God in my own heart. Thank you for holding the line!

- David, you've always believed in the big dreams and projects I come up with and make them your own. You are a great friend and brother. You're also good at everything you put your hands to and this book would not exist without you!

- Pastor Jim and Charlene, and the entire team at Refuge City Church, thank you for your steadfastness and for always championing my dreams. My hope is this book can be helpful to our collective ministries for years to come. Let's continue to be "a refuge, embracing people".

- Nicole, your tireless work has resulted in something truly beautiful. Your skillful editing and formatting, along with the wealth of wisdom you've acquired in your own writing pursuits have made *Foundation Stones* what it is. You've made this project your own and I know many lives will be impacted because of it! Thank you for putting together a gifted team of editors to verify the integrity of the doctrine as well as making sure this book reads well! Jodi and Adam, thank you for your time and skill. I really appreciate it!

Together, we present to you *Foundation Stones, Volume 1*!

-Jim Weaver

TABLE OF CONTENTS

	INTRODUCTION	01
01	BUILD UPON THE ROCK: Why We Read the Bible	05
02	SALVATION: What Does it Mean to be Saved?	19
03	THE CROSS: Punishment That Should Have Been Ours	31
04	THE BLOOD: The Price for Covering	45
05	COVENANT: God's Promise to Man	57
06	REPENTANCE: Go and Sin No More	71
07	THE CONFESSION OF OUR FAITH: Speak It Out-loud	83
08	SANCTIFICATION: The Process of Becoming More Like Him	95
09	WATER BAPTISM: A Public Declaration of Faith	107
10	COMMUNION: Proclaim Until He Comes	119

11	BAPTISM IN THE HOLY SPIRIT: Filled With Power	139
12	FORGIVENESS: Being Set Free by Freeing Others	159
13	PRAYER AND INTERCESSION: Communing With God	177
14	FASTING: A Holy Discipline	189
15	THE TRINITY: Three In One	205
16	WORSHIP: The Fortress of God's Presence	219
17	THE RAPTURE: Jesus' Return For His Bride	235
18	BIBLICAL GIVING: Displaying God's Generosity	249
19	CRUCIFIED WITH CHRIST: I No Longer Live	267
20	THE GREAT COMMISSION: If Not You, Then Who?	279
	CLOSING REMARKS	291
	RESOURCES	293

INTRODUCTION

Matthew 28:18-20 NKJV [1]
18 And Jesus came and spoke to them, saying, "All authority has been given to Me in heaven and on earth. 19 Go therefore and make disciples of all the nations, baptizing them in the name of the Father and of the Son and of the Holy Spirit, 20 teaching them to observe all things that I have commanded you; and lo, I am with you always, even to the end of the age." Amen.

Welcome to the journey of building a solid foundation for your faith in Jesus Christ! I love to see people turn to Christ by confessing their faith in Him and repenting of their sins.

During my years of ministry, I have rejoiced as many have come to a saving knowledge of Jesus Christ. Maybe they met Him in a service I was honored to be a part of or on an individual level as the result of a relationship and conversation I was able to share with them. Some people seem to launch straight into victorious living. Their hearts are consumed with love for God and they permanently turn their back on evil, the deceptions of the world, and their old lives. Others fall away from God and reject the faith. They may have started well, but they withered on the vine and are still not serving Jesus. What is the difference? Why do some thrive, and others falter?

I believe the difference is whether or not a solid foundation has been built for their faith, and ultimately their lives, to rest on. Strong foundations result in strong houses. Weak foundations result in collapse. I take Jesus' instructions to His disciples very seriously, and His instructions weren't to *only* get people to say a salvation prayer. His instructions included making disciples. Disciples are "disciplined ones" who take to heart their responsibility of serving Jesus every day by growing in knowledge, practice, and the heartbeat of God. His instructions included baptizing people in the name of the Father, Son, and Holy Spirit. This is a sure sign of repentance. Repentance is a turning away from the world and our sin nature and turning toward God. His instructions also included teaching people to observe all He commanded us to do.

So it's with this conviction in my heart that I embarked on the journey of creating this devotional book. On behalf of Refuge City Church, the great fellowship I am honored to serve with on pastoral staff, I want to commend you for taking this step in building your foundation in Jesus. My hope in this building process is that, when the wind and waves push against your life, your foundation in Christ is solid enough that you will withstand in solidarity, outlast the storm, walk in victory, and step into eternity to hear the precious words of Jesus: "Well done, good and faithful servant." Each chapter is like a stone in your foundation, making you ever stronger in your faith. I encourage you to take your time and study each topic thoroughly, not treating this book as something to be conquered, but as a tool to help you deeply understand these important concepts. You'll find extensive scripture references, carefully placed to ensure proper context. I encourage you not to

INTRODUCTION

skim past the scripture as God's Word speaks for itself! My heart's desire is to only teach concepts that you can find thoroughly embedded in scripture. You'll also find reflection questions to respond to. Don't feel you have to finish reading each chapter in a single sitting. Read, ponder, pray, and write. Enjoy the process of deepening your faith!

I'm the first to admit that my attempt to teach each topic only scratches the surface. I'm a fellow student. I look forward to exploring God's Word with you as I've tried to distill them in a way that will be helpful to you. I can't learn for you, and you can't learn for me, but when each of us builds on our foundation, the Body of Christ grows, strengthens, and thrives in a contrary world. I don't claim to be an expert by any means. All of the lessons in this book have come from extensive study of the Word, but we are on this journey together. We're growing and strengthening each other *until we all become the mature Body of Christ* as stated in Ephesians 4. What an amazing privilege to walk and grow together in the knowledge of our Savior! It's to this victory that you are called. You're not called simply to be saved, but to be in relationship with God every day. And it's this relationship that will help others find the goodness of God through the salvation of Jesus Christ as well!

I have carefully selected each topic in this study. Many will seem basic, and some will seem very deep, but all these lessons will lay one stone at a time in your foundation of faith. The goal is for you to know God, His Word, and His expectations–and to ultimately finish this race of life strong and victorious!

Let's start adding stones to our foundation!
-Jim Weaver

CHAPTER 1
BUILD UPON THE ROCK

Why We Read the Bible

Matthew 7:24-25 [2]
24 "Therefore whoever hears these sayings of Mine, and does them, I will liken him to a wise man who built his house on the rock: 25 and the rain descended, the floods came, and the winds blew and beat on that house; and it did not fall, for it was founded on the rock."

The Bible is the most printed, highly distributed, and sold book of all time. One estimate from *thebibleanswer.org* [3] is that over 100 million Bibles are printed every year, with over 20 million Bibles sold per year in the United States alone. One survey mentions that approximately 87% of American households have at least one Bible in their home, with most homes having an average of four Bibles in possession.

Recently, I received a correspondence from our Fellowship Headquarters of the Assemblies of God with some shocking statistics. The Assemblies of God partnered with the Barna Group, a research firm, to interview hundreds of Pastors and congregants in 2019. They found that most people have access to a Bible, but few regularly engage with it. Only 21% of Assemblies of God adherents regularly read their Bibles.

FOUNDATION STONES

This shocked me deeply. Even with the access that Bible Apps like YouVersion have provided, and having volumes of Bible translations on our mobile devices, only 21% are regularly reading the Word of God. At the time of the writing of this devotional, YouVersion had over 500 million downloads worldwide. This means we are full of great intentions, but somehow we have missed the most important part of having a Bible—reading it and getting to know God through it!

We also live in one of the most divided and contentious times in the history of the world. I think I can declare this very confidently: we are seeing evil and dark agendas abound in our time. We are watching as lives are destroyed, cultures are swayed against God, the education of the next generation is crumbling, and the Church is wandering around in aimless confusion and divisive arguments. And yet, our antidote tends to be to watch more news, scroll for more YouTube videos to support our viewpoints, argue with more people, and complain to those we feel are on our side. I wonder how much of what we are saying and doing actually reflects the heart and will of God.

Without engagement in the truths of God's Word, our motives and the content of our hearts are not being filtered and refined. God's truth has restricted access to the deep places of our soul and spirit. Then we wonder why His voice is distant and His presence in our homes is missing. When our diet of God's truth is dependent upon a forty-five-minute sermon on a Sunday, we can't be surprised when our faith is thin and our courage wanes. We can't be surprised that we don't know what to do, how to behave, or what to say in a dark time when the Word of God is not hidden deep inside our hearts.

"You can't say God has been silent if your Bible has been closed."
- **Unknown**

CHAPTER 1

The Bible is the primary way we hear from God. I've discovered that when I don't sense an answer to a question or direction from God, it's likely because the answer is already found in God's Word, and I must dig for it. I need to be listening by opening God's Word to hear Him. Truly, we are personally responsible for getting God's Word into our hearts. Read it. Listen to it. Memorize it. Talk about it. Study it. All of this is because when we read God's Word, we are not simply reading pages out of an old book. We are literally getting to know God Himself. God's Word teaches us that His Word was sent to us through Jesus and now when we read His Word, we are actually fellowshipping with Jesus Christ Himself. Jesus *is* the Word.

WE READ THE BIBLE TO GET TO KNOW JESUS

John 1:1-5, 14 [4] (emphasis added)
1 In the beginning was the Word, and the Word was with God, and the Word was God. 2 He was in the beginning with God. 3 All things were made through Him, and without Him nothing was made that was made. 4 In Him was life, and the life was the light of men. 5 And the light shines in the darkness, and the darkness did not comprehend it.

*14 And **the Word became flesh** and dwelt among us, and we beheld His glory, the glory as of the only begotten of the Father, full of grace and truth.*

Jesus *is* the Word. The Word of God is not simply words scribbled on a page. The Word of God was sent to us through the embodiment of Jesus Christ.

The Word is His heart toward humanity.

We need to understand that we can't know God without knowing the Word. I understand many have come to a saving knowledge of God who didn't have a Bible or maybe couldn't even read. However, *we do* have the Word of God today. We can't let it go unread! The Bible is a beautiful gift God has given to us so we can get to know Him. His Word is His heart toward humanity. It's important that we know it!

Some might argue that there are individuals who can't read or have a hard time with reading comprehension. In that case, listen to the Word as much as you can. However, stretch yourself to actually read it. (I've personally found that using the Bible in its book form with real pages, and not on a device, keeps me from getting distracted by the other things on my device.) In our culture, most people can read–even if slowly. We can't give ourselves an excuse to not be in the Word. If we can mindlessly scroll through the content on our phones every day, we can spend time with God in His Word!

ABIDE IN HIS WORD

Abide: *to continue in a place. To wait. To remain stable or fixed in a state of being.*[5]

John 8:31-32 [6]
31 Then Jesus said to those Jews who believed Him, "If you abide in My word, you are My disciples indeed. 32 And you shall know the truth, and the truth shall make you free."

Abiding in the truth of God can take many forms on any given day. Establishing a pattern of regularly opening the Bible to receive its truth helps us cultivate a hunger for God's voice. Abiding is generally established through how we spend our time. Every person may approach this according to their own daily schedule, but for me, it looks like this: first thing in the morning, with a cup of coffee at the ready, I begin a conversation with God with my prayer journal open, writing down things I'm praying about. Then, I often use a Bible reading schedule to read certain chapters and books in a progression, allowing things to rise to the surface that may be highlighted to me as I read. I might even write down a scripture that stands out to me in my prayer journal. This often helps me memorize that verse or section of scripture. The idea is that every morning I'm feeding my spirit with God's truth. The things I pray about, read, and contemplate stay at the forefront of my mind throughout the day. It's not uncommon for something from my morning time with God to resurface in a conversation with someone later in the day. In this way, I'm daily abiding in God's Word. His Word is shaping my faith, my thoughts, my attitudes, and my actions throughout the day.

CHAPTER 1

WE READ THE BIBLE TO KNOW GOD'S STANDARD

We have to understand that God has a standard. His ways are right, whether we like them or not and whether we acknowledge them or not. Creation itself says the Creator has a standard. Gravity works. The seasons always occur. We reap what we sow. The point is, why would all of creation operate out of unarguable standards, and then there not be any standards for our salvation and our conduct? How good is God that He would give us an instruction manual to know how to live according to His standard? What a beautiful gift to us from our Heavenly Father!

Imagine trying to put together a complicated machine with no instructions. We'd spend a lot of time guessing with trial and error (likely more error), and end up with a machine that may look something like it's supposed to but probably doesn't work. With every complicated assembly comes thorough instructions. But what good is an instruction manual if we don't read it and do what it says? Psalm 119 describes this concept perfectly:

Psalm 119:1-8[7]
1 Blessed are the undefiled in the way,
Who walk in the law of the Lord!
2 Blessed are those who keep His testimonies,
Who seek Him with the whole heart!
3 They also do no iniquity;
They walk in His ways.
4 You have commanded us
To keep Your precepts diligently.
5 Oh, that my ways were directed
To keep Your statutes!
6 Then I would not be ashamed,
When I look into all Your commandments.
7 I will praise You with uprightness of heart,
When I learn Your righteous judgments.
8 I will keep Your statutes;
Oh, do not forsake me utterly!

Why would all of creation operate out of unarguable standards, and then there not be any standards for our salvation and our conduct?

THE BIBLE ESTABLISHES RIGHT FROM WRONG

We keep our ways pure by 'taking heed' to God's Word. But the only way to 'take heed' is to have the Bible pouring into our hearts so it can speak to us when we face a situation where its standard is needed. Look again at Psalm 119:

Psalm 119:9-16[7]
*9 How can a young man cleanse his way?
By taking heed according to Your word.
10 With my whole heart I have sought You;
Oh, let me not wander from Your commandments!
11 Your word I have hidden in my heart,
That I might not sin against You.
12 Blessed are You, O Lord!
Teach me Your statutes.
13 With my lips I have declared
All the judgments of Your mouth.
14 I have rejoiced in the way of Your testimonies,
As much as in all riches.
15 I will meditate on Your precepts,
And contemplate Your ways.
16 I will delight myself in Your statutes;
I will not forget Your word.*

CHAPTER 1

READING THE BIBLE HELPS US NOT TO SIN

Many times it seems like sin creeps up on us and we get tangled up in something we didn't see coming. While that may be true from time to time, if we are in God's Word, His standard will be woven into the fiber of our souls. Any argument against that standard will have quite a fight on its hands because the Word of God in us will resist temptation's activity. The warning bells in our spirit will go off! Our souls will know better. The Word must be in our hearts to shield us from walking away from God and sinning against Him. The more we hide God's Word inside us, the more ammunition we have against the tidal wave of temptation that is always beating on the door of our hearts, trying to deceive us and steal us away from God.

WE READ THE BIBLE TO REFINE OUR MOTIVES

*Jeremiah 17:9-10[8] (**emphasis added**)*
9 The heart is deceitful above all things and beyond cure. Who can understand it? ***11 "I the Lord search the heart and examine the mind,*** *to reward each person according to their conduct, according to what their deeds deserve."*

*Hebrews 4:12-13[9] (**emphasis added**)*
*12 For the word of God is living and powerful, and sharper than any two-edged sword, piercing even to the division of soul and spirit, and of joints and marrow, and **is a discerner of the thoughts and intents of the heart.** 13 And there is no creature hidden from His sight, but all things are naked and open to the eyes of Him to whom we must give account.*

God's Word *reads* us back! It penetrates our hearts to the division of soul and spirit, which is our spiritual life, aligning us with truth and pointing out errors. God's Word also divides between joints and marrow which are the good and bad motives, temptations, and weaknesses of the flesh. The Bible discerns the thoughts and intentions of our hearts and gets to the core of who we are. This refines us if we are obedient students of God's Word with our whole being. This causes us to live *from* the Word of God, not from *our own* intellect.

WE READ THE BIBLE TO RECEIVE GOD'S DIRECTION

Psalm 119:97-106 [7] *(emphasis added)*
97 Oh, how I love Your law!
It is my meditation all the day.
98 You, through Your commandments,
make me wiser than my enemies;
For they are ever with me.
99 I have more understanding than all my teachers,
For Your testimonies are my meditation.
100 I understand more than the ancients,
Because I keep Your precepts.
101 I have restrained my feet from every evil way,
That I may keep Your word.
102 I have not departed from Your judgments,
For You Yourself have taught me.
103 How sweet are Your words to my taste,
Sweeter than honey to my mouth!
104 Through Your precepts I get understanding;
Therefore I hate every false way.
105 Your word is a lamp to my feet
And a light to my path.
106 I have sworn and confirmed
That I will keep Your righteous judgments.

The Psalmist is so hungry for the instruction of the words of God and dependent on their direction that he keeps them in the forefront of his heart and mind throughout his day. He uses scripture for understanding and wisdom. He describes God's Word as sweet to the taste. He describes it as a lamp to his path. He is determined to keep these words close to his heart just like he would protect precious treasure!

God's Word is sweet to the taste...

CHAPTER 1

GOD'S WORD SHINES A LIGHT ON OUR PATH

I want you to consider this truth with me: when we know God's heart and the direction of His Word, most of our decisions are already made! If a decision has to do with discerning between right and wrong, ethics and morals, the Bible has already given us most guidelines for things like this. Our decisions are already made and so our response is to simply obey what we've already learned! The more we get to know the Word of God, verses of instruction will often rise in our hearts when we face a fork in the road. We can then make a quality decision based on the fact that we already know God's heart.

God's Word is compared to a lamp that illuminates the path in front of us. We might not see years down the road, but we can see for the next few steps when we have the Word of God living inside our hearts. Let's make sure we keep our spiritual batteries charged so when we're in a dark night, we don't have a dim light. Let's fill up our hearts with God's Word every day!

Psalm 119:105 [7]
105 Your word is a lamp to my feet
And a light to my path.

The key to Godly decision-making is knowing God's Word in *advance.* While sometimes God's Word will be highlighted to us in a special moment of revelation, most of the time His Word comes alive to us when we need it *after* we've already allowed it into our hearts during studying we have done in the past. We need to make sure we're hiding His Word in our hearts. We need to keep pressing it into our souls so our toolbelt is full when we need the right tool for the job! God's Word gives us principles to help us make Godly decisions in varying, biblically unmentioned circumstances. If a decision has to do with the future of our life—who to marry, what to do for a living, what ministry calling to pursue—most of these things are given guidelines or principles in the Word of God. God's Word may not mention these situations specifically, but we can find His principles to guide us by making sure God's Word is resonating in our hearts *in advance!*

FOUNDATION STONES

Psalm 119:98-99 [7] (emphasis added)
*98 You, through **Your commandments**,*
make me wiser than my enemies;
For they are ever with me.
99 I have more understanding than all my teachers,
For Your testimonies are my meditation.

Meditation: *to engage in contemplation or reflection.*[10]

Meditation is a beautiful word that has been hijacked by the world. What does meditation in God's Word look like? Meditation simply means that we chew on the truth of God's Word! Just like you savor a fancy meal, chew on God's Word, getting all the flavors of God's truth rolling around in your spirit! I like to think of God's Word as a masterfully prepared spiritual feast that is sweet to the taste. Meditation can be broken down in the following way:

- **Ruminate.** Just like livestock will lay down in the cool of the day to chew their cud, which is literally "bringing it back up", so we too need to bring the Word "back up" to chew on it again. We can't think that because we've read it once we've gotten all we can get out of it. We must return to what we've read and give it another pass.

- **Think.** Much can be said about being thoughtful with God's Word. God gave us a mind. We need to think about what we read, maybe even writing scripture down, so we can think about it slowly. The more intentional we are with thinking about God's Word, the more likely it will be to stick in our hearts.

- **Pray.** Praying over what we are reading and asking God to teach us what He is speaking through the Bible will help us understand His heart and intention. He loves when we pursue Him in prayer over what He has spoken in His Word.

God is a Good Father. When we seek Him, the Word says we will find Him! When we seek revelation from His Word, He eagerly gives it. Why wouldn't He, after all, want to give us every spiritual blessing contained in His Living Book?

CHAPTER 1

Matthew 7:9-11[2]

9 Or what man is there among you who, if his son asks for bread, will give him a stone? 10 Or if he asks for a fish, will he give him a serpent? 11 If you then, being evil, know how to give good gifts to your children, how much more will your Father who is in heaven give good things to those who ask Him!

We should set aside a specific time every day to read God's Word. We have it available to us. Now it's time to use it. Maybe it needs to replace Facebook scrolling first thing in the morning or right after dinner. Maybe we can read the Bible during our lunch hour. Maybe a few times a week we can read it out loud with our family before we watch our favorite television program. Many people find it hard to sit down and read the Bible every day. The excuse of not having enough time is invalid because the truth is that we will *make time* for what is really important to us. We need to make it our daily top priority. Let's decide that nothing else matters until we've read God's Word.

I want to bring a challenge to you because you can't afford not to read it. Read the Bible on purpose every day. The Bible is quite literally our road map. It's our instruction manual. If we don't use it, we'll end up off track, deceived, and building on the wrong foundation.

REFLECTION QUESTIONS

1. We talked about being intentional in thinking about the Word of God. Take Psalm 1 below and really take some time to think about what these verses actually mean. Sometimes it's beneficial to read the same portion of scripture in two different translations. In the lines provided next to Psalm 1, write down what each line or verse means to you.

Psalm 1[11]   Psalm 1 (Your Notes)

1 Blessed is the man
Who walks not in the counsel of the ungodly,
Nor stands in the path of sinners,
Nor sits in the seat of the scornful;

2 But his delight is in the law of the Lord,
And in His law he meditates day and night.

3 He shall be like a tree
Planted by the rivers of water,
That brings forth its fruit in its season,
Whose leaf also shall not wither;
And whatever he does shall prosper.

4 The ungodly are not so,
But are like the chaff which the wind drives away.

5 Therefore the ungodly shall not stand in the judgment,
Nor sinners in the congregation of the righteous.

6 For the Lord knows the way of the righteous,
But the way of the ungodly shall perish.

REFLECTION QUESTIONS: CHAPTER 1

2. Not everyone's "Bible Time" looks the same. Some people are able to sit in one spot, drink their coffee, and read the physical Bible with no problem. Others have a more difficult time sitting still, or prefer to listen to the Bible. It's most important that the Word of God is getting into our hearts and minds. What is your preference and how can you set aside time daily to be with Jesus and His Word?

_____
_____
_____
_____
_____
_____
_____
_____
_____
_____

3. Meditation is a beautiful practice that gets the Word deep into our hearts and spirits. Pick a verse of scripture that you can focus on this week and follow the three principles we talked about in this chapter. **Ruminate. Think. Pray.**

Use the space below to write down anything that comes to mind as you go through your week. "It is the glory of God to conceal a matter and the glory of kings to search it out." (Proverbs 25:2) The Lord is eager to reveal Himself and His mysteries to us. What revelations has He shown you this week about this scripture?

_____
_____
_____
_____
_____
_____
_____
_____
_____
_____

CHAPTER 2
SALVATION

What Does It Mean to be Saved?

Christianity is more than a world religion or a framework with which to live our lives. Christianity *is* those things, of course. But it is *so much more* than that! To be a Christian means that we are becoming "Christ-like". We are becoming more *like* Christ. This is not just like mimicking our favorite celebrity or hero based on some random knowledge of their character traits. Christianity is actually supposed to be the process by which we get to know Jesus Christ in relationship with Him. We're not interacting with a concept. We are interacting with God Himself, who is alive and present in our midst every moment of every day!

To be a Christian means that
we are becoming "Christ-like".
We are becoming more like Christ.

God has always intended to walk with His people in a daily relationship. Conversations, called prayers, mark the son and daughter of God and these conversations have revealed the heart of connection that God intended for mankind from the beginning. This kind of connection is seen from the moment God breathed into the nostrils of Adam at creation and began a conversation with mankind that has never stopped. God regularly met with Adam and his wife, Eve, in the garden of Eden–to the point that when Adam and Eve rebelled against God by eating the forbidden fruit they hid from their daily appointment with God because they recognized their flaws for the first time. They felt the shame that sin brings, which exposed their nakedness and their need for God to cover them. What once covered them was the glory of God and the blessing of a clean conscience. There was no sin. There was no reason to hide anything from God.

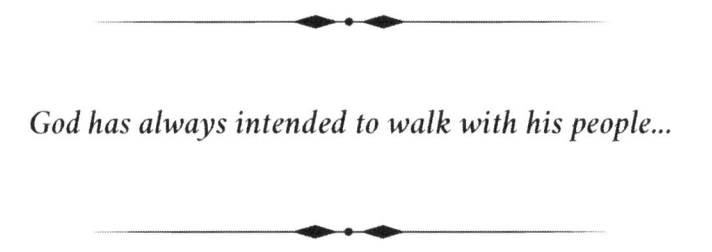

God has always intended to walk with his people...

Afterward, they had an inexplicable urge to hide from God when He showed up. We read about this encounter in Genesis 3. Mankind was in deep need of a rescue. They were hopelessly lost and had marred their perfect relationship with God. They were drowning in a sea of despair and judgment and they needed a life ring that only God Himself could send. They were in need of *salvation.*

Salvation is a word that we associate with Christianity, but without defining it, salvation can be misunderstood and taken for granted. So what does it really mean? The Webster's Dictionary defines salvation as *"deliverance from danger or difficulty"*.[13] This brings to light the spiritual meaning of salvation from our Christian perspective: *"deliverance from the power and effects of sin"*.

What is sin? Sin is a *"transgression of the law of God"*.[14] In essence, sin is anything we do that is contrary to what God has instructed us in His Word. The Ten Commandments are a good place to start as we define biblically what sin is.

CHAPTER 2

Exodus 20:3-17 [15]

3 "You shall have no other gods before Me. 4 "You shall not make for yourself a carved image—any likeness of anything that is in heaven above, or that is in the earth beneath, or that is in the water under the earth; 5 you shall not bow down to them nor serve them. For I, the Lord your God, am a jealous God, visiting the iniquity of the fathers upon the children to the third and fourth generations of those who hate Me, 6 but showing mercy to thousands, to those who love Me and keep My commandments. 7 "You shall not take the name of the Lord your God in vain, for the Lord will not hold him guiltless who takes His name in vain. 8 "Remember the Sabbath day, to keep it holy. 9 Six days you shall labor and do all your work, 10 but the seventh day is the Sabbath of the Lord your God. In it you shall do no work: you, nor your son, nor your daughter, nor your male servant, nor your female servant, nor your cattle, nor your stranger who is within your gates. 11 For in six days the Lord made the heavens and the earth, the sea, and all that is in them, and rested the seventh day. Therefore the Lord blessed the Sabbath day and hallowed it. 12 "Honor your father and your mother, that your days may be long upon the land which the Lord your God is giving you. 13 "You shall not murder. 14 "You shall not commit adultery. 15 "You shall not steal. 16 "You shall not bear false witness against your neighbor. 17 "You shall not covet your neighbor's house; you shall not covet your neighbor's wife, nor his male servant, nor his female servant, nor his ox, nor his donkey, nor anything that is your neighbor's."

We live in a fallen world and these types of trespasses happen all the time. However, God is not unclear as to what His standard is. He is perfect. He is Holy. He is eternal. God expects holiness because sin–literally the antithesis of God's character–cannot be present with Him in His perfection. This is why Adam and Eve hid. Like water and oil, sin and holiness shun one another! They repel against each other! Only by God's great rescue can a hopeless mankind have any possibility of coming back to God.

God is not unclear as to what His standard is. He is perfect.

1 Peter 1:15-16 NIV [16]
15 but as He who called you is holy, you also be holy in all your conduct,
16 because it is written, "Be holy, for I am holy."

We need to recognize a few important points about sin, separation from God, and our need for a Savior.

Only by God's great rescue can a hopeless mankind have any possibility of coming back to God.

SIN CREATES SEPARATION FROM GOD

Sin causes us to run away and hide from God. When we fall short of the standard, our heart grieves, and we'll do any number of things to hide from the Standard-Bearer! Sometimes it feels like we need to run from God. Or maybe we do our best to try not to believe in God because of sin. That's an interesting strategy to avoid sin's grief, but it happens all the time. In this case, because we're not willing to admit our sin could cost us eternity, we'd rather try to convince ourselves that God doesn't exist, or that if He does, He is unjust in His standard. This gives us an unfounded excuse to justify our behaviors. However, we can't get away from the fact that our very conscience knows there is a standard. If there is a standard, there is One who established the standard:

Romans 1:18-20 [17]
18 For the wrath of God is revealed from heaven against all ungodliness and unrighteousness of men, who suppress the truth in unrighteousness, 19 because what may be known of God is manifest in them, for God has shown it to them. 20 For since the creation of the world His invisible attributes are clearly seen, being understood by the things that are made, even His eternal power and Godhead, so that they are without excuse...

We can observe the evidence of God and His standard all around. God's word is not unclear: *everyone has sinned.* Not one person is innocent of breaking God's law. This is both terrifying and strangely comforting. It's terrifying that no one is exempt from His judgment. His judgment will result in our eternal separation from Him by a sentence to hell unless something else transpires to reroute the sentence. The definition of hell is not exclusively flames and torment–hell is eternal banishment from God's presence. *That* is terrifying! Even living unbelievers have not yet experienced that kind of hell–existing without God's presence available to them at any moment. Even non-believers have not experienced existence without a measure of His peace. But, being aware we are all sinners, we can find comfort that we are not alone in our struggle and we're not alone in our need to repent. We're not the *one poor soul* who is under God's judgment. *Humanity* is under His judgment until we accept His rescue plan—His plan of salvation. We must remember what salvation is: "deliverance from the power and effects of sin".

Romans 3:22-24 NIV [18]
22 even the righteousness of God, through faith in Jesus Christ, to all and on all who believe. For there is no difference; 23 for all have sinned and fall short of the glory of God, 24 being justified freely by His grace through the redemption that is in Christ Jesus,

Romans 6:23 NIV [19]
23 For the wages of sin is death, but the gift of God is eternal life in Christ Jesus our Lord.

NO ONE CAN PAY THE PRICE EXCEPT CHRIST

One of our greatest struggles is understanding that we are living in a death sentence and can do nothing to reverse it short of surrendering to God. We have this innate desire to fix our problems ourselves. Especially in our very independent culture, the thought of surrendering our whole being to God and admitting our standards have failed is the *last* thing we want to do. Admitting defeat and that we cannot fix ourselves tends to be one of our greatest fears. We like to know we can make it happen on our own. Or sometimes people have a strange, but common, response to our destitution: somehow we can believe the lie that being separated from God in hell will provide us with some crazy eternal party devoid of morals and restrictions for the rest of eternity. We have to understand that eternal bliss is not the inheritance of sin. Eternal torment separated from God is the inheritance of sin. Existing in a Godless void should be our single greatest terror. To live in an environment where God is not present is something none of us has experienced. Even in the terrible things we've experienced on this Earth, God has always been near. Eternity without Him should be the one thing that moves us to repentance and His gift of salvation more than anything else.

Realizing we cannot be good enough for God and understanding we can do nothing to earn His gift, we must simply believe in Jesus Christ. We must repent of our sins and find rest for our souls, rest from our concerns, limitations, and human attempts to get to Him. Rest for our souls looks like an end to the striving that we so often engage in as humans to try to come into right standing with God. To repent is to completely turn away from sin and move in a different direction (toward God). When we finally submit to the Lord and give up relying on our own power and strength, we become truly free.

Even in the terrible things we've experienced on this Earth,
God has always been near.

Here is the thing: *salvation starts with faith in what Jesus Christ has done for us by giving His own life as a ransom for us on the Cross.* We can't earn this salvation. It's not available to us through "works", which are our man-made attempts to get saved. Salvation means we simply receive what Jesus already accomplished on the cross for us by believing it is true and receiving it as God's gift to us. Then we confess our faith with our mouth (Romans 10:9-10) that Jesus paid for our sin and then we receive His forgiveness. It looks like this:

Ephesians 2:8-9 [21]
8 For by grace you have been saved through faith, and that not of yourselves; it is the gift of God, 9 not of works, lest anyone should boast.

CHAPTER 2

GOD PAID THE PRICE

Romans 8:3-4 [22]
3 For what the law could not do in that it was weak through the flesh, God did by sending His own Son in the likeness of sinful flesh, on account of sin: He condemned sin in the flesh, 4 that the righteous requirement of the law might be fulfilled in us who do not walk according to the flesh but according to the Spirit.

What a gift! What an amazing God we serve! We were powerless to return to God. In our sin, we had demolished the bridge God made in the Garden of Eden. We rejected the Tree of Life and embraced the Tree of the Knowledge of Good and Evil. We forfeited Eternity with God for our own fleshly desires and had no way back. Yet, before the fruit was eaten, God had already set in motion His rescue plan. In Revelation 13:8 we find the sacrifice–God's perfect Lamb, Jesus–had already been slain since before the foundation of the world. This doesn't mean Jesus died before the foundation of the world. It means God's plan to rescue mankind with salvation was already in motion before Adam and Eve took their first breath. God wasn't surprised by the Fall of Man. He knew their free will would pull them away. The Fall set in motion God's perfect plan of salvation and His deliverance from the power and effects of sin!

Revelation 13:8 [23] *(**emphasis added**)*
*8 All who dwell on the earth will worship him, whose names have not been written in the Book of Life of the Lamb **slain from the foundation of the world**.*

SALVATION IS FOR EVERYONE WHO BELIEVES

John 1:12a [4]
12 But as many as received Him, to them He gave the right to become children of God…

FOUNDATION STONES

God did not stipulate between Jews and Gentiles, men or women, different ethnicities, adults or children. He simply said, "Come and receive. Salvation is My gift to you if you will believe." If salvation is God's deliverance from the power and effects of sin, then by receiving this salvation, we will be removed from the power and effects of sin. This doesn't mean we won't sin from time to time. It doesn't mean we won't experience sin's legacy on earth while we live in this fallen world. What it does mean is that our *soul* is secure and our *spirit* will spend eternity with God when this life on earth is over. Our sins have been washed away! Our punishment was put on the shoulders of Jesus when He died on the cross, and our victory was secured when Jesus was raised to life again from the grave!

So, how do we receive this beautiful gift of salvation? *It's really very simple!*

> *Romans 10:9-10 NIV* [24]
> *9 If you declare with your mouth, "Jesus is Lord," and believe in your heart that God raised him from the dead, you will be saved. 10 For it is with your heart that you believe and are justified, and it is with your mouth that you profess your faith and are saved.*

> *John 3:16 NIV* [25]
> *16 For God so loved the world that he gave his one and only Son, that whoever believes in him shall not perish but have eternal life.*

Salvation is the Cornerstone of our foundation! Without God's victory over the effects and power of sin, we are eternally hopeless. We rejoice that God placed Jesus and His gift of salvation as our Chief Cornerstone! He set Jesus in place first and this is the Stone we will build the entire structure of our faith upon. Then we will be part of the foundation stones of His Church which He continues to build upon! This is the way the expansion of God's Kingdom on earth occurs:

> *Isaiah 9:7a* [26]
> *7 Of the increase of His government and peace*
> *There will be no end...*

CHAPTER 2

SALVATION TODAY

It's important to receive this free gift of salvation today! Knowing that life is fragile and we are not guaranteed another day, we have to make sure we're ready to meet Jesus *now*. We can't gamble with our lives. We can't procrastinate, thinking we may have ample opportunity to repent when we're older. We never know when our appointment with eternity will take place. Let's make sure to set this foundational cornerstone right now. Pray something like this:

"Jesus, I believe in You. I believe in Your gift of salvation–that You defeated the power and effect of sin. I ask You to be the Lord of my life and I receive You to save me. I admit I have sinned and fallen short of Your standard. I ask for Your forgiveness. Please help me live for You daily! I have an eternal mindset now, and I won't turn aside. You are my King! In Jesus' name, Amen!"

REFLECTION QUESTIONS

1. Salvation gives us the availability to be reunited with Father God, through Jesus' sacrifice. We have this priceless gift of being in relationship with Him. How would you like to see that relationship grow as you read this devotional? How has your perspective changed since you first became a Christian concerning the concept of religion versus relationship?

___
___
___
___
___

2. Have you ever thought about hell described as "total separation from God?" Is that description the same or different from what you were taught or understood?

___
___
___
___
___

3. There is nothing we can do to earn salvation. This concept is different from any other religion on the earth, where people are constantly working to appease their gods. How does this knowledge, that we literally just receive Jesus' gift by faith, make you feel? How might this knowledge change how you live your life from here on out?

___
___
___
___
___

CHAPTER 3
THE CROSS

Punishment That Should Have Been Ours

Christianity has a symbol. Wherever we find a believer in Christ in the world, we will likely find the symbol of a cross. A vertical beam that is crossed with a horizontal beam. In today's world, this symbol adorns beautiful church buildings, is used in jewelry, on bumper stickers, printed on t-shirts, and is even used in logos for relief organizations. Why is this symbol universally understood to represent Christianity? Why is The Cross so important?

As a point of reference for further study, I encourage you to read a potent article on christianity.com, written by Candice Lucey entitled *"What Is the Medical Account of the Crucifixion?"*[27] Much of this study on the cross and the act of crucifixion can be found in greater detail there.

THE CROSS AS A METHOD OF EXECUTION

The cross has not always been a beautiful symbol of religion. In fact, in the days of Jesus, the cross was a heinous Roman execution method. It was equivalent to today's electric chair used to execute criminals. It was so vile that very rarely was a Roman tizen crucified.

The Romans reserved this type of execution for the vilest offenders and those who would lead insurrections against the empire. This type of execution was intended to inflict the most suffering possible and the greatest degree of aversion because it was displayed publicly to dissuade future rebellion or disobedience by those who witnessed it. It was brutal and grotesque and was that way on purpose.

Jesus was a Jewish man, which means He was a part of the people group that was under the oppression of the Roman Empire in the land of Israel. The Hebrew people longed for liberty but were under the authority of Caesar. The Romans permitted a certain level of autonomy, which we can see in the power the High Priests operated in to implement trials such as the one Jesus was put through. However, legally, they still needed the Roman Empire to authorize a sentence of execution.

Jesus had been teaching in the land, healing the sick, feeding the multitudes, and attracting the common people for some time, and the High Priests were desperate to find a way to put a roadblock in Jesus' path. They found it with the betrayal of one of Jesus' loyal friends. Judas was willing to disown Jesus for the price of thirty pieces of silver, and the High Priests were willing to pay. They ambushed Jesus and His disciples in the Garden of Gethsemane on the weekend of Passover, arresting Jesus while He was praying.

The cross that Jesus endured was the pinnacle of a weekend of suffering. All of what Jesus encountered prepared Him to hang destitute on a Roman execution implement and every part of his suffering meant something. It all pointed to God's plan. It all accomplished the exact outcome God was working toward. The cross is the central symbol of the act of God's grace to set the soul of every man, woman, boy, and girl free from sin and eternal separation from God. If the enemies of Christ (Satan and his hoard) had any idea of what they were actually unleashing, they would have never crucified Christ (1 Corinthians 2:8)!

With the cross, the goal of the executioner was not simply death. If that were the case, criminals and those sentenced to death would have simply been beheaded or burned at the stake. What was the process that Jesus went through leading up to the moment of his death? Why did the death of Jesus require such terrible suffering?

CHAPTER 3

Jesus was arrested and sentenced to death on Passover weekend. This was a powerful parallel set up from before the foundation of the world (Revelation 13:8). His death was to be a mirror of the Passover Celebration. The Passover Lamb was sacrificed not only to provide a meal for the Hebrews before they were set free from Egypt during the time of Moses but, more importantly, to save their firstborn sons. The whole point of why the Passover Lamb was sacrificed was to drain its blood to paint the doorposts so the Angel of Death would "pass over". The homes that had the door posts covered with the lamb's blood were left alone and the Angel of Death would not take the life of their firstborn sons. They were granted mercy. Those without the blood-covering would suffer devastation. This was the tenth and final plague God used to set the captive Israelites free from Egypt.

JESUS IS OUR PASSOVER LAMB

John the Baptist was clear as to who Jesus was:

John 1:29 [4]
29 The next day John saw Jesus coming toward him, and said, "Behold! The Lamb of God who takes away the sin of the world!"

In order to fulfill the entirety of Passover as the Lamb, God established a process of sacrifice that included Jesus bleeding in several different ways. It began in the Garden of Gethsemane, after Jesus gave the Lord's Supper, or Communion, in the Upper Room. Notice, God returned to a garden–where He started–to take upon Himself the sins of mankind. God's provision of skins to cover the nakedness and sin of Adam and Eve in the Garden of Eden is pictured once again in the Garden of Gethsemane where He began to take on the sin of the world.

The shedding of blood has always been symbolic of the covering or remission of sins. God required life to be taken to cover the darkness of sin.

Romans 6:23 [29]
23 For the wages of sin is death, but the gift of God is eternal life in Christ Jesus our Lord.

Blood represents life.

Leviticus 17:1 [30]
1 For the life of the flesh is in the blood, and I have given it to you upon the altar to make atonement for your souls; for it is the blood that makes atonement for the soul.'

Atonement is the payment for sin. The payment for sin is *blood*.

Hebrews 9:22b [31]
22b ...without shedding of blood there is no remission.

Throughout Hebrew history, the blood had to come from a perfect lamb. It couldn't come from a blemished lamb. It had to be the best lamb of the flock. This has always been the picture of the kind of blood that would provide a final sacrifice, once and for all. Jesus was prepared to bleed as the perfect Passover Lamb.

God's provision of skins to cover the nakedness and sin of
Adam and Eve in the Garden of Eden
is pictured once again in the Garden of Gethsemane
where He began to take on the sin of the world.

JESUS' BLEEDING STARTED IN THE GARDEN OF GETHSEMANE

Luke 22:44 [32]
44 And being in agony, He prayed more earnestly. Then His sweat became like great drops of blood falling to the ground.

CHAPTER 3

Many believe this could have been a literal bleeding. Medically, this is known as *hematradosis*. It's the thinning of the skin and the mixing of the blood of the capillaries with sweat from the sweat glands. This condition is usually brought on by stress or anxiety. It is possible that Jesus' skin was literally bleeding, and also his skin was being prepared to bleed even more when He was arrested and abused by His accusers.

After Jesus was apprehended, He was put on trial in the middle of the night where He was struck again and again, beaten and tortured by an angry mob of jealous High Priests and their compatriots. The swelling and bruising that occurred prepared his body to bleed even more readily and sting with the full force of the punishment He was receiving.

The swelling and bruising that occurred prepared his body to bleed even more...

Next, Jesus was taken to the *praetorium*, a Roman courtyard of trial and punishment where He was mercilessly beaten. Not only did the Jewish council punish Him, but He was turned over to the Roman government for additional beating. Jesus was tied to a whipping post and was flogged over and over. Jewish tradition allowed for thirty-nine stripes during a flogging because the thought was any more than that would be fatal. But considering this was a Roman whipping, it's possible Jesus was not treated with the mercy of the Jewish custom. He was whipped by a Roman cat of nine tails, which was a leather hand-held whip. Each strand of leather or rope had pieces of bone, metal, and glass woven into it so that every stripe not only left a welt but tore the skin from the body. This would, many times, create so much bleeding and damage that the victim would not survive. Ribs and the vertebrae of the spine would be exposed, as well as the entrails. This form of punishment was meant to avert future criminals from following in the footsteps of the one being punished.

By this point in Jesus' ordeal, blood loss and strain would likely have created shock and dehydration so severe that His heart would have enlarged and begun to struggle against the fluid building up around it.

Next, the torturers put a robe of mockery and a crown of thorns on Jesus. Scripture says it was a purple robe that was put on the tattered back of Jesus and a crown of vicious thorns was driven into His scalp, which created more bleeding and severe pain. The Roman guards mocked Him and laughed at Him, jokingly calling Him their King before ripping the robe from His back. This would likely have opened the wounds of His scourging all over again, releasing His blood to flow once more.

After His scourging, Jesus had a cross beam placed on His shoulders and was paraded down the public street on His way to the site of execution. This roadway is still in existence today and has been named the "Via Dolorosa", or "Way of Suffering". After His punishment, blood loss, and shock, He was forced to carry His own wooden cross to the place of His death. He struggled along the street, being mocked and viewed by the townsfolk in utter disgrace. Just like Isaac from the book of Genesis, He carried the wood of the sacrifice up the mountain of Moriah where God had prepared the final sacrifice once and for all. This was the moment where humanity's sins—past, present, and future—would be washed away by every last drop of blood in Jesus' body.

When Jesus arrived at the place of execution, Jesus' wrists and feet were nailed to the cross with terrifying spikes. But these spikes were not the agent that killed Him. They were there to increase suffering while He pushed Himself up and down to try to exhale and inhale oxygen. Because of the upright position with arms extended overhead and the weight of His body pulling down on His ribcage and diaphragm, Jesus would have had trouble exhaling, causing a buildup of carbon dioxide in His system which would cause a severe poisoning of His body. Shock, blood loss, and the inability to breathe created one of the most agonizing deaths known to mankind.

He was forced to carry His own wooden cross to the place of His death...

Jesus didn't last long on the cross. Only a few short hours upon the cross and His body faded. He committed His Spirit to the Father and breathed His last. The guards pierced His side to verify He was dead and drew blood and water, a guarantee that He was dead and not simply unconscious.

CHAPTER 3

Truly, this must have been terrifying to witness, and brutal to endure. This sacrifice of a sinless, perfect Man drew every drop of blood from Jesus' body and took tremendous strength and submission to God the Father's will to perform. This was the moment time was split in two and the Old Covenant of Law and Symbolism was replaced by the New Covenant of Grace and Salvation available to every human being. One sacrifice for all. This sacrifice satisfied the justice of God while extending His mercy. This sacrifice was performed on a tool of torture we know today as The Cross. It's not such a beautiful picture once we know what it represents. But oh, how beautiful it is when we recognize what was accomplished for us on that terrible Cross!

Now, by receiving the sacrifice Jesus made, we don't have to endure the punishment our sins deserve. That cross should have been ours, but Jesus endured it in our place. What a miracle!

Interestingly, the cross was prophesied about before Roman crucifixion was ever invented. Roman crucifixion as Jesus experienced it had only been around for about three-hundred years by the time Jesus was executed. But many places in the Bible describe the crucifixion in stunning detail seven hundred to a thousand years before Jesus ever walked the earth. God knew what method of sacrifice Jesus the Messiah would endure and put it in the mouths of the prophets before the process was ever thought up by a human.

This was the moment time was split in two
and the Old Covenant of Law and Symbolism
was replaced by the New Covenant of Grace and Salvation
available to every human being.

One sacrifice for all.

FOUNDATION STONES

PROPHECIES ABOUT THE CROSS

Let's look at a few of these prophecies from the Old Testament to reveal to us that this moment had been foreordained before mankind even knew what crucifixion was.

Psalm 22:14 - 18 [33]
14 I am poured out like water,
and all my bones are out of joint.
My heart has turned to wax;
it has melted within me.
15 My mouth is dried up like a potsherd,
and my tongue sticks to the roof of my mouth;
you lay me in the dust of death.
16 Dogs surround me,
a pack of villains encircles me;
they pierce my hands and my feet.
17 All my bones are on display;
people stare and gloat over me.
18 They divide my clothes among them
and cast lots for my garment.

The Bible makes clear that a curse was the result of rebelling against God and His standard. Adam and Eve released the curse of evil in their disobedience. Shame and darkness entered the world and distance from God was the result. One of the places this curse was illustrated was in the way that a defeated foe was displayed after their demise. A dead person may be displayed by hanging them on a tree if they were defeated in battle or executed as a result of a sentencing from the justice system. In the time of the patriarchs, it was a curse to have someone hung from a tree. The picture was that the curse would be nailed to a tree as a public spectacle. It was a place of shame and humiliation and the Jewish people knew it. That's why Jesus was mocked so incessantly.

CHAPTER 3

Deuteronomy 21:22-23 [34]

22 "If a man has committed a sin deserving of death, and he is put to death, and you hang him on a tree, 23 his body shall not remain overnight on the tree, but you shall surely bury him that day so that you do not defile the land which the Lord your God is giving you as an inheritance; for he who is hanged is accursed of God.

Isaiah 53:5 [35]
*5 But He was wounded for our transgressions,
He was bruised for our iniquities;
The chastisement for our peace was upon Him,
And by His stripes we are healed.*

JESUS AND THE CROSS

No wonder the execution of Jesus was spurned by the Hebrew people! He was considered a curse and a criminal. Why is that so significant? What happened there that has continued to resonate thousands of years later?

Jesus provided for us what we could not provide for ourselves. He provided salvation, healing, deliverance, and restoration. And He did it in complete fulfillment of what the Word of God had been showing for thousands of years prior. Not a detail was lacking. Not a piece of the puzzle was missing. It was a complete fulfillment of the prophecies. Jesus has fulfilled 351 Old Testament Prophecies. [36] . Statistically speaking, there is only a 1 in 10^{17} chance (that's 10 with 17 zeros behind it) of someone fulfilling just *eight* biblical prophecies. And Jesus fulfilled 351! That is staggering. Even more than the statistics, his sacrifice resulted in complete forgiveness of mankind's sin for those who would confess their sin and receive what Jesus accomplished for them. It accomplished complete restoration with God and access to His Presence–the Presence that Adam and Eve forfeited when they rebelled in the Garden of Eden.

CHRISTIANS AND THE CROSS

Consider that Jesus referred His followers to the cross before He even went to the cross. *Before* He was crucified, Jesus told His disciples they must pick up their own cross and be willing to live dead (surrendered completely) for God!

Luke 9:23-24 [37]
23 Then He said to them all, "If anyone desires to come after Me, let him deny himself, and take up his cross daily, and follow Me. 24 For whoever desires to save his life will lose it, but whoever loses his life for My sake will save it.

Our salvation...is secure when we place our faith in Christ and His finished...sacrifice for us on the cross.

Other believers were crucified and martyred throughout the early Church, including, according to tradition, Peter. Though it was a terrible death, the picture of the cross is one of complete devotion to Jesus. The cross that is placed on the walls of our churches, on the bumper stickers of our cars, and around our necks as symbols of our religious affiliation, truly means more than we realize. It means we've surrendered our lives, died to ourselves, and fully bought into being disciples of Jesus Christ.

What does the cross mean for us today? It means several things! The most important is that our salvation—our ultimate forgiveness from sin and guarantee of eternity in Heaven with God—is secure when we place our faith in Christ and His finished, once-for-all sacrifice for us on the cross.

The cross also means we inherit some amazing promises while we're living on Earth. We can ask God for healing, deliverance from Satan and his bondage, freedom from sin, and the receiving of God's authority. This is not because we deserve it, but because of the vicious and terrible cross, Jesus brought us redemption through His blood (Isaiah 53).

CHAPTER 3

The cross is overwhelming in its cruel imagery, and yet, it's precious. It's beautiful. The cross is to be treasured–way more than a piece of jewelry we wear or a decoration we place on our wall. Our beautiful decoration was once the most feared and terrible sign of torture and execution the world had ever experienced up to that point. Now, we embrace it as the most incredible symbol of God's love ever given.

Isaiah 53[35]
1 Who has believed our report?
And to whom has the arm of the Lord been revealed?
2 For He shall grow up before Him as a tender plant,
And as a root out of dry ground.
He has no form or comeliness;
And when we see Him,
There is no beauty that we should desire Him.
3 He is despised and rejected by men,
A Man of sorrows and acquainted with grief.
And we hid, as it were, our faces from Him;
He was despised, and we did not esteem Him.
4 Surely He has borne our griefs
And carried our sorrows;
Yet we esteemed Him stricken,
Smitten by God, and afflicted.
5 But He was wounded for our transgressions,
He was bruised for our iniquities;
The chastisement for our peace was upon Him,
And by His stripes we are healed.
6 All we like sheep have gone astray;
We have turned, everyone, to his own way;
And the Lord has laid on Him the iniquity of us all.
7 He was oppressed and He was afflicted,
Yet He opened not His mouth;
He was led as a lamb to the slaughter,
And as a sheep before its shearers is silent,
So He opened not His mouth.

8 He was taken from prison and from judgment,
And who will declare His generation?
For He was cut off from the land of the living;
For the transgressions of My people He was stricken.
9 And they made His grave with the wicked—
But with the rich at His death,
Because He had done no violence,
Nor was any deceit in His mouth.
10 Yet it pleased the Lord to bruise Him;
He has put Him to grief.
When You make His soul an offering for sin,
He shall see His seed, He shall prolong His days,
And the pleasure of the Lord shall prosper in His hand.
11 He shall see the labor of His soul, and be satisfied.
By His knowledge My righteous Servant shall justify many,
For He shall bear their iniquities.
12 Therefore I will divide Him a portion with the great,
And He shall divide the spoil with the strong,
Because He poured out His soul unto death,
And He was numbered with the transgressors,
And He bore the sin of many,
And made intercession for the transgressors.

May we value the cross. May we cling to the cross. May we talk about the cross. May we celebrate the cross. And may we live a life thankful to God for the cross. We must live our lives as if the cross was supposed to be ours instead of His. He was our substitute. He took our punishment. He bore our cross. He received the chastisement for our peace. He is our hero, our Savior, our God, our forgiveness, and we must honor the cross with great reverence. Our salvation was purchased for much too high a price for us to haphazardly serve God. This one act–this one symbol–should cause us to consecrate our lives and live passionately for Jesus for all the days we're given on Earth.

REFLECTION QUESTIONS

1. What are some other examples you can think of from your knowledge of scripture that remind you of Jesus as the Lamb of God, or point to the cross that was to come? (Example: Abraham told Isaac that God Himself would provide the ram for sacrifice when they were walking up Mount Moriah where God had told him to sacrifice his son. This is a symbol of what Jesus would do for all mankind.)

2. Have you ever thought about the correlation between the Garden of Eden and the Garden of Gethsemane? What is something that stands out to you as you studied this portion of scripture today?

3. Read Isaiah 53 again. Pick out one verse that stands out to you and go deeper. (What is the scripture saying? What did it mean culturally when it was written? Look up any words you may not know, even what certain words meant in the original Hebrew, if you want to go even deeper. What is the Lord showing you about this specific scripture?)

CHAPTER 4
THE BLOOD

The Price for Covering

I remember growing up in the church hearing over and over the phrase "we need to plead the blood of Jesus". We sang songs with lyrics like "Oh the Blood of Jesus, it washes white as snow". I remember thinking as a child, "How can something so red make something white?" We sang "There's Power in the Blood", and I didn't understand how the fluid that flows from someone's veins could have any power at all. Every time I would fall from my bike or scrape my knee, my blood usually came out when I was hurting and injured. That didn't seem very powerful at all. It seemed messy and gross.

"How can something so red make something white?"

I didn't understand how the fluid that flows from someone's veins could have any power at all.

THE SIGNIFICANCE OF THE BLOOD

I can remember Christians praying over other Christians and "pleading the blood" for safety, healing, or breakthrough in a situation. If anything, it sounded extra spiritual, but I didn't understand its significance. But having a solid understanding of what the blood of Jesus really represents is a vital Foundation Stone.

The blood of Jesus is a very important part of our Christianity, but it's unfortunate how it's not understood very well in our post-Christian, modern era. It's probably viewed as barbaric if not archaic. This sentiment could be an accurate description of the blood of Christ–it *was* barbaric. And yes, it *is* archaic. But just because things are tough to understand, outside of our cultural context and beyond our modern actualization, doesn't mean it's not pertinent for us today. I would venture to say our understanding of the blood of Jesus Christ is one of the single most important things we need to understand as believers.

Christ's blood is the proof of our Lord's sacrifice. It is literally His "skin in the game" of our redemption. Many leaders throughout history have claimed to have the answers and the ability to save mankind. But only Jesus drained every drop of lifeblood from His body to prove it. I've heard it said all other world religions force man to attempt to get to God while Jesus was God coming to man. This sacrifice– the draining of Christ's blood and His death on the cross–was God completing the requirement of forgiveness of sin. This was a price we could not pay for our imperfections.

WHY BLOOD?

Why was death required for sin anyway? Why was the spilling of blood a prerequisite for forgiveness from God?

Romans 6:23 [29]
23 For the wages of sin is death, but the gift of God is eternal life in Christ Jesus our Lord.

CHAPTER 4

To understand the blood, we must understand what the price of sin is. The "paycheck" for sin is death. It always has been. God has never been unclear about what it costs to rebel against Him.

Genesis 2:16-17[38]
16 And the LORD God commanded the man, saying, "Of every tree of the garden you may freely eat; 17 but of the tree of the knowledge of good and evil you shall not eat, for in the day that you eat of it you shall surely die."

Adam and Eve did, in fact, eat from this tree. Their immediate instinct–the sin nature that was awakened in them–was to hide from God. Don't we still do that today? Guilt causes shame, which causes us to hide. We do this subconsciously because our awareness of God's standard is hardwired into our humanity. Deep down, we know we have fallen short and we withdraw to cover it up. When I've sinned and I know it, I get very pensive, embarrassed, and quiet. Even after my repentance, sometimes it takes some time for my condemnation to fizzle and melt off of my conscience. We know deep down when we are separated from God, just like Adam and Eve. They hid themselves. They were aware of their need to be covered up. The nakedness of their bodies was an illustration of the vulnerability of their eternal souls.

SIN = DEATH

This is where God stepped in. This is where the very first death for sin occurred. And as wild as it sounds, it was by God's hand that the first sacrifice was made. God's solution was to provide a covering so Adam and Eve's shame could be covered. Their attempt at clothing themselves was inadequate. The fig leaves they attempted to cover their bodies with were not sufficient. This was their *own* effort in attempting to cover their shame. But the truth was that God needed to provide the covering. He needed to provide the skin to cover the shame–which He did by performing the very first sacrifice. What an interesting revelation. God provided the skins of an animal for Adam and Eve. This means God Himself took life and shed blood for the initial covering.

Genesis 3:21[39] *(emphasis added)*
*21 "Also for Adam and his wife **the LORD God made tunics of skin**, and clothed them."*

God showed Adam and Eve a picture of what was required from this point forward in order to stay in right standing with God: the shedding of innocent lifeblood. For there to be right standing between God and man, death had to occur. Since the point of God creating man was for relationship, the blood of a perfect animal would suffice as a substitute so mankind could live.

This pattern of sacrifice was established in the Garden of Eden. Adam and Eve knew the only acceptable sacrifice was an animal from whose body blood could flow. It couldn't be vegetation—mankind's fig leaves. This is why God accepted Abel's sacrifice of an animal and rejected Cain's sacrifice of fruits and vegetables. It's not that there wasn't value in Cain's sacrifice. It was that there was no blood. There was no death. When Cain realized God had accepted Abel's sacrifice and rejected his, he became enraged with jealousy and murdered Abel, spilling his blood on the ground. Then he lied about his sin to God when God confronted him about the location of his brother, asking God, "Am I my brother's keeper? (Genesis 4:9)

God says something very telling in His response to Cain:

Genesis 4:10[40]
10 "And He said, "What have you done? The voice of your brother's blood cries out to Me from the ground."

God was very aware that Abel's blood had been shed, and the Bible takes great pains to reveal that, from a spiritual standpoint, blood has a voice that God can hear.

For there to be right standing between God and man, death had to occur.

CHAPTER 4

BLOOD = LIFE

What is it about blood that God responds to? Without blood, life fades away. A human cannot live without blood. Blood carries the oxygen and nutrients the body tissues need, and carries waste away from those tissues. Literally, blood is the flowing source of life. When blood is spilled–when life is taken–the life God created ebbs away. This gets God's attention because He is the Author of Life! He notices the shedding of blood:

Leviticus 17:11[30]
11 "For the life of the flesh is in the blood, and I have given it to you upon the altar to make atonement for your souls; for it is the blood that makes atonement for the soul.'"

It is, in fact, an act of grace that God would accept the blood of an animal as a substitution in the first place. Many people think grace is only present in the New Testament. But I believe by recognizing that God would actually accept a substitute, He demonstrated He wanted mankind to live and be forgiven. What kindness! What mercy! Even before Jesus came, God extended grace. By sacrificing an animal, a human's life could be saved. This was how God ensured His beloved mankind could survive the Old Covenant period. It was the assurance that we would recognize His ultimate fulfillment of the requirement of death and blood for sin when Jesus came as our substitute, the final sacrifice for all. How would we recognize the final sacrifice if we had not seen the first iteration of God's requirement in the sacrifice of animals upon an altar?

We have to understand and recognize that God has a currency, a pattern, and a system that is ultimately *His* decision and under *His* control. We use the currency of our country to engage in commerce. It is simply understood that this is the way it works. In the same way, we must operate under God's system for heaven. God requires the shedding of blood for the forgiveness of sins. He just does. That's His way.

Hebrews 9:22 [31]

22 And according to the law almost all things are purified with blood, and without shedding of blood there is no remission.

The absolute sanctity, heaviness, and sobering nature of the death of one life for the freedom of another causes those who are forgiven to realize how deep the activity of sin goes into the soul. Without the substitute, the person is destined to eternal separation from God! Even the holy items in the Tabernacle and later, the Temple, were to be set apart by the sprinkling of blood. Everything holy unto the Lord on earth must be set apart by the blood of the sacrifice. There is a heavy price that must be paid for holiness. No one could haphazardly trot into God's presence. Everything must be set apart under the weighty price of the blood of life.

Without the substitute, the person is destined to eternal separation from God! Even the holy items in the Tabernacle and later, the Temple, were to be set apart by the sprinkling of blood. Everything holy unto the Lord on earth must be set apart by the blood of the sacrifice.

For generations, this pattern of animal sacrifice as substitution was ingrained in the hearts and minds of God's people. There was an understanding of what it cost to be God's children. And there was a reason for this. Prophets throughout the Old Testament told of a coming sacrifice that would be God's *final* installment of His holy requirement for blood. We see one of those portions of scripture in Isaiah 53. This is a portion of scripture written approximately 700 years before Christ, but eerily accurate regarding the death of the coming Messiah on a cross. Let's look at it:

CHAPTER 4

Isaiah 53:4-10 [35]

4 "Surely He has borne our griefs And carried our sorrows; Yet we esteemed Him stricken, Smitten by God, and afflicted. 5 But He was wounded for our transgressions, He was bruised for our iniquities; The chastisement for our peace was upon Him, And by His stripes we are healed. 6 All we like sheep have gone astray; We have turned, every one, to his own way; And the LORD has laid on Him the iniquity of us all. 7 He was oppressed and He was afflicted, Yet He opened not His mouth; He was led as a lamb to the slaughter, And as a sheep before its shearers is silent, So He opened not His mouth. 8 He was taken from prison and from judgment, And who will declare His generation? For He was cut off from the land of the living; For the transgressions of My people He was stricken. 9 And they made His grave with the wicked— But with the rich at His death, Because He had done no violence, Nor was any deceit in His mouth. 10 Yet it pleased the LORD to bruise Him; He has put Him to grief. When You make His soul an offering for sin, He shall see His seed, He shall prolong His days, And the pleasure of the LORD shall prosper in His hand."

Jesus, who is God's only begotten Son, was given as a sacrifice for the sin of mankind. He was called "The Lamb of God" by John the Baptist and was positioned before the foundation of the world to be the final installment in God's plan for salvation for mankind according to Revelation 13:8.

In the previous chapter on the cross, we talked about how Jesus was literally prepared in body and soul to bleed every last drop of His lifeblood for us. He bled in the Garden of Gethsemane where blood mingled with His sweat as He prayed. He bled while the priests and crowd beat Him at Caiaphas' house during His unlawful trial. He bled at the whipping post under the torture of the Romans. He bled when the crown of thorns was placed on His head. He bled under the weight of His heavy cross down the Via Dolorosa–the Way of Suffering. He bled when the spikes were driven through His wrists and feet. He bled as He hung on an Old Rugged Cross. And He bled one more time after His death as the Romans pierced His side to verify He was no longer alive. Jesus' blood was spilled out in its entirety. He was stricken. He was afflicted. He was wounded. He was bruised. He was ridiculed. He was scourged. He was tortured–all in our place. This was the punishment of a sinner.

But this punishment was insidiously administered to a pure and sinless man. A pure Lamb. The selfless Messiah–the Lamb who would take away the sin of the world.

He bled in the Garden of Gethsemane where
blood mingled with His sweat as He prayed...
He was stricken, afflicted, wounded, bruised,
ridiculed, and scourged. He was tortured–all in our place.
This was the punishment of a sinner.

WHAT IT MEANS TO "PLEAD THE BLOOD"

So when we "plead the blood", or "ask for a blood covering" in our life, it's a picture of us staying submitted under the covering of God's atoning sacrifice for our sin and receiving the benefits of His way and purpose. We "plead the blood" in prayer when we ask for the salvation of a loved one because we acknowledge Jesus is the only way they can receive eternal life. We "plead the blood" when we pray for healing, because of Isaiah's statement that by the stripes of Christ, we are healed. We "plead the blood" when we pray for protection because we know the chastisement for our peace was upon Him.

The term "pleading the blood" has no special magic qualities in prayer. It is simply our acknowledgment that without the shedding of the blood of Christ, we have no access to the Father, let alone to ask Him for answers to our needs.

One of the greatest chapters of the protection of God for His children can be found in Psalm 91. I believe Jesus is the fulfillment of this scripture. When we run to Him and acknowledge His way, His sacrifice, and His price, we can experience the promises of this scripture.

CHAPTER 4

Psalm 91:1-16 [41]

1 He who dwells in the secret place of the Most High
Shall abide under the shadow of the Almighty.
2 I will say of the Lord, "He is my refuge and my fortress;
My God, in Him I will trust."
3 Surely He shall deliver you from the snare of the fowler
And from the perilous pestilence.
4 He shall cover you with His feathers,
And under His wings you shall take refuge;
His truth shall be your shield and buckler.
5 You shall not be afraid of the terror by night,
Nor of the arrow that flies by day,
6 Nor of the pestilence that walks in darkness,
Nor of the destruction that lays waste at noonday.
7 A thousand may fall at your side,
And ten thousand at your right hand; But it shall not come near you.
8 Only with your eyes shall you look,
And see the reward of the wicked.
9 Because you have made the Lord, who is my refuge,
Even the Most High, your dwelling place,
10 No evil shall befall you,
Nor shall any plague come near your dwelling;
11 For He shall give His angels charge over you,
To keep you in all your ways.
12 In their hands they shall bear you up,
Lest you dash your foot against a stone.
13 You shall tread upon the lion and the cobra,
The young lion and the serpent you shall trample underfoot.
14 "Because he has set his love upon Me, therefore I will deliver him;
I will set him on high, because he has known My name.
15 He shall call upon Me, and I will answer him;
I will be with him in trouble; I will deliver him and honor him.
16 With long life I will satisfy him,
And show him My salvation."

FOUNDATION STONES

What is so important about the blood of Jesus? The life of God is in the blood of Jesus! Our forgiveness is in the blood of Jesus! Our healing is in the blood of Jesus! Our protection is in the blood of Jesus! Our eternal salvation is in the blood of Jesus! Remember, without the shedding of blood, there is no remission of sin.

Remission:
1. *The cancellation of a debt, charge, or penalty.*
2. *Forgiveness of sins* [42]

When we ask Jesus into our life and make Him our Lord, we step under His priceless blood which provides for salvation, healing, deliverance, protection, and hope! As Christ-followers, now we must *stay* under His blood. We must live as if what Jesus did for us matters immensely. And as we do, we receive the benefits of His finished work of redemption. The blood of Jesus is our *life*!

If you've been running your Christian life haphazardly and not honoring the price of Christ's blood with your decisions, today is the day to be transformed. Get alone with God and receive His salvation and all the other promises He provided through His sacrifice. Then stay in that place, under His blood. When we walk through difficult things or when we are crying out for God's promises, pleading the blood of Jesus simply acknowledges to God that we want Him, His presence, and His answers–*His way!*

REFLECTION QUESTIONS

1. What is your response (or trigger) when you have sinned? What is your go-to response when you know you have fallen short of God's standard? Is there a place of "comfort" you try to run back to?

_____
_____
_____
_____
_____
_____
_____
_____
_____

2. What would be a better response to your sin according to Scripture?

_____
_____
_____
_____
_____
_____
_____
_____

3. Ask the Lord to show you how He sees you, even when you mess up. The enemy will always come in with a lie to create that response of separation or of hiding. Allow the Lord to show you His love and for you to see it with fresh eyes today.

_____
_____
_____
_____
_____

CHAPTER 5
COVENANT

God's Promise to Man

I have become more and more aware that as Christians, we tend to use words that don't show up in everyday language. Have you noticed that? Things like "salvation", "baptism", and "sanctification", among other things. It's easy to go through an entire church service and feel like we're hearing a foreign language. Inevitably, we leave not knowing how to apply anything that we've heard. It's important to understand what many of these words mean. These are our Foundation Stones and having an understanding of these things is important! Let's break down some of that big vocabulary and take the "teeth" out of it so we can grow in Christ. I hope that each topic we explore will equip us to know what is being taught from the Bible, form a good understanding of the backdrop for it, and grow in our walk with God as a result.

Let's wrestle today with a concept that comes up regularly in our study of God's Word. Its premise is what divides the Bible into its parts: the Old Testament and the New Testament. It is the word *covenant*.

Another couple of words that usually mean the same thing as a covenant in the Bible and the context of Christianity are *testament* and *promise*.

FOUNDATION STONES

Covenant:
1: *a usually formal, solemn, and binding* **agreement**
2a: *a written* **agreement** *or promise usually under seal between two or more parties especially for the performance of some action* [43]

Testament:
1a: *a tangible proof or tribute*
2a: *an act by which a person determines the disposition of his or her property after death*
2b: *WILL*
3b *archaic : a covenant between God and the human race* [44]

Promise:
1a: *a* **declaration** *that one will do or refrain from doing something specified*
1b: *a legally binding declaration that gives the person to whom it is made a right to expect or to claim the performance or forbearance of a specified act* [45]

In today's culture, a covenant can be understood by looking at solid marriage vows. My wife and I stood at an altar before God and our loved ones and pledged our lives to one another. The vows affirmed that no matter what happened, we would remain faithful until death parts us. We exchanged rings that we wear to this day to remind us of this promise. We invited our loved ones as witnesses to our promise and to hold us accountable to that promise should we struggle with our faithfulness at any point in our union. Consider that God created man and woman and placed them in the Garden of Eden in a state of sinless perfection with only one instruction.

A covenant can be understood by looking at solid marriage vows.

Genesis 2:17 [38]
17 "...but of the tree of the knowledge of good and evil you shall not eat, for in the day that you eat of it you shall surely die."

58

CHAPTER 5

God's original intention was that mankind would live in a complete, unrestricted relationship with Him and not be tainted with sin. Like a small child, there would be no guilty conscience and there would be no separation between us and Him. This was God's original promise. Mankind would live forever in perfect relationship with God! This was the original agreement or covenant that God had in mind. In its simplicity, this covenant could be paraphrased like this: "Live here in perfection with God, and don't eat from *that* tree."

However, Adam and Eve disobeyed God when they were tempted by Satan and surrendered their promise. This started God's plan of restoring His desire for eternal life to his children. You see, God always has a plan! God always has it taken care of from the beginning to the end. Even with our free will, God has a way of rolling out His plan before us. He began our restoration by establishing the definition of sin and what it would cost to pay for it. We see throughout Genesis, and into the first several books of the Bible, how God has defined sin as rebellion and defiance of *His* standard. Essentially, anything in our heart and behavior that displeases God and goes contrary to His instruction is sin.

What is sin? Sin is missing the mark. Sin is doing what displeases God. Sin is doing anything that God's Word, the Bible, says we should not do. (Or for that matter, *not* doing what it says we *should* do!) It's been said that sin is like an archer aiming at a target, releasing his arrow, and completely missing the bullseye.

---

*Sin is like an archer aiming at a target,
releasing his arrow, and completely missing the bullseye.*

But why doesn't God want us to sin? Is He sitting up in Heaven, looking down on us with glee until we sin so He gets to punish us? No! Sin hurts us. It hurts His kids and He does not want that for us. When we are in pain, His heart hurts. Imagine being a parent (if you aren't already) and how you would feel if you told your kids not to touch a burning stove. If they went ahead and did it anyway and burned their hands, you would feel for them because they're your child and you love them. You don't like to see them in pain, right? It's the same with our Good Father.

On an even deeper level, the penalty that resulted from sin is death. Sin invites the curse of evil. Sin incurs the death penalty and eternal separation from God. Because sin had entered the hearts of the man and woman, there was nothing they could do to root it back out. It became lodged in their heart. It was passed on to their children (Psalm 51:5). The only way the curse of sin could be broken is if God Himself demolished it and so God made a way! The first picture of this provision was in the covering that God made for Adam and Eve by giving them skins to cover their nakedness. God performed the first sacrifice to cover the shame of sin. He began, as a Master Artist, to paint the picture of His redemption that He would tell through the lineage of Adam and Eve for the benefit and restoration of everyone who would now be tainted with the sin nature.

God prepared a lamb, or a variety of other animals, that could be slaughtered in the place of a man to pay the man's penalty while God patiently prepared His ultimate Sacrifice through the generations that would take mankind's sin once and for all. We see this picture of substitution throughout the first part of the Bible, which is traditionally called "The Old Testament", or even "The First Covenant". The first two-thirds of your Bible is the story of God setting up the pitch for His ultimate Home Run! But, to receive His Sacrifice by faith, God's people would have to recognize His Master Plan for what it was. Had God just immediately provided the Final Sacrifice, mankind would not have recognized the severity of the price. They had to see the result of sin in the blood of the animal, and experience the heavy price of sin–even economically, as their best lamb was required–and then witness the pain of sin through the death of their sacrifice in their place.

In essence, God was telling mankind that He would temporarily accept a substitute to cover mankind's trespass until a suitable sacrifice was provided. God was carefully painting a picture, telling a story of His plan of restoration to generations of mankind as He was preparing the ultimate Sacrifice once and for all. This way, mankind would recognize His provision.

Had God just immediately provided the Final Sacrifice, mankind would not have recognized the severity of the price.

CHAPTER 5

THE SACRIFICIAL SYSTEM

This sacrificial system is called the Old Covenant, which is the beginning of God's story where He promises to restore mankind. Let's explore this First Covenant a little bit.

There was a man named Abram, later known as Abraham. God called him out of his native land of Ur and drew him to a land of promise, called Canaan. He and his wife were unable to have children of their own, but through a series of miraculous interventions, God provided a son to Abraham and his wife, Sarah, in their old age. God then asked Abraham for this son back as a test of Abraham's faith:

Genesis 22:1-2 [47]

1 Now it came to pass after these things that God tested Abraham, and said to him, "Abraham!" And he said, "Here I am." 2 Then He said, "Take now your son, your only son Isaac, whom you love, and go to the land of Moriah, and offer him there as a burnt offering on one of the mountains of which I shall tell you."

God asked Abraham for his son back as a test of Abraham's faith.

Isaac, Abraham's son, was responsible for carrying his sacrificial wood up the Mountain of Moriah. He didn't know he would be the sacrifice–only that God would provide a sacrifice when they arrived.

Abraham and Isaac arrived at the place of sacrifice and Abraham bound his son. Imagine the tears streaming down his face and the look of horror on his young son's face. He rose the dagger above the body of Isaac, ready to take the life of his son in obedience to God. When Abraham was faithful and obedient, God stopped Abraham short of sacrificing his son. He told Abraham to look nearby and he saw a ram with its horns stuck in a thicket.

FOUNDATION STONES

Genesis 22:12-18 [47]

12 And He said, "Do not lay your hand on the lad, or do anything to him; for now I know that you fear God since you have not withheld your son, your only son, from Me." 13 Then Abraham lifted his eyes and looked, and there behind him was a ram caught in a thicket by its horns. So Abraham went and took the ram, and offered it up for a burnt offering instead of his son. 14 And Abraham called the name of the place, The-Lord-Will-Provide; as it is said to this day, "In the Mount of the Lord it shall be provided." 15 Then the Angel of the Lord called to Abraham a second time out of heaven, 16 and said: "By Myself I have sworn, says the Lord, because you have done this thing, and have not withheld your son, your only son— 17 blessing I will bless you, and multiplying I will multiply your descendants as the stars of the heaven and as the sand which is on the seashore; and your descendants shall possess the gate of their enemies. 18 In your seed all the nations of the earth shall be blessed, because you have obeyed My voice."

Throughout the generations, from Abraham until now, God has always honored faithfulness. He was preparing his people, the Hebrews, to recognize the satisfaction of His justice and mercy. It's important to see that God would provide another lamb on the same mountain–the mountain of Moriah. The mountain on which Abraham was offering Isaac is present-day Jerusalem and the Temple Mount, where another Son carried His own sacrificial wood up the mountain of Moriah.

The picture of Abraham leading his son up a lonely hill carrying his sacrificial wood was the picture God would use in leading His only Begotten Son, Jesus Christ, to the same mountain carrying His cross. At that moment, the Covenant shifted from the sacrificial system to the pouring out of grace, as Jesus became the final Sacrifice, once for all destroying sin and providing a bridge back to God. God's story had reached a climax and mankind could return to His presence again.

The mountain on which Abraham was offering Isaac is present-day Jerusalem ...where another Son carried His own sacrificial wood up the mountain...

CHAPTER 5

THE COMPLETED PROMISE

As an artist, God knows exactly what color to add during each stroke of His brush. There was a moment in time that was poised for absolute effectiveness for God to release His ultimate promise. You see, there was a time when God's nation, Israel, was being held captive by the domineering regime of the Roman Empire. Just before Christ arrived, a road system had been created that connected the known world and provided easier transportation to outlying locations because of the rule of Rome. Nations and cultures were beginning to mingle like never before and technology and information were accessible to larger swaths of society. The world was ready for the dispersion of the message God had been preparing for millennia.

The Jewish nation *hated* the Roman Empire. They considered the Romans oppressive and abusive. Rome taxed the Hebrew people excessively. They persecuted the Jews and considered the Middle Eastern nation the refuse dump of the world. The Hebrew people were severely oppressed and longed for deliverance. Throughout the books of the Bible, you will find prophecies of a coming hero, and the Israelites *longed for* this promised Savior. They looked for Him to overthrow the Roman Empire in His grandeur and power.

Scriptures telling of God's Man can be found in writings hundreds and even a thousand years before this time. Scriptures like Isaiah 9 and 61 foretell His coming:

Isaiah 9:6-7 [26]
6 For unto us a Child is born, Unto us a Son is given;
And the government will be upon His shoulder. And His name will be called
Wonderful, Counselor, Mighty God,
Everlasting Father, Prince of Peace.
7 Of the increase of His government and peace
There will be no end,
Upon the throne of David and over His kingdom,
To order it and establish it with judgment and justice
From that time forward, even forever.
The zeal of the Lord of hosts will perform this.

FOUNDATION STONES

Isaiah 61:2 [48]
2 To proclaim the acceptable year of the Lord,
And the day of vengeance of our God;
To comfort all who mourn.

Scriptures foretelling the brutal crucifixion of the Messiah can be found in Psalm 22 and Isaiah 53, describing the details of Christ's suffering in stunning detail and accuracy, written almost a thousand years before the events happened.

So what is the point of a covenant, or a promise, of God? Why did God start with one promise and replace it with a new one? The answer is simply this: God will always fulfill His Word and His Word declares He loves us and has created us to be with Him forever. The Bible says this about God's Word:

Psalm 138:2 [49] *(emphasis added)*
2 I will worship toward Your holy temple,
And praise Your name
For Your lovingkindness and Your truth;
For **You have magnified Your word above all Your name.**

God is perfect in fulfilling His Word which includes His vow to send a Savior, provide a sacrifice for all mankind, and allow us to inherit eternal life again through our faith in Jesus Christ. We need to realize God's plan of salvation was told through the Hebrew people, but from the beginning of His story, He *always* intended to extend the invitation of salvation to the whole world, even to non-Jews called "gentiles".

God is perfect in fulfilling His Word which includes
His vow to send a Savior...

CHAPTER 5

> *Isaiah 11:10* [50] *(emphasis added)*
> *10 "And in that day there shall be a Root of Jesse,*
> *Who shall stand as a banner to the people;*
> ***For the Gentiles shall seek Him,***
> *And His resting place shall be glorious."*

Why is there a New Covenant? Why is there a New Promise? Why is there a New Testament from God? Simply because the Old Covenant was available to the Hebrews only to paint the base layers of God's story. But now, because of Jesus Christ fulfilling that Covenant, the Gentiles–those who are not of Jewish descent–have access to receive salvation and eternal life as well!

Paul the Apostle talks about the mystery of the ages that was veiled until Christ came. And Paul revealed the mystery to us in Ephesians:

> *Ephesians 2:14-16* [21]
> *14 For He Himself is our peace, who has made both one, and has broken down the middle wall of separation, 15 having abolished in His flesh the enmity, that is, the law of commandments contained in ordinances, so as to create in Himself one new man from the two, thus making peace, 16 and that He might reconcile them both to God in one body through the cross, thereby putting to death the enmity.*

> *Ephesians 3:1-6* [51]
> *1 For this reason I, Paul, the prisoner of Christ Jesus for you Gentiles— 2 if indeed you have heard of the dispensation of the grace of God which was given to me for you, 3 how that by revelation He made known to me the mystery (as I have briefly written already, 4 by which, when you read, you may understand my knowledge in the mystery of Christ), 5 which in other ages was not made known to the sons of men, as it has now been revealed by the Spirit to His holy apostles and prophets: 6 that the Gentiles should be fellow heirs, of the same body, and partakers of His promise in Christ through the gospel...*

The mystery Paul is referring to is God creating in mankind "One New Man". God was extending forgiveness and salvation to everyone, Jew and Gentile alike, making one Body–the Body of Christ!

It's amazing to me that this story of all stories, the mystery of the ages, has been revealed to us who have received Jesus Christ as Lord and Savior! God was not sending a political hero to overthrow Rome. He was sending a Savior who would defeat Satan, our sin, and then give us eternal life. We have been given a New Promise. This is a New Covenant. It's a New Contract! Those of us who are not Hebrew by descent have been given equal access to God because of His free gift of salvation. And we must simply believe to receive it.

Romans 10:9 [20]
9 "...that if you confess with your mouth the Lord Jesus and believe in your heart that God has raised Him from the dead, you will be saved.

Remember, Adam and Eve were never supposed to die. They were supposed to live in perfection forever with God in the Garden of Eden. They invited death with their rebellion and lost their eternal life. Salvation, which is our opportunity to receive God's New Covenant, is now God's free gift to us! This is His new contract. It's His New Covenant! Through the blood of Jesus Christ, the contract has been signed, sealed, and delivered, and we are heirs to God's promise because of His free gift. What an amazing God we serve! His plan is so thorough and so powerful. We must never take it for granted.

WE ARE SEALED BY THE HOLY SPIRIT IN BELIEVING

Through faith, we believe and are saved according to Ephesians 2:8-9. Now, by receiving His Holy Spirit, we are sealed for the day of His coming:

2 Corinthians 1:21-22 [52]
21 Now He who establishes us with you in Christ and has anointed us is God,
22 who also has sealed us and given us the Spirit in our hearts as a guarantee.

CHAPTER 5

In our exploration of Covenant, we realize that this beautiful plan of God includes a contract written in the very blood of His Son, Jesus Christ, whom we receive for salvation. When we receive Christ as Lord, we receive the gift of the Holy Spirit as a seal–a guarantee–of His promised eternity when this life on earth is over. Why is this important to us today? Why should we understand these covenants? Because we must understand we would not have the New Covenant without God starting with the Old Covenant.

We must also realize that God's current promise is where we live. Today, we are living in the time of the New Covenant which is the Covenant of Grace. His forgiveness is available to us at this very moment. Relationship with God has been restored because of God's finished work of the sacrifice of Jesus and His resurrection. The Old Covenant revealed what sin was and showed us the *standard* of God. The New Covenant shows us Jesus fulfilling the requirements of the Old Covenant and then granting us grace to live forgiven, even in our imperfections. Now we comply with God's Word out of relationship rather than out of a fear of punishment. You can't earn God's promise. You must receive it. This means your lifestyle of obedience becomes an act of worship and love rather than an act of slavery. To me, this makes the need for obedience that much greater! I *want* to obey God, not because I fear punishment, but because I *love* Him and I'm *so grateful* for His goodness to me!

We don't know what the full love of God is without understanding *both* covenants. This is why it's important to read the *entire Bible*. God's truth is truth on *both* sides of the cross. And to understand one side of the cross is to understand the other side of the cross. Make sure to understand the *fullness* of God's Word and Promises. Just make sure you live on the New Side of the Finished Work of Christ through the cross! That's where it all makes sense! That's where the artist has signed His masterpiece and has allowed us to step back in awe and say, "Wow! God is so good to us!"

REFLECTION QUESTIONS

1. After reading the definitions for "covenant", "testament", and "promise", how has your perception changed when it comes to looking at the Old and New Covenants?

___

2. What was the purpose of the Sacrificial System?

___

3. Isn't it amazing how God brings His plan full-circle? For example, God told Abraham to take Isaac up Mount Moriah to sacrifice him, and instead of God making Abraham go through with killing his son, He provided a ram. Jesus sacrificed his life on that same mountain. Can you think of any other parallels connecting the Old and New Testament where God brought the promise full-circle in this way through Jesus?

___

CHAPTER 6
REPENTANCE
"Go and Sin No More"

My first real memory of the sting of guilt happened when I was about five years old and my brother, Eric, was three. One beautiful summer morning, he and I were out in the front yard playing. We noticed my mom's tiny yellow Toyota Corolla in the driveway with the trunk still open. My mom had taken something out of the trunk and disappeared inside the house, which left us with something new to explore! We couldn't resist the pull of messing around with my mom's car. Somehow our exploration of the trunk turned into a game where Eric got in the trunk and I lowered the trunk lid as close to latching as possible before it latched. I can remember peeking through the crack and seeing his little eyes lighting up with adventure as we both realized we were risking locking him in the trunk. It was exhilarating! We went several cycles of lowering the lid and raising it back up, giggling all the way!

Of course, the inevitable happened. There came a fateful moment when we heard the dreaded 'click' of the latch. It surprised me! I thought I was getting away with coming 'just close enough' and, when the realization hit that I had locked my brother in the trunk of my mom's car, I understood I was probably in trouble for the rest of my life!

I was caught in a dilemma. There was no mistaking the fact my brother was locked in the trunk. I couldn't make up a story that left me innocent! Obviously, someone had done it, and I was the only one around. At five years old, I wasn't sure if he would even survive in there! Maybe he'd run out of air! Then it would be my fault that my brother died in the trunk! I was desperate to get Eric out, terrified of being *found* out, and the clock was probably ticking on his very life. I was caught. My mom had the only solution–the key to the trunk!

I weighed my options, gathered my courage, and came up with a plan that I thought might provide me with the least amount of punishment, and I ran into the house in a flurry. My heart was beating fast, my script was rehearsed and it was now or never! I rounded the corner to the kitchen where my mom was standing and quickly blurted out, "Mom, I locked Eric in the trunk and now I'm going to my room to think about it for a while!" With that, I pivoted quickly on my heels and ran for my room, not looking back to see if Mom was chasing me down to give me a spanking! I made it to my room in a panic, closed the door, and laid down on my bed expecting that at any moment my deserved punishment was coming. After all, I *was* guilty.

I waited a long time and didn't hear anything. After a while, I could hear my brother playing again, and it seemed like my mom wasn't coming. I sheepishly opened the door to my bedroom to see the house in relative normality. I slinked out, trying to blend into the surroundings. Everything was at peace and I didn't hear a word from my mom. Never did I hear a word from my mom about this situation until much later, when, as an adult, I recounted the story. She was quite amused! She thought it was funny. My guilt had been punishment enough, and come to find out, a human can live for quite a while in the trunk of a car. Eric, of course, wasn't ever in danger of death.

GODLY SORROW LEADS TO REPENTANCE

Repentance: to turn from sin and dedicate oneself to the amendment of one's life [53]

What I felt that day at five years old is my first recollection of guilt and a primitive version of repentance, though I didn't know what I was doing! See, I was caught!

CHAPTER 6

I knew I couldn't lie my way out of this one. The only way to save my brother (and myself) was to admit my fault and run to the only one who had the key. And while it makes for a funny story, I think we can all relate. Sin makes us want to make excuses, run from God, and blame someone else for our mistakes. But God tells us in His Word that true freedom comes from confessing our sins and running *to* the One who has the key!

1 John 1:9 [54]
9 If we confess our sins, He is faithful and just to forgive us our sins and to cleanse us from all unrighteousness.

Sin has been defined in its simplest form as "missing the mark". It's like pulling a firearm up on a target, and then completely missing the bullseye. And the fact of the matter is, all of us have sinned. We've all missed the target God has set for us–the target of His perfection.

Isaiah 53:6 [35]
6 "All we like sheep have gone astray;
We have turned, every one, to his own way;
And the LORD has laid on Him the iniquity of us all."

YOU CAN'T MOVE THE BULLSEYE

Now, just because we are all guilty of sin doesn't mean God is all right with sin. His standard is holiness. God is holy and without holiness, we cannot see the Lord. Many people in today's culture think they can have their own version of truth, but this essentially is like shooting an arrow and then drawing a bullseye around it wherever it hits. It just doesn't work that way.

Hebrews 12:14 [55]
14 Pursue peace with all people, and holiness,
without which no one will see the Lord...

FOUNDATION STONES

> *Psalm 24:3-4* [56]
> *3 Who may ascend into the hill of the Lord?*
> *Or who may stand in His holy place?*
> *4 He who has clean hands and a pure heart,*
> *Who has not lifted up his soul to an idol,*
> *Nor sworn deceitfully.*

Because we are guilty of sin, we have been disqualified from eternal life. Sin is what separated Adam and Eve from their eternal life with God in the Garden of Eden when they ate the fruit God commanded them not to eat.

> *Genesis 2:16-17* [38]
> *16 And the Lord God commanded the man, saying, "Of every tree of the garden you may freely eat; 17 but of the tree of the knowledge of good and evil you shall not eat, for in the day that you eat of it you shall surely die."*

Jesus was clear during His Sermon on the Mount:

> *Matthew 5:20* [57]
> *20 "For I say to you, that unless your righteousness exceeds the righteousness of the scribes and Pharisees, you will by no means enter the kingdom of heaven."*

It would be a natural response for hopelessness and despair to overcome our hearts when we see that punishment for sin is eternal separation from God. Much like my five-year-old heart panicked at the thought of going to the one person who had my answer, I resisted going to them because they also held the authority to dole out my punishment! But the good news is that Jesus paved a narrow way for us to return to God, as is talked about in Matthew:

> *Matthew 7:13-14* [2]
> *13 "Enter by the narrow gate; for wide is the gate and broad is the way that leads to destruction, and there are many who go in by it. 14 Because narrow is the gate and difficult is the way which leads to life, and there are few who find it."*

CHAPTER 6

John 14:6 [58]

6 "Jesus said to him, "I am the way, the truth, and the life. No one comes to the Father except through Me."

GOD HOLDS JUDGEMENT & THE KEY TO DELIVERANCE

While it is true that God is the One who has the authority to judge and punish us, He is also the only One with the key to our deliverance! We must turn away from sin and run toward God, falling on His great mercy when we recognize our sin. Asking God for forgiveness is where we start. Asking for forgiveness is our appeal to the mercy of God. We confess that we know we broke God's standard.

What comes next is what is incredibly important for us to understand. Once we've been forgiven, then comes *our* part in the relationship. Repentance.

Repentance is what we do *after* forgiveness to amend our ways. Repentance is our response to God's forgiveness. It's the 'turning away' from the sin that caused us to appeal to God's forgiveness in the first place! Repentance is the running away from ever doing that sin again. Repentance is the one-hundred-and-eighty-degree turn away from what got us in trouble to begin with. We see this example laid out for us in the story of the woman caught in adultery.

John 8:10-11 [6]

10 "When Jesus had raised Himself up and saw no one but the woman, He said to her, "Woman, where are those accusers of yours? Has no one condemned you?" 11 She said, "No one, Lord." And Jesus said to her, "Neither do I condemn you; go and sin no more.""

Repentance is the one-hundred-and-eighty-degree turn away from what got us in trouble to begin with.

When authentic confession and repentance happens in our hearts, something amazing unfolds. God gives salvation and refreshing after we repent. He rescues us. He wipes away our sins, makes our hearts white like snow again, and gives us a fresh opportunity to serve Him! God doesn't *have* to do this. But He does it nonetheless. He isn't a cosmic tyrant searching for ways to punish mankind. He's a Father who longs to see His sons and daughters operating in complete victory and freedom and aligned with their original created value. Much like my mom, who patiently took the key out of her purse and unlocked the trunk to rescue my brother, our Heavenly Father longs to take the key, His Son Jesus who defeated sin at the cross, and unlock our mess so we can find freedom, deliverance and a fresh start! The part we play is coming to Him to ask for the key!

Acts 2:37-38 [59]

37 "Now when they heard this, they were cut to the heart, and said to Peter and the rest of the apostles, "Men and brethren, what shall we do?" 38 Then Peter said to them, "Repent, and let every one of you be baptized in the name of Jesus Christ for the remission of sins; and you shall receive the gift of the Holy Spirit."

Acts 3:19 [60]

19 "Repent therefore and be converted, that your sins may be blotted out, so that times of refreshing may come from the presence of the Lord,"

2 Chronicles 7:14 [61]

14 "If My people who are called by My name will humble themselves, and pray and seek My face, and turn from their wicked ways, then I will hear from heaven, and will forgive their sin and heal their land."

NO ONE HAS IT "ALL FIGURED OUT"

It's easy to think there are those 'super Christians' who have everything figured out and have no need to repent anymore. We compare ourselves with people we think have it all figured out. But no one is exempt from repentance. Even King David, the "man after God's own heart", fell into sin and had to be restored through God's mercy because of his own repentance.

CHAPTER 6

*Though David loved God, the temptations of his flesh
overwhelmed him and one day, he used his authority as
king to commit adultery with Bathsheba...
It would have likely been easiest on his monarchy to cover it up...
But...his heart was so convicted that he confessed
and cried out to God in deep repentance.*

King David started his life as a shepherd boy, learning to worship God in solitude while he tended his father's flock of sheep. God honored him and promoted him throughout his life until finally, he became the most powerful man of his day. He became king of Israel. Though David loved God, the temptations of his flesh overwhelmed him and one day, he used his authority as king to commit adultery with Bathsheba. That, in turn, also resulted in murder when he had Bathsheba's husband killed after she came to him and told him she was pregnant. In the end, David's sin caused the death of the child that had been conceived in sin and a murderous cover-up of the truth. You can read the story in 2 Samuel 11. In one sweeping act of the flesh, David broke many of God's commandments. Hoping it would go away, he kept silent until a prophet named Nathan confronted him about his sin. In this moment of conviction, David had two choices: either he could deny it and mock God's standard with his play-acting, or confess it humbly. It would have likely been easiest on his monarchy to cover it up. As a king, he would have a heavy price to pay should the nation find out he had done such terrible things. But David feared God more than people. His heart was so convicted that he confessed and cried out to God in deep repentance. His prayer of repentance was recorded for us in the book of Psalm, chapter 51:

FOUNDATION STONES

Psalms 51:1-4, 10-13 [46]
1 "Have mercy upon me, O God,
According to Your lovingkindness;
According to the multitude of Your tender mercies,
Blot out my transgressions.
2 Wash me thoroughly from my iniquity,
And cleanse me from my sin.
3 For I acknowledge my transgressions,
And my sin is always before me.
4 Against You, You only, have I sinned,
And done this evil in Your sight—
That You may be found just when You speak,
And blameless when You judge.

10 Create in me a clean heart, O God,
And renew a steadfast spirit within me.
11 Do not cast me away from Your presence,
And do not take Your Holy Spirit from me.
12 Restore to me the joy of Your salvation,
And uphold me by Your generous Spirit.
13 Then I will teach transgressors Your ways,
And sinners shall be converted to You."

As human beings, we live in a fallen world and are susceptible to mistakes. We can't escape that. But what we can do is stay humbly submitted to God and remain soft-hearted. We must admit our failures, ask for forgiveness, and then turn (repent) so we don't continue to replay the same mistakes again and again.

...stay humbly submitted to God and remain soft-hearted.

CHAPTER 6

Hebrews 3:7-15 [62]

7 Therefore, as the Holy Spirit says: "Today, if you will hear His voice, 8 Do not harden your hearts as in the rebellion, In the day of trial in the wilderness, 9 Where your fathers tested Me, tried Me, And saw My works forty years. 10 Therefore I was angry with that generation, And said, 'They always go astray in their heart, And they have not known My ways.' 11 So I swore in My wrath, 'They shall not enter My rest.'"

12 Beware, brethren, lest there be in any of you an evil heart of unbelief in departing from the living God; 13 but exhort one another daily, while it is called "Today," lest any of you be hardened through the deceitfulness of sin. 14 For we have become partakers of Christ if we hold the beginning of our confidence steadfast to the end, 15 while it is said: "Today, if you will hear His voice, Do not harden your hearts as in the rebellion."

The key is to stay sensitive to the voice of the Holy Spirit, the written Words in our Bible, and the conviction of our hearts so that we don't embody a hardened heart. We must live a daily lifestyle of repentance. It's our daily choice to turn *from* sin and run *toward* God! *That* is repentance.

REFLECTION QUESTIONS

1. Have you ever experienced something like the story at the beginning of the chapter where you knew you blew it and also knew there was no way you were getting out of it on your own?

_____
_____
_____
_____
_____
_____

2. Repentance is not just feeling sorry for something we've done–for getting caught. It's turning from that behavior and allowing the Holy Spirit to change us. What are some things you think the enemy puts in our way to keep us from true repentance? (Example: pride)

_____
_____
_____
_____
_____
_____

3. Is there anything in your life and heart that you need to repent for today? Ask the Lord to show you any areas of your heart that need to be given over to Him in complete repentance.

_____
_____
_____
_____
_____
_____
_____

CHAPTER 7
CONFESSION OF FAITH

Speak It Out Loud

The verbal "confession of our faith" is paramount in our walk with God. There are two parts to receiving salvation according to Romans 10:9-10. We must believe in our hearts, of course. This part can happen internally. But we've also got to confess our faith with our mouths in a way that others can hear. It's so important to let the reality of our "out loud" confession of Christ as Lord to become a part of our everyday lives, where our words are continually surrendered to the Lord, holding fast to our faith for our entire lifetime! Our confession of faith in Jesus represents the inward commitment of our hearts to God. Our "out loud" confession is the evidence of our "internal" belief. What comes out of our mouths is so important. Yet, in this day and age, we're seeing a very concerning carelessness in regard to our speech. People speak many things, but very little life and hope are being spoken. Our opinions, emotions, and even degrading insults are easier to speak than the Good News of Jesus Christ. Somehow it's not always understood that our speech is the *first and most revealing* indicator of the condition of our heart.

What comes out of our mouths is so important...

FOUNDATION STONES

Romans 10:9-10 [20]
9 ...if you confess with your mouth the Lord Jesus and believe in your heart that God has raised Him from the dead, you will be saved. 10 For with the heart one believes unto righteousness, and with the mouth confession is made unto salvation.

Why is it important what comes from the mouth of a Christian? Is it important that our verbal confession of faith and the content of our speech are different from non-believers?

First of all, we must understand that our faith can only start with a belief in our heart and a confession from our mouth. Out of the overflow of our hearts, our mouths speak, which means as soon as our hearts have been filled with faith, the natural progression of that faith is that it will spill over into our speech (Luke 6:45). Confession by its very nature is "out loud". You cannot make a confession silently. And there's a reason for that.

Confession: *a formal statement of religious beliefs, a creed. An admission or acknowledgement* [63]

In essence, confession is our statement of what we believe to be true. But what is the biblical definition of faith?

Hebrews 11:1-3 [64]
1 Now faith is the substance of things hoped for, the evidence of things not seen. 2 For by it the elders obtained a good testimony. 3 By faith we understand that the worlds were framed by the word of God, so that the things which are seen were not made of things which are visible.

Confession is our statement of what we believe to be true.

CHAPTER 7

Faith is another one of those words that Christians throw around often, but what does it mean? Where does faith come from?

Romans 10:17 [20]
17 "So then faith comes by hearing, and hearing by the word of God."

Once we believe what we've heard about Jesus, that faith naturally rises to the surface of our hearts to come back out of our mouths. According to scripture, this is the initiation of our salvation! We believe in our hearts and then confess with our mouths:

Romans 10:8-10 [20]
8 "But what does it say? "The word is near you, in your mouth and in your heart" (that is, the word of faith which we preach): 9 that if you confess with your mouth the Lord Jesus and believe in your heart that God has raised Him from the dead, you will be saved. 10 For with the heart one believes unto righteousness, and with the mouth confession is made unto salvation."

Amazingly, this is also the way that God empowers the Gospel Message to continue to reach more and more people. Salvation spreads like a wildfire. Someone confesses the Gospel, then someone hears it and believes and confesses it to the next hearer. Soon, the forest of humanity is consumed with the holy fire of God's Good News!

WHY WE SPEAK OUR FAITH OUT LOUD

God made it so our environment responds to sound. Creation responded to God's voice. The spoken Word of God is how creation came into being!

Genesis 1:3 [65] *(emphasis added)*
*1 Then God **said**, "Let there be light";*
and there was light.

God made our hearts like a vault that can accumulate important (or sometimes toxic) things. This vault makes up our character and personality which is why we must carefully tend to the content of our hearts. We've got to take responsibility to ensure untruths and unhealthy things don't take root, and subsequently make sure good things are stored up in the center of our being. The heart is the description of the *core* of who we are as a person. Jesus said it this way:

Luke 6:45[66]
45 A good man out of the good treasure of his heart brings forth good; and an evil man out of the evil treasure of his heart brings forth evil. For out of the abundance of the heart his mouth speaks.

According to this verse, whatever comes from our mouths is a reflection of what is already in our hearts. If we truly want to know what we're made of, we need to do an audit of our speech.

The confession of our faith in Christ is the verbal acknowledgment of what we know to be true–that Jesus Christ is Lord and we are surrendered to Him. But, when we're ashamed or insecure about things, we can hide them inside to prevent being held to them later. Speaking our confession of faith out loud holds us accountable to live for Christ during the hard times, especially in front of the people who heard our confession. Jesus was adamant that our faith in Him was something we were not to be ashamed of. If we withhold our confession and are unwilling to acknowledge Jesus verbally and publicly, our faith is aborted.

Matthew 10:32-33[67]
32 Therefore whoever confesses Me before men, him I will also confess before My Father who is in heaven. 33 But whoever denies Me before men, him I will also deny before My Father who is in heaven.

Jesus was adamant that our faith in Him was something we were not to be ashamed of.

CHAPTER 7

GOD EMPHASIZES THE SPOKEN WORD

Throughout scripture, it is confirmed time and again that God uses speech–the actual, out-loud truth being spoken–to create, shape, and change the world around us. God used speech to create, then He created us in His image with a heart to receive and a mouth to proclaim! If God spoke to create and we're created in His image, we are designed by God to do the same thing.

Romans 4:16-18 [68] *(emphasis added)*
16 Therefore it is of faith that it might be according to grace, so that the promise might be sure to all the seed, not only to those who are of the law, but also to those who are of the faith of Abraham, who is the father of us all 17 (as it is written,"I have made you a father of many nations") in the presence of Him whom he believed—God, who gives life to the dead and **calls those things which do not exist as though they did;** *18 who, contrary to hope, in hope believed, so that he became the father of many nations, according to what was spoken, "So shall your descendants be."*

God creates with His words. When He created the universe, He spoke it into being. When He told the story of salvation, He "called those things that were not as though they were." Jesus Himself is even called "The *Word* of God"!

John 1:1-4 [4] *(emphasis added)*
1 In the beginning was the Word, and the Word was with God, and **the Word was God. 2 He was in the beginning with God.** *3 All things were made through Him, and without Him nothing was made that was made. 4 In Him was life, and the life was the light of men.*

The tongue...is an instrument of blessing to continue the advance of God's Kingdom.

Because God spoke the universe into existence, He established the truth that the power of life and death is in the auditory declarations of our mouth. God gave us the same creative power in our words. What we speak from our mouths is reflective of the life we begin to live. This is why, just like with God, there is power even in our words:

Proverbs 18:21[69]
21 Death and life are in the power of the tongue,
And those who love it will eat its fruit.

The tongue with which we have a casual conversation, and the tongue with which we can sometimes say terrible things, is the *same tongue* God wants us to use to bring our public confession of faith in Jesus Christ to the world. It's an instrument of blessing to continue the advancement of God's Kingdom. That's why it must be redeemed with our confession of faith in Jesus and be submitted daily to God as an instrument of life, holy unto the Lord. It can't be salt water and fresh at the same time:

James 3:5, 10-11[70]
5 Even so the tongue is a little member and boasts great things. See how great a forest a little fire kindles!

10 Out of the same mouth proceed blessing and cursing. My brethren, these things ought not to be so. 11 Does a spring send forth fresh water and bitter from the same opening?

WE MUST SUBMIT OUR WORDS TO CHRIST

Surrendering our speech is a tremendous feat, possible only in surrender and submission to Christ. This is why the first step in redeemed speech is our confession of faith in Jesus. Our confession should start us on a journey where our words begin to reflect Heaven's priorities and not Earth's priorities.

CHAPTER 7

James 3:3-10 [70]

3 Indeed, we put bits in horses' mouths that they may obey us, and we turn their whole body. 4 Look also at ships: although they are so large and are driven by fierce winds, they are turned by a very small rudder wherever the pilot desires. 5 Even so the tongue is a little member and boasts great things. See how great a forest a little fire kindles! 6 And the tongue is a fire, a world of iniquity. The tongue is so set among our members that it defiles the whole body, and sets on fire the course of nature; and it is set on fire by hell. 7 For every kind of beast and bird, of reptile and creature of the sea, is tamed and has been tamed by mankind. 8 But no man can tame the tongue. It is an unruly evil, full of deadly poison. 9 With it we bless our God and Father, and with it we curse men, who have been made in the similitude of God. 10 Out of the same mouth proceed blessing and cursing. My brethren, these things ought not to be so.

Submitted speech marked by holy confession demonstrates true faith in Christ whereas an uncontrolled tongue demonstrates a lack of faith in Christ. An unrestrained tongue is rebellious and disobedient to God.

It's amazing to ponder what the Apostle James clearly teaches us. He says if we can tame the tongue we can be perfect. This shows how important it is to God that we submit our Words to Christ. Does this mean we never make a mistake? Of course not! It means we rely on Christ through His Holy Spirit to help our words become more and more reflective of Jesus. This is why our faith starts with an out-loud confession of Christ as Lord. This is our lips–our tongue–speaking holy words. Our confession and surrender begin to build an accountability to our heart attitudes. This is a filter between our carnal mind and our outward expression. Our confession that provides accountability permits God's Holy Spirit to whisper into our ears before we spew something evil from our mouths so we can catch it and submit it to Him.

Submitted speech marked by holy confession demonstrates true faith in Christ...

True and undefiled worship before God is our verbal confession of faith erupting from a heart that is full of the goodness of God. Our lips and tongues submitted to God become a beautiful filter system for our hearts. By prayerfully listening to our speech–our confession–we will begin to hear what our heart condition is and can continue to lay it down before God to be cleansed and refined. Being surprised by what pours out of our mouths can be a refining tool in God's hand to help us become more like Christ.

REFLECTION QUESTIONS

1. Today, let's start taking inventory of what we speak. Ask yourself some questions about your words:

Have I verbally (out-loud) acknowledged Jesus Christ as my Lord, and as the only Way, Truth and Life?

_____
_____
_____
_____

Can I imagine Jesus speaking the words I'm speaking?

_____
_____
_____
_____

If Jesus were standing right next to me in the flesh, would I still say this?

_____
_____
_____
_____

If what I am saying was said to me by someone else, how would I feel?

_____
_____
_____

Do these words create life and hope, or death and discouragement?

_____
_____
_____
_____

REFLECTION QUESTIONS - CHAPTER 7

2. Have you recently been in a situation where you were able to share your faith with someone out-loud? What was that experience like for you?

3. If you have not recently (within the last few weeks or months) been able to share your faith with someone, do you feel there may be something holding you back? (i.e. fear, excuses of busyness, etc.) Take some time to pray today and ask the Lord to change your heart and help you overcome those things that are holding you back, and give you a heart to share your faith with others.

CHAPTER 8
SANCTIFICATION

Becoming More Like Him

Once we've given our hearts to the Lord, the Bible makes it very clear we have started a relationship with God. This is not a relationship with religion, with endless rules and regulations, but rather a relationship with a very present God. His Word gives us instructions on how to relate with God in the way He desires, which leads to pleasing Him and growing in friendship with Him just like we see many of the central figures of the Bible do. When we do not do what God's Word says we should, or when we do not change the way God's Word wants us to change, we are walking in rebellion. There comes a point as we consider ourselves a believer in Christ and a follower of God where change should be the result of our affiliation with Him. To be a "Christian" without being like Christ is a deviation from the very definition of our faith.

When the early disciples were scattered from Jerusalem due to severe persecution, a group of them who lived in Antioch were called "Christians" for the first time:

Acts 11:26b [71]
26...And the disciples were first called
Christians in Antioch.

FOUNDATION STONES

Christian: GREEK - *christianos* - a follower of Christ.[72]

This name was originally used by Gentiles (non-Jewish people), to describe a person's affiliation with Christ. It was quite possibly considered an insult. In some settings, this name could be translated as "little Christs" or "Christ-like". Into the second century, the word "Christian" was adopted as a title of honor by followers of Jesus. They considered this description of their passion for Christ as "Christ-like" to be a fitting framework within which to live their lives. What an amazing compliment to someone's character, to be called by the name of the person they are choosing to model their life after. May it be true, even today, that those who call themselves "Christian" actually live like Jesus did.

How did a group of random people from so many different cultural backgrounds become such a force to be reckoned with, so much so that the people around them created a title with which to label them that is still used today? They didn't just embody a system of rules and regulations. They literally *became like the one they followed* to such an extent that they became recognizable by how they lived. They became like Jesus. They were sanctified.

Sanctify: *to set apart to a sacred purpose or to religious use* [73]

Sanctification: *the state of growing in divine grace as a result of Christian commitment after baptism or conversion* [74]

Sanctification is the process of becoming more like Christ—a child of God!

Process: *a natural phenomenon marked by gradual changes that lead toward a particular result* [75]

Become: *to undergo change or development* [76]

They literally became like the one they followed...

CHAPTER 8

As believers in Jesus, we are not supposed to only be a part of a worldwide religion. We have started a relationship with God Himself because of the work of Jesus on the cross. This means we're not just to attend church, sing lyrics presented on a screen, and listen to someone speak behind a pulpit once a week. We need to live in such a way that the world could mistake us for Jesus Himself. Our life becomes His life lived through us and looks less and less like who we *used* to be.

John the Baptist was the cousin of Jesus and his ministry was to declare the coming of the Messiah. Though he had his critics and skeptics, his ministry was incredibly effective and John had become very famous. It was evident there was a touch of God on his life and the multitude of people he was attracting confirmed his message. But there came a moment when Jesus began to rise to greater prominence and John's disciples tried to point this out to John to retain John's fame. John, however, understood something in his walk with God that it would do us good to understand as well:

John 3:30 [77]
30 He must increase, but I must decrease.

John was assuring his followers that the way to live was in full surrender to Jesus Christ, which is the will of God. To fight for a position when God is looking for our surrender is to fight a losing battle. God wants His people to become more like Christ—even John the Baptist. Our religious practices are less important to God than us becoming like Christ in our hearts, character, and our behaviors.

In understanding that our Christianity is less about formula and more about our relationship with God through Jesus Christ, where does our journey in becoming Christian (like Christ) begin?

SALVATION IS WHERE SANCTIFICATION BEGINS

When we received Jesus Christ as our Lord and Savior, God *made us* holy so we could *become* holy.

FOUNDATION STONES

Hebrews 10:14 [78]
14 For by one offering He has perfected forever those who are being sanctified.

Consider this question: if we have been perfected, why do we need to be sanctified? Or even simpler, if we are perfect, why do we need to be further perfected? The answer lies in the completed work of God through the sacrifice of Jesus Christ on the cross.

Hebrews 10:12 [78]
12 But this Man (Jesus), after He had offered one sacrifice for sins forever, sat down at the right hand of God...

When we receive salvation by faith in full repentance of our sins and surrender to Jesus Christ, we are immediately forgiven, and perfected in God's eyes. This washing of our lives is the gift of God to us because we cannot cleanse ourselves. We are immediately made right with God when we put our faith in Jesus! Our perfection starts with faith.

Acts 2:21 [59]
21 ...Whoever calls on the name of the Lord shall be saved.

Romans 10:9 [20]
9 ...If you confess with your mouth the Lord Jesus and believe in your heart that God has raised Him from the dead, you will be saved.

John 14:6 [58]
6 Jesus said to him, "I am the way, the truth, and the life. No one comes to the Father except through Me.

Praise be to God that we don't have to start from scratch and hope to get to the finish line as a holy person in God's eyes through our own efforts. Jesus allows us to start from the place of being holy already when He frees us from sin at the time of salvation!

CHAPTER 8

1 John 1:9 [54]
9 If we confess our sins, He is faithful and just to forgive us our sins and to cleanse us from all unrighteousness.

With this in mind, sanctification (our becoming more like Jesus) can only start with salvation. When we confess our sins and receive Jesus Christ as our Savior and Lord, we begin the journey of becoming like Christ in heart and character. It is completely abnormal to become a Christian and then not change to be more like Christ. Refusal to change to become like Jesus is a refusal to adopt the very nature of what being "Christian" is all about: Christ-likeness!

Once we are saved, we then begin the journey of becoming like Christ from a place of being forgiven and cleansed. As long as there is breath in our lungs, we have the opportunity to become more like Jesus. So while we're cleansed at salvation, we now *live* from that position, wanting to get better and better at being like Jesus.

Once we are saved, we then begin the journey of becoming like Christ from a place of being forgiven and cleansed.

Being sanctified is only available to a true believer in Jesus Christ. You cannot be set apart as holy if you refuse to submit to the only One who can make you holy. It is impossible to be sanctified if you aren't saved. This is where religious works come from. Humans have been trying to be good enough for God, outside of surrender to Him, for as long as time has been! Trying to become something noteworthy without a relationship with God is fruitless. In our flesh, it's easy to try to get to God through good works–doing enough things to impress God and man resulting in us being accepted. But this is the ultimate idol of "self". This idol lies to us by convincing us that if we do enough good things, we'll earn our way to God. But the simple fact is that the only way we're made holy is by receiving the gift of holiness God gave us through Jesus Christ. And we receive this gift through faith in Him!

NOW THAT WE *ARE* SAVED, WE ARE IN THE PROCESS OF *BEING* SAVED

Let me assure you when you received Christ as your Lord and Savior, you were saved at that very moment! But we are still living in a fallen world. On this side of heaven, while we're still breathing, growing, aging, interacting with other people, and trying to hold our character to the standard of God's Word, we need to continue to *be* saved. Remember what it says in Hebrews 10:14. Let's look at it in the NIV version this time:

Hebrews 10:14 NIV [79] *(emphasis added)*
14 For by one sacrifice he **has made perfect** *(salvation) forever those who are* **being made holy** *(salvation).*

After we have *been* saved, now we live our lives *being* saved, so that ultimately we can be saved at the moment this life ends and our new life in heaven with God begins! This is the *process* of sanctification!

After we have been saved, now we live our lives being saved...

SALVATION AND SANCTIFICATION ARE YOUR CHOICE

When we are willingly saved by faith in Jesus, we will begin to desire to become more like Christ. We are led to salvation by the Holy Spirit, we receive Christ willingly, and now our desire shifts away from carnal things and toward being set apart for God! Literally, we start to develop an appetite for God, His Presence, His Word, and the changes He wants to make in our lives. No longer do we have an appetite for sin and rebellion against God. Our gratitude toward God's forgiveness causes us to want to change to become more like Him. Let's look at it in a powerful chapter in the book of Romans:

CHAPTER 8

Romans 6:1-19 [29]

1 What shall we say then? Shall we continue in sin that grace may abound? 2 Certainly not! How shall we who died to sin live any longer in it? 3 Or do you not know that as many of us as were baptized into Christ Jesus were baptized into His death? 4 Therefore we were buried with Him through baptism into death, that just as Christ was raised from the dead by the glory of the Father, even so, we also should walk in newness of life.

5 For if we have been united together in the likeness of His death, certainly we also shall be in the likeness of His resurrection, 6 knowing this, that our old man was crucified with Him, that the body of sin might be done away with, that we should no longer be slaves of sin. 7 For he who has died has been freed from sin. 8 Now if we died with Christ, we believe that we shall also live with Him, 9 knowing that Christ, having been raised from the dead, dies no more. Death no longer has dominion over Him. 10 For the death that He died, He died to sin once for all; but the life that He lives, He lives to God. 11 Likewise you also, reckon (decide) yourselves to be dead indeed to sin, but alive to God in Christ Jesus our Lord.

12 Therefore do not let sin reign in your mortal body, that you should obey it in its lusts. 13 And do not present your members as instruments of unrighteousness to sin, but present yourselves to God as being alive from the dead, and your members as instruments of righteousness to God. 14 For sin shall not have dominion over you, for you are not under law but under grace. 15 What then? Shall we sin because we are not under law but under grace? Certainly not! 16 Do you not know that to whom you present yourselves slaves to obey, you are that one's slaves whom you obey, whether of sin leading to death, or of obedience leading to righteousness? 17 But God be thanked that though you were slaves of sin, yet you obeyed from the heart that form of doctrine to which you were delivered. 18 And having been set free from sin, you became slaves of righteousness. 19 I speak in human terms because of the weakness of your flesh. For just as you presented your members as slaves of uncleanness, and of lawlessness leading to more lawlessness, so now present your members as slaves of righteousness for holiness.

FOUNDATION STONES

Hebrews 4:15-16 [9]

15 "For we do not have a High Priest who cannot sympathize with our weaknesses, but was in all points tempted as we are, yet without sin. 16 Let us therefore come boldly to the throne of grace, that we may obtain mercy and find grace to help in time of need."

Of course, we will fail from time to time. There will be moments of weakness and the occasional mistake. But in our sincere surrender, sanctification becomes fruitful because we're surrendered to, and led by, the Holy Spirit.

Sanctification, the process of becoming more like Christ, begins in relationship with Christ and the guidance of the Holy Spirit. Any attempt at becoming godly, absent of a relationship with God, is meaningless. It's religious, but not authentic. Satan will hijack fleshly attempts at godliness. He did so with the Pharisees who contended against Jesus every chance they got. In John 8, the Pharisees wanted to kill Jesus thinking it was their service to God. Their religion had blocked their love and they were not like Christ at all. They were behaving like Satan and trying to call it holiness. Be careful not to do that! Get in the Bible every day and find out what the authentic love of God looks like. Model your life after Jesus Christ and His character to find out what it truly means to be Christ-like. It's imperative that your desire to become like Christ is rooted in a genuine relationship with God and the humility of a son or daughter–not in the arrogance of religious duty and self-imposed piety.

You'll sense when your desire for sanctification turns into a religious duty by the language you use and the judgment you feel toward other believers. If you start to measure your holiness against your perception of another person's holiness, you are embracing a sinful measuring rod for your own qualifications. When cynicism and arrogance aimed at other people around you rise up in your heart and thoughts of your own self-righteousness prevail, it is time to repent and get back to the business of humbly growing in Christ. If you stop *serving* and start wanting ***to be served***, you are no longer walking in authentic sanctification. Instead, you have embraced a self-righteous and self-important view. If you are growing in knowledge but not growing in *love*, you are simply becoming more religious without becoming more like Christ. Remember, Jesus' definition of following God's commands is summed up like this:

CHAPTER 8

Matthew 22:34-40 [80]
34 But when the Pharisees heard that He had silenced the Sadducees, they gathered together. 35 Then one of them, a lawyer, asked Him a question, testing Him, and saying, 36 "Teacher, which is the great commandment in the law?" 37 Jesus said to him, "'You shall love the Lord your God with all your heart, with all your soul, and with all your mind.' 38 This is the first and great commandment. 39 And the second is like it: 'You shall love your neighbor as yourself.' 40 On these two commandments hang all the Law and the Prophets."

We must grow in loving God and loving people to truly be sanctified. This is when we are truly becoming more like Christ.

SANCTIFICATION IS AUTHENTICATED THROUGH OBEDIENCE

Learning and embracing God's Word in order to grow in Christ is the cornerstone for true sanctification. But remember once again: embracing the Word of God is more about encountering the Savior, Jesus Christ, and less about acquiring more head knowledge. God's Word illuminates our hearts and exposes the truth of who we really are.

Hebrews 4:12 [9]
12 For the word of God is living and powerful, and sharper than any two-edged sword, piercing even to the division of soul and spirit, and of joints and marrow, and is a discerner of the thoughts and intents of the heart.

God's Word illuminates our hearts and exposes the truth of who we really are.

The Word of God judges the thoughts and intents of the heart. The point of sanctification is to become more like Christ in every part of our being: our actions, our thoughts, and our motives. God is after your heart, not just your form of religion on the surface of your life.

Our prayer needs to become, "Lord, search my heart and know me. See if there is any wicked way in me." (Psalm 139:24) In this way, we are able to grow in the reputation and fruitfulness of God because He is leading us into greater righteousness.

Guard against self-righteousness. Guard against Christian arrogance. The true Christian lives his or her life to the benefit of other people: Christian and non-Christian alike. Your life should point to Jesus. The true Christian doesn't have to point to his or her own accomplishments. If you do that, that's all the reward you will ever receive. Love God and love people. And progressively get better at it as you grow! God will help you! He will heal, deliver, teach, and empower you, until one day, you can stand before His throne and hear Him say, "Well done, good and faithful servant".

REFLECTION QUESTIONS

1. What do you think about this notion that you can be saved, and are continually being saved all at once? What does that mean to you?

2. How have you experienced this transformation in your own life?

3. What does it look like to be "Christ-like"? Cite scripture as you explain.

CHAPTER 9
WATER BAPTISM

Your Public Declaration

In the Bible, water has always represented cleansing and refreshing. In an arid place, like the desert places in the Middle East, water is priceless and vital for life. In Bible times it represented hope and sustenance. Without water, human despair set in. Water was needed for crops to thrive and for animals and people to drink. A spring, a flowing source of water, was important in order to keep waters from being stagnant and infected.

Clean water was to be used for ceremonial cleansing before a sacrifice in the days before Christ went to the cross. This was to wash oneself after indulging in sin or after some kind of illness so a person could once again rejoin the camp and be in community with the rest of their people.

A spring, a flowing source of water, was important in order to keep waters from being stagnant and infected.

After the years of the Exodus when the people of Israel settled in villages and cities, ceremonial cleansing continued, but this time in a structure called a *mikvah*. A *mikvah* was like a large bathtub that the people would step into to ceremonially wash away the filth of their sin. Men and priests had to ceremonially cleanse themselves before they could ever approach God with a sacrifice or step into the Temple area. Many of these *mikvahs* can still be seen in ruins around Israel's ancient worship sites to this day.

God had established a picture of baptism before Jesus ever came on the scene so the idea of cleansing and change through a repentant heart could be understood with Christ's sacrifice. Before Jesus rose to prominence, his cousin, John the Baptist, started baptizing people in the Jordan River in the arid Israeli desert. Because of his message and unorthodox delivery style, people began to flock to the desert in droves wanting to hear what John had to say. He would preach, call for repentance, and invite people into the waters of the Jordan River to be immersed as a symbol of their changed hearts. He was fulfilling prophecy with his actions:

Isaiah 40:3 [81]

3 The voice of one crying in the wilderness: "Prepare the way of the Lord; make straight in the desert a highway for our God."

Baptize: GREEK - baptizo - *to dip repeatedly, to immerse, to submerge (of vessels sunk)*
1. *to cleanse by dipping or submerging, to wash, to make clean with water, to wash one's self, bathe*
2. *to overwhelm* [82]

John the Baptist was using the imagery of the cleansing that happened when people approached the Holy Place in the Temple to reveal that hearts needed to be changed for the coming of the Messiah. John the Baptist established a baptism of repentance. This baptism demonstrated a life change. Immersion, dipping the entire body under the surface of the water, demonstrated submission and humility. It represented a moment in the life of a believer where their mind, will, emotions, hopes, dreams, and every other part of their lives were submitted to God. Past mistakes were confessed and repented of, and their future was committed to God.

CHAPTER 9

Even in the Old Testament, there were prophetic pictures preparing people to recognize the New Testament act of baptism by revealing the *humility* it takes to go under the water in full view of other people. In our flesh, humans tend to resist standing in front of other humans in humility and surrender. No one wants to be that vulnerable. Our flesh resists it so much that we will talk ourselves out of doing it in any way possible. And yet, the Bible calls us to it.

One such Old Testament picture of baptism and wrestling against our flesh can be found in 2 Kings 5:

> *2 Kings 5:9-14* [83]
>
> *9 Then Naaman went with his horses and chariot, and he stood at the door of Elisha's house. 10 And Elisha sent a messenger to him, saying, "Go and wash in the Jordan seven times, and your flesh shall be restored to you, and you shall be clean." 11 But Naaman became furious, and went away and said, "Indeed, I said to myself, 'He will surely come out to me, and stand and call on the name of the Lord his God, and wave his hand over the place, and heal the leprosy.' 12 Are not the Abanah and the Pharpar, the rivers of Damascus, better than all the waters of Israel? Could I not wash in them and be clean?" So he turned and went away in a rage. 13 And his servants came near and spoke to him, and said, "My father, if the prophet had told you to do something great, would you not have done it? How much more then, when he says to you, 'Wash, and be clean'?" 14 So he went down and dipped seven times in the Jordan, according to the saying of the man of God; and his flesh was restored like the flesh of a little child, and he was clean.*

The act of baptism, which is confessing you are a sinner and going under the water in full view of other people, is very humbling. But humility is the key to this symbol of baptism. Without a willingness to be brought low in the eyes of others, your pride will work against you throughout your relationship with God. Pride says, "I can do it myself". Humility says, "I need to surrender to God in baptism, and allow other people to see me do it. In this way I am held accountable in my decision to follow Jesus." This is the point where you publicly repent of your own ways and turn to Jesus' way!

Baptism is very much like a wedding ceremony. Sure, you and your fiancée can go down to the courthouse and elope. In the eyes of the State, you'd be legally married. But a big part of a wedding is to share the experience with your friends and family so you have witnesses to keep you accountable to your wedding vows. It is a celebration of two lives coming together in holy union. Baptism is similar to standing at the altar with your husband or wife-to-be and declaring your promise to love, honor, and cherish them, no matter what happens. Jesus laid His life down for the Church, His Bride, in the most vulnerable, degrading, and terrifying way on the cross. Should we not also lay down our pride and publicly declare our faith in Him?

The symbolism of washing is such a beautiful reminder of what Jesus does for us when we repent of our sins and ask for forgiveness. His blood cleanses us from our sin, our hearts are made new, and our consciences are healed. What a beautiful experience!

Baptism is a public declaration of our faith. It shows that we are not ashamed of being associated with Jesus and living our lives for Him! God is insistent that we openly confess Him as our God. He's not interested in indulging our desire to be "private" Christians. If salvation is a gift to us, the way God chooses to extend that gift to other people is through you giving it away once again. How can someone else know about how to be restored to God if you and I are silent about our relationship with Him? This is what is at stake when we are called to make a public confession of our faith. Defeating the fear and humiliation of being seen in the water in full vulnerability begins to set us free to declare the Good News of Jesus Christ openly with our lives! We've already been in the waters of baptism! Now we are bold to speak about our transformation to those who have not yet received Jesus! If we are unwilling to confess Jesus in the waters of baptism in front of friends, family, and the Church, how are we going to be ready to confess Jesus in the hostile environments of the world?

Baptism is very much like a wedding ceremony...

CHAPTER 9

Think about it. How did you find out about Jesus? Most likely you heard about Him from someone else who was unashamed to tell you about Him. Don't let the gift of salvation and forgiveness from God stop with you! Baptism is an aggressive way to train your heart to live for and confess Jesus publicly as a regular part of your life.

Though this scripture isn't only talking about baptism, it shows the importance that Jesus places on our willingness to openly confess Him as Lord:

Matthew 10:32-33 [67]
32 "Therefore whoever confesses Me before men, him I will also confess before My Father who is in heaven. 33 But whoever denies Me before men, him I will also deny before My Father who is in heaven."

On the Day of Pentecost, Peter preached to the crowd about the "turning" of our lives toward God which is repentance. Turning from the world and toward God is necessary in surrendering our lives to Christ. When you confess your faith in Christ, you repent (turn) from your sin, and you are "baptized *into*" the name of Jesus. Many say, "I'm just not ready to be baptized". One very important question surfaces with this resistance. When, then, *will* you be ready? In Acts 8, Philip sat on the chariot with the Ethiopian Eunuch and once the Eunuch was saved, his question was "What is keeping me from being baptized right now?" Think of this: the longer you wait to do something important, the more excuses you'll find to never do it. Jump in! Why wait? What's the real reason for waiting? It's usually fear. Fear of being seen, fear of crowds, fear of embarrassment, or even fear of messing up and sinning after baptism.

Another protest that often arises is, "I don't need to be baptized to be saved." This is true. You *can* be a confessing Christian without being baptized. Baptism is *not* a heaven issue. The thief on the cross made heaven without baptism. **But, baptism *is* an *obedience* issue.** If you refuse to be baptized when you *can* be baptized, you are *willingly disobeying* God's instruction in scripture *to be* baptized. If we are grateful for God's salvation and fully submitted to Him as our Lord, why would we willingly disobey *anything* He asks us to do?

FOUNDATION STONES

In Acts 22, Paul gave a testimony of his conversion. A man named Ananias was called by God to minister to Paul to get him started in his new relationship with Jesus. Ananias asked him a very important question that we must also consider:

> *Acts 22:16* [84] *(emphasis added)*
> *16 "And now **why are you waiting?** Arise and be baptized, and wash away your sins, calling on the name of the Lord."*

If you have not yet been baptized, maybe this same question is resonating in your heart as well. "Why are you waiting?"

When He was preparing to return to heaven, Jesus gave His followers this instruction that believers now call "The Great Commission":

> *Matthew 28:18-20* [1] *(emphasis added)*
> *18 And Jesus came and spoke to them, saying, "All authority has been given to Me in heaven and on earth. 19 Go therefore and make disciples of all the nations, **baptizing them in the name of the Father and of the Son and of the Holy Spirit**, 20 teaching them to observe all things that I have commanded you; and lo, I am with you always, even to the end of the age." Amen.*

What does baptism represent? Let's look for a moment at the symbolism.

Baptism represents being one with Jesus in His death, burial, and resurrection to new life! Water baptism is first the symbol of repentance. What is repentance? Repentance is the intentional act of turning from sin (the wrong direction of our life), and turning *toward* Jesus. Remember, John the Baptist began to baptize people into a baptism of repentance. This was a symbol of the life that was to come in relationship with Christ the Messiah. To fulfill the example of God's desire for His people to be baptized, even Jesus allowed Himself to be baptized:

> *Matthew 3:13* [85]
> *13 Then Jesus came from Galilee to John at the Jordan to be baptized by him.*

CHAPTER 9

What is the picture we are painting when we are obedient to God to be baptized? We are replicating in our own lives the death, burial, and resurrection of Jesus!

- **Death** - the public confession of our need for Him, humbling ourselves before others to proclaim we want to serve Him.

- **Burial** - We "go under" the water, representing the burial of our flesh–our human sin nature–into the grave.

- **Resurrection** - the bringing back to life of a new person as we come up and out of the water in victory!

The victorious part of baptism is when people are *raised to new life* when they come up out of the water! The old has passed away and the new has been raised up!

Romans 6:1-11[29]
1 What shall we say then? Shall we continue in sin that grace may abound? 2 Certainly not! How shall we who died to sin live any longer in it? 3 Or do you not know that as many of us as were baptized into Christ Jesus were baptized into His death?

4 Therefore we were buried with Him through baptism into death, that just as Christ was raised from the dead by the glory of the Father, even so, we also should walk in newness of life. 5 For if we have been united together in the likeness of His death, certainly we also shall be in the likeness of His resurrection, 6 knowing this, that our old man was crucified with Him, that the body of sin might be done away with, that we should no longer be slaves of sin.

7 For he who has died has been freed from sin. 8 Now if we died with Christ, we believe that we shall also live with Him, 9 knowing that Christ, having been raised from the dead, dies no more. Death no longer has dominion over Him. 10 For the death that He died, He died to sin once for all; but the life that He lives, He lives to God. 11 Likewise you also, reckon yourselves to be dead indeed to sin, but alive to God in Christ Jesus our Lord.

The Great Commission in Matthew 28 makes it clear that Jesus expects people to be baptized:

Matthew 28:19[1]
19 "Go therefore and make disciples of all the nations, baptizing them in the name of the Father and of the Son and of the Holy Spirit..."

Baptism is not considered an option by Jesus. It's a part of the process of serving Him! We believe, are baptized, and then filled with the Holy Spirit. We are forgiven, cleansed, empowered, and sent out–a full equipping to prepare us to continue the message of Jesus to the next person Jesus loves!

Baptism is expected. Baptism is not a prerequisite for salvation. It's not a salvation issue. But if we are alive and breathing, Jesus has given us a command to do it. Why would we *not* do something Jesus told us *to* do? He must know something about the act of baptism that we need to learn. Baptism is a key to our Christian victory! It's an intimate, bold, and powerful part of our walk with God that Jesus *expects* we will do.

Let's not look for excuses in order to get out of being baptized. Let's just do it.

Maybe the best question to ask yourself is, "What is hindering me from being baptized?" If you've never been baptized, ask yourself why and contend with the answer to the question until you experience the victory of breakthrough. A powerful action of faith and victory is to just do it by faith and courage and then watch victory and strength come into your life as a result of your obedience! Do it scared! Watch God fill you up as you obey!

Baptism is to help us remember the price that Jesus paid. It represents Jesus' death, burial, and resurrection. And it represents the resurrection life He gives to us. These reminders keep us focused, solid, and full of victory in our walk with Jesus!

Baptism is expected...
Why would we not do something Jesus told us to do?

CHAPTER 9

Baptism establishes a Foundation Stone we always return to–keeping us solid in our faith. When you are baptized, you'll never forget that day! It's a memorial you can point back to when you are tempted, confused, tired, or discouraged and you can say, "On *that* day, I proclaimed Jesus was who I was living for! I won't turn back!" Similarly, God had Joshua instruct the leaders of the twelve tribes of Israel to take rocks from the middle of the Jordan River and build a pillar when they entered the Promised Land. His reasoning? To make sure the next generation of Israelites would have something to look back on and remember that God's faithfulness brought them to their promise (Joshua 4). In the same way, baptism is a figurative memorial pillar, reminding us that we have committed our entire lives to Jesus.

Paul, in giving his testimony of conversion in Acts 22, says it this way:

Acts 22:12-16 [84] *(emphasis added)*
12 "Then a certain Ananias, a devout man according to the law, having a good testimony with all the Jews who dwelt there, 13 came to me; and he stood and said to me, 'Brother Saul, receive your sight.' And at that same hour I looked up at him. 14 Then he said, 'The God of our fathers has chosen you that you should know His will, and see the Just One, and hear the voice of His mouth. 15 For you will be His witness to all men of what you have seen and heard. 16 ***And now why are you waiting? Arise and be baptized, and wash away your sins, calling on the name of the Lord.***'

Today's question for every believer not yet baptized is, "What are you waiting for?"

REFLECTION QUESTIONS

1. How can you openly confess Jesus in front of friends, family, and the Church on a daily basis? If you are not in the practice of sharing what the Lord has done for you, what is one way you can start now?

_____
_____
_____
_____
_____
_____

2. If you have been baptized, think back on that "memorial stone". What were you feeling? What was the Lord speaking to you?

_____
_____
_____
_____
_____

3. Testimony is a powerful tool to share the Gospel with others. Oftentimes, people are asked to share their testimony before getting baptized, why they are making their commitment to the Lord, and what they plan to do in the future–a wedding vow–of sorts. Take some time today to write down your testimony as if you were speaking it in front of your family, friends, and church before you got baptized. (And if you haven't yet been baptized, this would be a great way to "practice" what you might say on that day!)

_____
_____
_____
_____
_____

CHAPTER 10
COMMUNION

Proclaim Until He Comes

There is an act of worship that is so powerful and so intimate with the Heavenly Father's heart that we are instructed to do it regularly. This one act of worship has remained throughout the ages since Jesus walked the earth in His physical form. It has outlived the styles of songs that church culture has moved through. It's outlived the liturgy of church services. It's overflowed into every nation in the world through the ages regardless of ethnicity and worship style. And while there may be some unique ways to participate throughout the cultures of the world, this act of worship has remained largely unchanged for two millennia since Jesus died and rose again. This is the practice of receiving what we call "communion". Your Bible headings will many times call this "The Lord's Supper". This is the symbolic act of a group of believers in Jesus Christ receiving a bite of bread to represent Jesus' body, and a sip of the fruit of the vine to represent His blood.

Communion is an act of worship that has remained throughout the ages since Jesus walked the earth in His physical form.

While all of us today receive communion *after* the death, burial, and resurrection of Jesus Christ, there was one moment in history when communion was received *before* the body of Christ was broken and His blood was spilled. It was the moment when history was pivoting on the hinge of Jesus' impending death on the cross. Before Jesus performed what He came to do, He wanted to demonstrate to His disciples what His sacrifice on the cross meant and how to keep it sacred and in the forefront of their minds through the generations. He gave the disciples an illustrated message. He revealed to them the heartbeat of what He was going to do *before* He did it.

Luke 22:14-20 [32]

14 When the hour had come, He sat down, and the twelve apostles with Him. 15 Then He said to them, "With fervent desire, I have desired to eat this Passover with you before I suffer; 16 for I say to you, I will no longer eat of it until it is fulfilled in the kingdom of God." 17 Then He took the cup, and gave thanks, and said, "Take this and divide it among yourselves; 18 for I say to you, I will not drink of the fruit of the vine until the kingdom of God comes." 19 And He took bread, gave thanks and broke it, and gave it to them, saying, "This is My body which is given for you; do this in remembrance of Me." 20 Likewise He also took the cup after supper, saying, "This cup is the new covenant in My blood, which is shed for you.

Before Jesus performed what He came to do, He wanted to demonstrate to His disciples what His sacrifice on the cross meant...He revealed to them the heartbeat of what He was going to do before He did it.

To understand why Jesus chose this particular meal, you have to back up a little in scripture. It's more than just a "last meal" before His execution. This meal had major significance in the overall picture of what God was painting in His masterpiece of salvation for mankind. This was Passover for Jesus and His disciples:

CHAPTER 10

Luke 22:7-13 [32]

7 Then came the Day of Unleavened Bread, when the Passover must be killed. 8 And He sent Peter and John, saying, "Go and prepare the Passover for us, that we may eat." 9 So they said to Him, "Where do You want us to prepare?" 10 And He said to them, "Behold, when you have entered the city, a man will meet you carrying a pitcher of water; follow him into the house which he enters. 11 Then you shall say to the master of the house, 'The Teacher says to you, "Where is the guest room where I may eat the Passover with My disciples?"' 12 Then he will show you a large, furnished upper room; there make ready." 13 So they went and found it just as He had said to them, and they prepared the Passover.

WHAT IS PASSOVER, AND WHY IS IT IMPORTANT?

Passover was the festival that God instituted for the Israelites after their deliverance from slavery in Egypt during the time of Moses. You can read this story in the book of Exodus. The Israelites had been in captivity in Egypt for four hundred years and God used Moses and a series of plagues to pry the fingers of bondage off the Hebrew people. The final of the ten plagues was the Angel of Death hovering over the nation of Egypt and taking the life of every firstborn male. God had warned the Israelites this was going to happen, and through Moses, they received instructions that every family was to prepare for their deliverance and departure, make a very simple meal, eat it in haste so they could remain mobile, and wait for their exodus the next morning. Passover was their simple meal. Exodus 12 describes this moment in history:

- The Israelites were instructed to take one lamb per household on the tenth day of the month. It was to be a yearling male without blemish (Exodus 12:5).

- Each family was to bring their lamb in or near their home and care for it until the fourteenth day of the month when they were to slaughter it at twilight (Exodus 12:6).

- Once the lamb was slaughtered, they were to take its blood and paint it on the doorposts of their home with a branch of hyssop to display obedience to God so the Angel of Death would pass them over and not touch their firstborn (Exodus 12:7).

- After they spread the blood, they were to prepare the meat by roasting it in fire and eating unleavened bread with bitter herbs. Leaven, also known as yeast, works through the bread dough and takes too much time to prepare the bread for baking. Its effect on the bread causes it to rise, but because of this, leaven usually represents sin in God's imagery in the Bible. No leaven, or yeast, was to be used on this night of deliverance (Exodus 12:8). (This is also the reason why it's possible that the 'wine' that was received was non-alcoholic. Wine has gone through a process of fermentation that includes yeast. If yeast was not permitted in the bread, why would it be permitted in the wine?)

- God wouldn't allow the Israelites to keep any leftovers, meaning this meal was sufficient for this one night (Exodus 12:10).

- The Hebrews were to eat the Passover meal with their belt fastened, sandals on, and staff in their hand, ready for swift departure in obedience to God's leading when they were told to exit Egypt (Exodus 12:11).

- This meal was their preparation for God's judgment on Egypt and God's deliverance for Israel. God was about to "pass over" and anyone on whom the sign of the blood of the lamb was not present would reap the destruction of their firstborn (Exodus 12:12-13). Passover was a picture of God's protection, provision, redemption, and salvation for the people He was in covenant with according to Genesis 12:3. God asked them to receive this Passover meal annually on the same day of the year to remember what God had done and to remind them of how God wanted to continue to be with them.

Exodus 12:14 ESV [86]
14 *"This day shall be for you a memorial day, and you shall keep it as a feast to the Lord; throughout your generations, as a statute forever, you shall keep it as a feast.*

CHAPTER 10

Why do we need this understanding of an Old Testament story when talking about the act of Communion in the New Testament? It's because *this* was the meal that Jesus and His disciples were receiving when we first see the Lord's Supper in Luke 22. The symbolism that God had hidden in the Passover meal, (also called Seder, which the Jewish people still celebrate today), was playing out before the disciples' very eyes.

In Luke 22, the Hebrew people made their annual pilgrimage to Jerusalem for the festival of Passover, like they had every year since they inherited the Promised Land. The city was bustling with people and festivities. Lambs were being slaughtered, unleavened bread was being prepared, and bitter herbs were set on tables–all in remembrance of how God had delivered the Israelites so many generations before. The disciples knew that Jesus would want to receive Passover, so they asked Him where He would want to partake. They followed His instructions and they prepared the meal that was prescribed in Exodus 12. When Jesus and the rest of the disciples arrived, the table was set for the anticipated yearly feast of Passover.

The symbolism that God had hidden in the Passover meal...was playing out before the disciples' very eyes.

Throughout the Gospels (Matthew, Mark, Luke, and John), you will find that the story of Jesus played out over approximately three and a half years. Jesus made many pilgrimages to Jerusalem throughout His life to remain true to the Hebrew traditions and laws. But there was something significant about *this* journey during *this* Passover. Jesus had risen in prominence consistently. People knew who He was. He had just raised Lazarus from the dead and the Bible says that the chief priests and scribes were looking for a way to put Jesus to death. To them, He was a nuisance and they feared what His fame would do to the people they were responsible for leading.

Luke 22:2 [32]
2 And the chief priests and the scribes sought how they might kill Him, for they feared the people.

FOUNDATION STONES

As Jesus sat down with His disciples that fateful night, He played out everything prescribed in Exodus 12 to the smallest detail. But then, He did something very powerful. He held up the Unleavened Bread and told them what it represented. Through this revelation, we find out the unleavened bread had always represented the sinless body of our Savior:

> *Luke 22:19* [32]
> *19 And He took bread, gave thanks and broke it, and gave it to them, saying, "This is My body which is given for you; do this in remembrance of Me."*

Then He took the cup of wine and told the disciples what it represented (again, yes, from the beginning):

> *Luke 22:20* [32]
> *20 Likewise He also took the cup after supper, saying, "This cup is the new covenant in My blood, which is shed for you.*

Understand, there are some denominations in Christianity that will teach that when we receive communion the bread and the drink actually *become the real and actual* Body and Blood of Jesus. But when we read the Gospel accounts and Paul's instruction in 1 Corinthians 11, what we see is an act of worship *symbolizing* what Jesus did. It was something to do *"in remembrance of"*. It's a picture. It's an illustration. It's a *reminder* so we can stay aligned with God in reverence!

There's another piece to this puzzle, another layer to the symbolism of Passover. It's how Jesus is described prophetically in scripture. He is "Immanuel, God with us" (Isaiah 7:14, Matthew 1:23). He is the "Bread of Life" (John 6:35). He is the "I AM" (John 8:58), where Jesus used the same title God the Father used to describe Himself to Moses at the burning bush in Exodus 3. And He is "the Lamb who takes away the sin of the world" (John 1:29).

> *John 1:29* [4]
> *29 The next day John saw Jesus coming toward him, and said, "Behold! The Lamb of God who takes away the sin of the world!*

CHAPTER 10

Jesus, the Lamb of God. The Passover Lamb.

That fateful Passover night, Jesus and His disciples received their meal and then went to the Garden of Gethsemane, where Jesus prayed earnestly and cried out to the Father in preparation for His execution. He was arrested, put on trial, beaten and abused, paraded through the common market, bleeding all the way, and then hung on a cross for all to see. He was crucified at approximately *nine o'clock in the morning*, which would have been described in Jewish timekeeping as the third hour of the day:

Mark 15:25 [87]

25 Now it was the third hour, and they crucified Him.

At noon, the darkness of death covered the land and remained that way for three more hours.

Mark 15:33 [87]

33 Now when the sixth hour had come, there was darkness over the whole land until the ninth hour.

At the ninth hour, Jesus cried out and died–three o'clock in the afternoon.

Mark 15:34 [87]

34 And at the ninth hour Jesus cried out with a loud voice, saying, "Eloi, Eloi, lama sabachthani?" which is translated, "My God, My God, why have You forsaken Me?"

Mark 15:37 [87]

37 And Jesus cried out with a loud voice, and breathed His last.

Something significant happened at this exact moment that we can't miss. It has everything to do with Passover, and subsequently what Jesus did around the table with His disciples when He had them drink the cup representing His blood:

FOUNDATION STONES

Mark 15:38 [87]

38 Then the veil of the temple was torn in two from top to bottom.

Why is this so significant? First of all, you'll remember that God had ordained for a Lamb to be slaughtered to eat it at dark during Passover. The Passover Lamb was traditionally slaughtered at 3 PM. The high priest would have likely been in the Holy Place to present the Blood of the Passover Lamb the moment Jesus died. We also find in a survey of scripture that the Ark of the Covenant had not been in the Holy of Holies for many hundreds of years up to this point. It had been hidden away when Jerusalem was sacked in history and hadn't been seen since. This means that every time a priest went into this place, it was in religious duty and show, but the presence of God was not there. When the mighty earthquake hit at 3 PM the day Jesus was crucified, at the very moment He died, the curtain–a strong, thick fabric woven with great care–tore from top to bottom. It exposed the Old Covenant as a pattern *pointing* to a New Covenant. The Blood of the true Passover Lamb had released the New Covenant of God Almighty which included all the nations of the world—not just the Hebrews!

The Blood of the true Passover Lamb had released the New Covenant of God Almighty which included all the nations of the world...

Luke 22:20 [32]

20 Likewise He also took the cup after supper, saying, "This cup is the new covenant in My blood, which is shed for you.

No wonder when we receive communion and remember what Jesus did, it's so powerful and important! We can never forget what Jesus did for us, how He included us in His story of redemption, and how He wants to continue to release His delivering power and grace over our lives! Communion as an instruction is for us to never forget the massive sacrifice, the eternal breakthrough, and the never-ending glory of what God has done for us through the death, burial, and resurrection of His Son Jesus Christ!

CHAPTER 10

PRESERVING THE PURITY OF COMMUNION

As often happens when we lose the heart of why something was instituted, we find that, over time, communion had become a religious ritual without the awe in some places in the early church. Paul the Apostle was appalled. He went to great lengths to correct this travesty in his description of what communion was all about:

> *1 Corinthians 11:23-32* [88]
> *23 For I received from the Lord that which I also delivered to you: that the Lord Jesus on the same night in which He was betrayed took bread; 24 and when He had given thanks, He broke it and said, "Take, eat; this is My body which is broken for you; do this in remembrance of Me." 25 In the same manner He also took the cup after supper, saying, "This cup is the new covenant in My blood. This do, as often as you drink it, in remembrance of Me." 26 For as often as you eat this bread and drink this cup, you proclaim the Lord's death till He comes. 27 Therefore whoever eats this bread or drinks this cup of the Lord in an unworthy manner will be guilty of the body and blood of the Lord. 28 But let a man examine himself, and so let him eat of the bread and drink of the cup. 29 For he who eats and drinks in an unworthy manner eats and drinks judgment to himself, not discerning the Lord's body. 30 For this reason many are weak and sick among you, and many sleep. 31 For if we would judge ourselves, we would not be judged. 32 But when we are judged, we are chastened by the Lord, that we may not be condemned with the world.*

As often happens when we lose the heart of why something was instituted, we find that...communion has become a religious ritual without the awe in some places in the early church. Paul...went to great lengths to correct this travesty in his description of what communion was all about.

The Corinthian church had lost the depth and meaning of what the Lord's Supper, Communion, was all about. They were operating in 'classes' where people who had greater importance or affluence than others were treated better than the poor or afflicted. They used the Lord's Supper as an opulent feast, a way to display their wealth, and a way to push those of lesser net worth to the side. Division was fueled by a religious spirit. Communion had become a symbol of religious arrogance rather than a display of Christian humility, family, and equal standing before God. And Paul had had enough. He instructed them on the heartbeat of why Jesus instituted communion in the first place. He then warned the Corinthians that they were actually eating and drinking judgment on themselves if they didn't retain the reverence toward what Jesus did by taking communion *together* in humility, unity, and self-reflection.

With this understanding, what is the point of communion? What are the reasons we are to continue to partake in communion as an act of worship throughout our earthly lives and service to Jesus?

REMEMBER THE PRESENCE OF JESUS

This is not simply a religion we are following. There are two times Jesus instructed us to receive communion in *remembrance* of Him: when we break and eat the bread representing His broken body, and when we receive the cup representing His shed blood. Jesus said when we come together in agreement, He is there in our midst!

Matthew 18:20 [89]
20 For where two or three are gathered together in My name, I am there in the midst of them."

While communion *can* be received alone, there is *power* in communion being received together as a church family, which is the family of God. We're to remember that Jesus gave us the ultimate sacrifice and the ultimate example of selflessness. Paul was shocked that the Corinthians were receiving communion while they were so divided! They intentionally put up barriers of social status between one another and used communion to do it!

CHAPTER 10

> *1 Corinthians 11:18-22 ESV* [90]
>
> *18 For first of all, when you come together as a church, I hear that there are divisions among you, and in part I believe it. 19 For there must also be factions among you, that those who are approved may be recognized among you. 20 Therefore, when you come together in one place, it is not to eat the Lord's Supper. 21 For in eating, each one takes his own supper ahead of others; and one is hungry and another is drunk. 22 What! Do you not have houses to eat and drink in? Or do you despise the church of God and shame those who have nothing? What shall I say to you? Shall I praise you in this? I do not praise you.*

Paul is pulling the rug out from underneath pride and arrogance–those things that trigger separation and division. He's saying that the receiving of communion is the ultimate display of oneness that supersedes our financial standing, racial standing, and social status. You'll find in John 15-17, right after the Lord's Supper, Jesus spends a long time praying that the disciples would "be one" as He and the Father were one. It's not an accident that this was His prayer right after the Lord's Supper!

...Jesus spent a long time praying that the disciples would "be one" as He and the Father were one...

Communion refocuses our hearts when we've become distracted or discouraged. In 1 Corinthians 11, Paul relays to the Corinthian believers that Jesus instructed them to "do this in remembrance of Me". The reason he instructed them to do this is because when Christians remember what Jesus did, we keep our focus on what we believe, how we live, how we treat others, and where we're going as His disciples on earth:

> *1 Corinthians 11:26* [90]
>
> *26 For as often as you eat this bread and drink this cup, you proclaim the Lord's death till He comes.*

What an interesting phrase. When we receive communion, we "proclaim the Lord's death until He comes". Communion reminds us of the price Jesus paid for our forgiveness. The longer we are Christians, the more we run the risk of taking for granted what Jesus did for us in His ultimate sacrifice. It becomes commonplace for us to know that Jesus saved us, forgave us, and set us free to live for Him. We take for granted that our names are written down in heaven. Communion returns us to the sober recognition that Jesus paid a price none of us could have paid, and we've been given a gift worth immeasurably more than we can fathom:

2 Corinthians 5:14-15 [91]
14 For the love of Christ compels us, because we judge thus: that if One died for all, then all died; 15 and He died for all, that those who live should live no longer for themselves, but for Him who died for them and rose again.

Communion is an act of continual surrender reminding us that we need Jesus because we can't be holy and acceptable to God on our own. We need His finished work of the cross. Communion causes us to examine our hearts. Where am I today? Is my heart fully surrendered? Am I in full compliance with God's Word, His gift, and His standards? In 1 Corinthians, Paul continues his correction of the abuses the Corinthian church was involved in regarding communion:

1 Corinthians 11:28 [90]
28 But let a man examine himself, and so let him eat of the bread and drink of the cup.

Is my heart fully surrendered?
Am I in full compliance with God's Word, His gift,
and His standards?

As we examine our hearts and begin to repent and acknowledge Jesus' Lordship in our lives again, we proclaim the Lord's death to ourselves, our Church Family, and to the world. We declare through this act of worship, "What Jesus did is enough! Receive Him!" This declaration of Jesus' sacrifice keeps us motivated to share the Good News! When we have a regular reminder of God's great love for us, it ignites our hearts again to tell other people the good news that Jesus can forgive them, too! Consider, when you proclaim the death of Christ, you also proclaim His resurrection power of forgiveness of sins!

Because of this surrender to Jesus, we are compelled by the love of God. We can't help but share the Good News! We *proclaim* the Lord's death! We speak the Good News of Jesus Christ. We have the passion and commission of the Good News restarted in our hearts as we remember Christ and His sacrifice during the act of communion.

Because of this surrender to Jesus, we are compelled by the love of God...to share the Good News!

WHEN WE RECEIVE COMMUNION, WE RECEIVE THE NEW COVENANT

Paul is reminding the church that we are under a New Covenant. Jesus told us that His blood shed on the cross was the cup of the New Covenant. No longer are we under the weight of the law–the do's and don'ts of scripture. Our correct behavior becomes an overflow of our relationship with God and not just our human effort fueled by religion. We're under the New Covenant of grace that empowers us to live as sons and daughters of God! We're no longer just religious drones. We're activated to partner with God and His plan of redemption for the world. We have been given salvation and freedom in Jesus. Communion reminds us that we're living in *God's grace*. What Jesus did by shedding His blood is the hinge of all history. Jesus pivoted the world from the letter of the law to the open heaven of grace that the law pointed to all along!

COMMUNION HELPS US REMAIN REPENTANT AND CLEANSED

Communion returns us to the revelation of forgiveness and causes us to seek God in humble surrender and repentance so that we can walk in continual freedom and grace! God's grace is not a license to sin. It's empowerment to live for Christ free from sin!

Romans 6:1-4 ESV [92]
1 What shall we say then? Shall we continue in sin that grace may abound? 2 Certainly not! How shall we who died to sin live any longer in it? 3 Or do you not know that as many of us as were baptized into Christ Jesus were baptized into His death? 4 Therefore we were buried with Him through baptism into death, that just as Christ was raised from the dead by the glory of the Father, even so, we also should walk in newness of life.

Communion causes us to remain dependent on Jesus for salvation and not ourselves. We can't earn God's attention or forgiveness. We can only receive what has already been given. Communion is our regular reminder of this Biblical fact:

Ephesians 2:8-9 [21]
8 For by grace you have been saved through faith, and that not of yourselves; it is the gift of God, 9 not of works, lest anyone should boast.

As a result of this perspective on the importance of communion, Paul emphasizes that we must examine ourselves. We must approach God humbly and allow the Holy Spirit to shine His light and conviction into our hearts. While we receive communion, we allow God access to every deep place of our hearts so we come out cleansed, refocused, humble, and empowered to declare the Gospel!

...we allow God access to every deep place of our hearts...

CHAPTER 10

> *1 Corinthians 11:27-32 ESV* [90]
>
> *27 Therefore whoever eats this bread or drinks this cup of the Lord in an unworthy manner will be guilty of the body and blood of the Lord. 28 But let a man examine himself, and so let him eat of the bread and drink of the cup. 29 For he who eats and drinks in an unworthy manner eats and drinks judgment to himself, not discerning the Lord's body. 30 For this reason many are weak and sick among you, and many sleep. 31 For if we would judge ourselves, we would not be judged. 32 But when we are judged, we are chastened by the Lord, that we may not be condemned with the world.*

Our personal holiness is dependent on Jesus and our surrender to Him. One of the great traps of being a "Good Christian" is becoming impressed with our own piety. We're easily impressed with ourselves. Our spiritual arrogance can quickly replace reverence and humility. We can begin to excuse sin and pacify fleshly compromises. Communion returns us to the *Source of our freedom* and reminds us of our great need for Jesus!

COMMUNION PREPARES US FOR RESTORED RELATIONSHIPS WITH OTHERS

Again, we *can* receive communion alone, between us and God. But, notice how often communion is displayed scripturally in a *corporate setting*. I believe communion has an equalizing effect on the Body of Christ. It doesn't matter who you are, we're all in need of the grace of Jesus. Communion reminds us that we *need one another* under the Lordship of Jesus Christ. One of the things that will rise to the surface quickly when we examine our hearts in communion is division with other people. God expects forgiveness. He expects love, respect, and honor between His followers. Communion reminds us that Christ died for everyone, not just one individual. The people all around us are *just as valuable* in God's eyes as we are, which causes our spiritual pride to crumble. If God can forgive them, why can't we?

Communion is a great *revealer*. It will expose our true motives and intentions. Notice on the night Jesus implemented the Lord's Supper, it was immediately afterward that the disciples argued about who was greater than who:

FOUNDATION STONES

Luke 22:24-27 [32]

24 Now there was also a dispute among them, as to which of them should be considered the greatest. 25 And He said to them, "The kings of the Gentiles exercise lordship over them, and those who exercise authority over them are called 'benefactors.' 26 But not so among you; on the contrary, he who is greatest among you, let him be as the younger, and he who governs as he who serves. 27 For who is greater, he who sits at the table, or he who serves? Is it not he who sits at the table? Yet I am among you as the One who serves.

Is it any wonder that a dispute arose among them as soon as they received communion together? Communion tends to uncover the true motives of our hearts. Their pride boiled to the surface when they were faced with the holiness of communion. This gave Jesus the opportunity to expose the mission of the Kingdom: "I did not come to be served, but to serve" (Vs. 27).

What a powerful sacrament Jesus gave us in communion! What a gift of recalibration that He gave us! What reverence we should walk in as we receive it. If we want our lives to be regularly transformed and aligned with God, we've got to make sure communion is something we take very seriously.

Communion tends to uncover the true motives of our hearts...

It's important to receive communion without mindless religious motion attached to it. We must retain its sacredness, meaning, and depth. Don't let it become an empty religious ritual. Communion can retain its meaning if we preserve our sincerity, but beware of making it robotic by ensuring it's always done mindfully. We always want to safeguard the genuineness of our worship. It's important to plan communion as a corporate act of worship when we feel moved by the Holy Spirit. That way we can give the proper reverence communion deserves. We never want it to become a religious ritual that loses its richness. We want it to retain great reverence and depth. We want to embark on a moment of corporate worship that will help center us and transform our lives!

CHAPTER 10

As interesting as it sounds, some in Christianity decry the 'ordinances of the faith', as we call them. They argue that we don't *have* to do them. Some even contend that we *shouldn't* do them because we're embarking on 'works' for salvation. There is a big difference between attempting to earn our salvation through religious rituals and engaging in a sacrament as a memorial that helps keep us aligned with God in our relationship. There are two ordinances that scripture points to that are important to implement in our walk with Jesus: Baptism and Communion. Since we've studied both baptism and communion now, let's look at the importance of both of these acts as ordinances.

Ordinance: *a prescribed usage, practice, or ceremony* [93]

Ordinance is a fancy word that describes something Jesus wants us to do in our walk with Him. It's not a prerequisite for salvation. But it *is* a practice that reminds us who God is and who *we* are in light of Him. Ordinances keep us connected to the heart of God, and testify to others of His greatness! Why would we ever resist this? So while ordinances are not salvation issues, we do them to remind our hearts of what is occurring *in us* in relationship with Jesus Christ! Like a beautiful wedding band we give our spouse, an ordinance is a declaration of allegiance and obedience to the One we love, and the One who saved us. Our resistance to these ordinances reveals more about our hearts than we think! Why would we drag our feet to do something Jesus has very clearly told us to do?

Consider the symbolism of these two ordinances: water baptism and communion.

WATER BAPTISM HAPPENS *ONE TIME* AS A SYMBOL OF NEW LIFE

Matthew 28:19-20 [1] *(emphasis added)*
19 Go therefore and make disciples of all the nations, **baptizing them in the name of the Father and of the Son and of the Holy Spirit,** *20 teaching them to observe all things that I have commanded you; and lo, I am with you always, even to the end of the age." Amen.*

Baptism is a part of the instructions Jesus gave about our Great Commission. We're not *just* to preach, but baptize, too! Those who respond to the preaching have been made a new creation through faith in Christ! The old man has died and the new has been resurrected! We baptize into the death of Christ, and a person is raised to new life in Jesus Christ! It's a symbol that testifies to the heart and the world around us!

Water Baptism happens once. But, communion happens *regularly* as a remembrance symbol of sanctification, transformation, and a lifetime of dependence on what Jesus did!

Luke 22:19b [32]
19 "...Do this in remembrance of me."

1 Corinthians 11:26 [90] *(emphasis added)*
26 For ***as often*** *as you eat this bread and drink this cup, you proclaim the Lord's death till He comes.*

The beautiful act of worship in communion is exciting to our hearts and prepares us to want to partake of it with great reverence! Let there be gratitude in your heart for what Jesus made available to you in salvation. Maybe even today, you can receive communion in your living room by yourself or with a loved one, and remember all Jesus has done for you. If not today, the next time you receive communion in a corporate setting of a church service, may your heart overflow with gratitude, repentant examination, and a renewed sense of unity with your brothers and sisters in Christ.

REFLECTION QUESTIONS

1. Do you ever feel like you take communion for granted? If so, how has this chapter helped refocus your mindset on the importance of communion?

___

2. Has communion ever revealed someone to you that you needed to reconcile with? Perhaps there is someone right now that you realize you need to ask forgiveness from or have an honest, loving conversation with. Ask the Lord to show you how to approach them and the words to speak to bring healing in your relationship with that person.

___

3. Communion is a time of reverent remembrance and thanks. Take a moment and write down a few things that you are thankful for, perhaps that the Lord has blessed you with or done for you.

___

CHAPTER 11
HOLY SPIRIT BAPTISM

Filled With His Power

Baptism in water is a public declaration of our faith, a memorial stone for our confession, and a proclamation of the truth of the Gospel of Jesus Christ through our own adherence to Jesus Christ as Lord and Savior.

> *Ephesians 4:1-6 [94] (emphasis added)*
> *1 I, therefore, the prisoner of the Lord, beseech you to walk worthy of the calling with which you were called, 2 with all lowliness and gentleness, with longsuffering, bearing with one another in love, 3 endeavoring to keep the unity of the Spirit in the bond of peace. 4 There is one body and one Spirit, just as you were called in one hope of your calling; 5 one Lord, one faith, **one baptism**; 6 one God and Father of all, who is above all, and through all, and in you all.*

Baptism in water is a public declaration of our faith...

FOUNDATION STONES

Paul is making clear to the Ephesian church that there is *one* Baptism into the Gospel of Jesus Christ. We are baptized into Jesus' name alone. We are baptized as a Christian in the name of Jesus no matter our culture, country, gender, or any other distinction. We're not baptized into the name of Paul, John, James, or any other individual. Your public confession and accompanying water baptism is into the Father, Son, and Holy Spirit–*no one else*! *That* is what is meant by one baptism. This baptism in water unites us all in heart and conduct and lifts up the message of the cross. It eliminates the divisions and personality-chasing that we are all so susceptible to.

The Trinity, the understanding of God in Three Persons, is the understanding that God the Father is the Source and Jesus is the Son, the Begotten of the Father. In other words, the Savior is the imprint of the Father, who is the Source (Hebrews 1). From there, then, the Holy Spirit is the Spirit of Jesus who was sent from the Father to make sure that we were not left as orphans when Jesus returned to heaven after His resurrection.

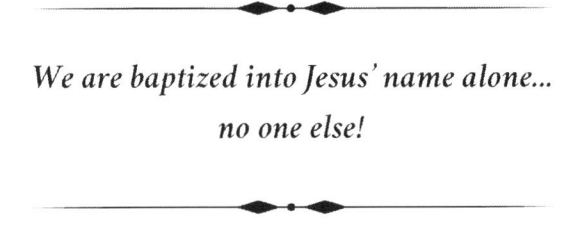

We are baptized into Jesus' name alone...
no one else!

I'd like you to consider this today: never at any time in the history of mankind has God left us alone as orphans. The Spirit of God hovered over the deep as creation began (Genesis 1:2). The Father was present with His People through the Exodus, the establishment of Judaism, and the nation of Israel. Jesus the Son, then, walked among us in the flesh on earth until His ascension after the cross. And *now* the Holy Spirit dwells among us for some very specific reasons as we prepare to meet God in eternity, whether by death or the rapture of the Church.

Old Testament and New Testament scriptures alike prophesy of a time when the Spirit of God would be released on God's people. Not only would the Holy Spirit be present *with* us, but He would dwell *within* us. Jesus told His disciples:

CHAPTER 11

John 14:15-20 [58] *(emphasis added)*
*15 "If you love Me, keep My commandments. 16 And I will pray the Father, and He will give you another Helper, that He may abide with you forever—17 the Spirit of truth, whom the world cannot receive, because it neither sees Him nor knows Him; but you know Him, for He dwells with you and **will be in you**. 18 I will not leave you orphans; I will come to you. 19 "A little while longer and the world will see Me no more, but you will see Me. Because I live, you will live also. 20 At that day you will know that I am in My Father, and you in Me, and **I in you.***

Joel the Prophet proclaimed these words, later echoed by Peter on the Day of Pentecost after the Resurrection of Jesus when he was explaining the sign and wonder of Spirit-infilling that everyone was witnessing:

Joel 2:28-30 [95]
*28 And it shall come to pass afterward
That I will pour out My Spirit on all flesh;
Your sons and your daughters shall prophesy,
Your old men shall dream dreams,
Your young men shall see visions.
29 And also on My menservants and on
My maidservants I will pour out My Spirit in those days.
30 And I will show wonders in the heavens and in the earth:
Blood and fire and pillars of smoke.*

**"If you love Me, keep My commandments...
the Spirit of truth, whom the world cannot receive,
because it neither sees Him nor knows Him;
but you know Him, for He dwells with you and will be in you."**

FOUNDATION STONES

While this chapter's Foundation Stone is about the infilling of the Holy Spirit, one question usually comes up about this gift from God when it is discussed:

DO WE HAVE HOLY SPIRIT IN US WHEN WE GET SAVED?

Let's be clear. It is the Holy Spirit who leads you to salvation. Jesus said we are drawn to Jesus by the Father. Since the drawing of the Father is not something visible to our eyes, we understand that we are being drawn by the Spirit of God toward the salvation of our souls. Jesus said:

John 6:44 [96]
44 "No one can come to Me unless the Father who sent Me draws him; and I will raise him up at the last day."

Romans 8:15-16 [22]
15 For you did not receive the spirit of bondage again to fear, but you received the Spirit of adoption by whom we cry out, "Abba, Father." 16 The Spirit Himself bears witness with our spirit that we are children of God...

It is the Holy Spirit who leads you to salvation...

We believe in Jesus Christ and are transformed in our identities to begin living out the fullness of salvation. This is the change of our actions being aligned with God's holiness. This is a work of the Holy Spirit.

Ephesians 4:20-24 [94]
20 But you have not so learned Christ, 21 if indeed you have heard Him and have been taught by Him, as the truth is in Jesus: 22 that you put off, concerning your former conduct, the old man which grows corrupt according to the deceitful lusts, 23 and be renewed in the spirit of your mind, 24 and that you put on the new man which was created according to God, in true righteousness and holiness.

CHAPTER 11

> *Titus 2:11-15* [97]
>
> *11 For the grace of God that brings salvation has appeared to all men, 12 teaching us that, denying ungodliness and worldly lusts, we should live soberly, righteously, and godly in the present age, 13 looking for the blessed hope and glorious appearing of our great God and Savior Jesus Christ, 14 who gave Himself for us, that He might redeem us from every lawless deed and purify for Himself His own special people, zealous for good works. 15 Speak these things, exhort, and rebuke with all authority. Let no one despise you.*

The transformation of our lives from living in sensual, sinful self-indulgence, to a life of Godly character and submission to Christ is the work of the Holy Spirit who is our Teacher, our Counselor, and our connection in relationship to God the Father. So, yes, we receive the Holy Spirit at salvation. We cannot walk as a genuine Christian without the Holy Spirit.

With this understanding established, we can now turn to the understanding that in our relationship with God through His Holy Spirit, **there is a gift we can receive.**

THE INFILLING OF THE HOLY SPIRIT

This infilling, or baptism, in the Holy Spirit, is revealed in many places throughout the counsel of God's Word. Jesus painted a beautiful picture of what is meant by "baptism" in this statement He made to His disciples. Jesus was on a mission. It is the Holy Spirit who leads you to salvation.

> *Luke 24:45-49* [98] *(emphasis added)*
>
> *45 And He opened their understanding, that they might comprehend the Scriptures. 46 Then He said to them, "Thus it is written, and thus it was necessary for the Christ to suffer and to rise from the dead the third day, 47 and that repentance and remission of sins should be preached in His name to all nations, beginning at Jerusalem. 48 And you are witnesses of these things. 49 Behold, I send the Promise of My Father upon you; but **tarry** in the city of Jerusalem **until you are endued with power from on high.**"*

FOUNDATION STONES

The word "until" here is pointing us toward an event. Jesus was telling His disciples that they would recognize this moment when it occurred. Something about this future moment would be unmistakable–everyone would know something supernatural had happened. What was the signal of this event? What would be the confirmation that this moment had arrived? The prophet Joel describes the event of the infilling, or baptism, in the Holy Spirit by prophesying what would happen to empower God's people in the last days:

Joel 2:28-29 [95]
28 And it shall come to pass afterward
That I will pour out My Spirit on all flesh;
Your sons and your daughters shall prophesy,
Your old men shall dream dreams,
Your young men shall see visions.
29 And also on My menservants and on
My maidservants I will pour out My Spirit in those days.

The distinction of the Baptism in the Holy Spirit is that this experience is a *gift that is received* like salvation. This is something additional to having the Holy Spirit in us to draw us to salvation and help us live a Godly life. This is an indwelling of God living in us to *empower* us to effectively and powerfully advance the Gospel of Jesus Christ. Yes, you receive the Holy Spirit at conversion. But you receive the Baptism in the Holy Spirit, which is His empowerment and supernatural fuel–the 'clothing with power from on high'–as a gift that is given by God. This gift is directly connected to the Great Commission Jesus gave to His disciples right before He ascended to heaven:

Matthew 28:18-20 [1]
18 And Jesus came and spoke to them, saying, "All authority has been given to Me in heaven and on earth. 19 Go therefore and make disciples of all the nations, baptizing them in the name of the Father and of the Son and of the Holy Spirit, 20 teaching them to observe all things that I have commanded you; and lo, I am with you always, even to the end of the age." Amen.

CHAPTER 11

Jesus was clear there was a very distinct experience that would prepare His disciples for effective witness. Jesus spoke of a "clothing" of His power. He prophesied about an experience that was the direct result of waiting for the Father's gift. And Jesus was clear that this experience was in order to empower His followers to witness and minister in the power of God.

> *Acts 1:4-8[99] (emphasis added)*
>
> *4 And being assembled together with them, He commanded them not to depart from Jerusalem, but to wait for the Promise of the Father, "which," He said, "you have heard from Me; 5 for John truly baptized with water, but you **shall be baptized with the Holy Spirit** not many days from now." 6 Therefore, when they had come together, they asked Him, saying, "Lord, will You at this time restore the kingdom to Israel?" 7 And He said to them, "It is not for you to know times or seasons which the Father has put in His own authority. 8 But **you shall receive power when the Holy Spirit has come upon you; and you shall be witnesses to Me in Jerusalem, and in all Judea and Samaria, and to the end of the earth.**"*

[Holy Spirit Baptism] is an indwelling of God living in us to empower us to effectively and powerfully advance the Gospel of Jesus Christ...This gift is directly connected to the Great Commission Jesus gave to His disciples right before He ascended to heaven...

You see, the result of this clothing of power–the baptism of the Holy Spirit in your life–is the courage, power, and demonstration of the Gospel of Jesus Christ throughout the world, accompanied by powerful and bold declarations, signs, and wonders.

Let's consider a question. What are the chances of a movement started by a man during a three-and-a-half-year stint of ministry two millennia ago so radically revolutionizing the world that the world's calendar shifted, every corner of the earth was impacted, and every generation since has heard His name? Consider that the movement and expansion of Christianity has not ceased over two millennia. It's actually *increased* in momentum and influence! We have to admit this is no ordinary faith. We have to ask the question–was there something *supernatural* behind this man, Jesus Christ, and *His followers?*

The disciples of Jesus were so fearful during Jesus' crucifixion that they fled for their lives. Fifty days later they were so emboldened that they spent the rest of their lives willing to die for Jesus. And as a matter of fact, almost all of them *did* give their lives for Jesus Christ. What happened to these disciples that transformed them from timid fishermen and tax collectors to inflamed megaphones for the message of the man who died on the cross in just a few week's time?

Let's look at the result of their obedience to wait in Jerusalem until "The Gift" that God promised came:

> *Acts 2:1-21* [59] *(emphasis added)*
> *1 When the Day of Pentecost had fully come, they were all with one accord in one place. 2 And suddenly there came a sound from heaven, as of a rushing mighty wind, and it filled the whole house where they were sitting. 3 Then there appeared to them divided tongues, as of fire, and one sat upon each of them. 4 And* ***they were all filled with the Holy Spirit and began to speak with other tongues, as the Spirit gave them utterance.*** *5 And there were dwelling in Jerusalem Jews, devout men, from every nation under heaven. 6 And when this sound occurred, the multitude came together, and were confused, because everyone heard them speak in his own language. 7 Then they were all amazed and marveled, saying to one another, "Look, are not all these who speak Galileans? 8 And how is it that we hear, each in our own language in which we were born? 9 Parthians and Medes and Elamites, those dwelling in Mesopotamia, Judea and Cappadocia, Pontus and Asia,*

CHAPTER 11

*10 Phrygia and Pamphylia, Egypt and the parts of Libya adjoining Cyrene, visitors from Rome, both Jews and proselytes, 11 Cretans and Arabs—we hear them speaking in our own tongues the wonderful works of God." 12 So they were all amazed and perplexed, saying to one another, "Whatever could this mean?" 13 Others mocking said, "They are full of new wine." 14 But Peter, standing up with the eleven, raised his voice and said to them, "Men of Judea and all who dwell in Jerusalem, let this be known to you, and heed my words. 15 For these are not drunk, as you suppose, since it is only the third hour of the day. 16 But this is what was spoken by the prophet Joel: 17 'And it shall come to pass in the last days, says God, That **I will pour out of My Spirit on all flesh;** Your sons and your daughters shall prophesy, Your young men shall see visions, Your old men shall dream dreams. 18 And on My menservants and on My maidservants I will pour out My Spirit in those days; And they shall prophesy. 19 I will show wonders in heaven above And signs in the earth beneath: Blood and fire and vapor of smoke. 20 The sun shall be turned into darkness, And the moon into blood, Before the coming of the great and awesome day of the LORD. 21 And it shall come to pass That whoever calls on the name of the LORD Shall be saved."*

Let's look at some marks of what happened with this experience:

- They were waiting together in unity in obedience to Jesus.

- A wind from heaven came, bringing what appeared to be flames that rested on each of them.

- They were filled with the Holy Spirit.

- They spoke in other tongues (languages).

- They were bold and spoke to other people about God!

FOUNDATION STONES

Several years ago, my wife and I, along with several from our church, were on a mission trip to the Philippines. We were ministering at a youth camp and were building relationships with teenagers from many walks of life. Some of them had a wholesome upbringing, but many of them grew up as outcasts and orphans and were being brought back into their God-given value by the churches we were partnering with. One night, my wife shared a very vulnerable story from her own past about feeling a sense of abandonment as a child. She emphasized the need to forgive those who had stepped out on her so that God could restore her heart. There was a powerful altar time of forgiveness where tears flowed and teenagers wept as God healed their hearts. It was incredibly powerful! However, we did not fully know what that cleansing and restoration would result in throughout the duration of the camp.

The next morning, as we spent time in worship, a holy hush came over the gathering of young people. It was reverent and almost uncomfortable to experience a group of teenagers that large get that quiet and expectant. We waited on God for quite some time, not really knowing why. Some teens were on their knees in the front, and others sitting or standing around the meeting area. One sixteen-year-old boy in particular was standing in the middle aisle with his eyes closed and his hands lifted. We had learned before that this boy was an orphan who was being raised by the church. He had no parents or family. The night before, he had surrendered the hurt he felt toward his absent parents and had received a healing in his heart that he desperately needed. And now, he stood in the presence of God, seeking the One who promised He would never leave.

All around him, other teenagers began
to experience the same thing.
Languages unknown to anyone were being spoken,
kids were surrendering and crying out to God,
and hearts were being filled as tears flowed...

CHAPTER 11

Suddenly, the silence was broken by this young man loudly crying out in a language nobody knew. It wasn't English, and it wasn't his native Philippine language, Cebuano. He cried out for several seconds in this new language, began to weep, and then suddenly collapsed to the ground, weeping and surrendering to God. His experience was like a lightning bolt to the gathering of teenagers. All around him, other teenagers began to experience the same thing. Languages unknown to anyone were being spoken, kids were surrendering and crying out to God, and hearts were being filled as tears flowed. There was a roar of adoration of God that was completely uncoached, unexpected, reverent, holy, and powerful! The amazing thing was that we had not even taught about baptism in the Holy Spirit. These teenagers had no idea what was happening but were being radically touched by the Holy Spirit.

From that moment forward, a move of God started happening in these teenagers and their churches. They were bold to proclaim the Gospel and lives were transformed. It was as if we were living with a front-row seat to the Book of Acts!

Some would say that tongues and the supernatural gifts of the Spirit were only for the times of the Apostles. Because of this, at times there is a religious ridicule of anything that could be construed as "weird" or "out of control" in our Christian experience. While I am an advocate for order (scripture tells us that God is not the author of confusion, but of order, 1 Corinthians 14:33), I challenge you to find a single scripture in the Bible that says the manifestations of the Spirit died out with the first generations of Christians and that we should no longer expect them. I have found quite the opposite to be true. Much of the New Testament is *filled* with instructions on exactly what the movement and gifts of the Holy Spirit are, why we should use them by describing what they accomplish, and *how* to use them. Not one time does the Bible say the Holy Spirit and His gifts are not necessary now that the Church is established.

Paul says to the Ephesian church:

Ephesians 5:18 NLT[100] (emphasis added)
*18 Don't be drunk with wine, because that will ruin your life. Instead, **be filled with the Holy Spirit**...*

Galatians describes the Fruit that will manifest in our lives through the Holy Spirit, which is love, joy, peace, patience, kindness, goodness, gentleness, faithfulness, and self-control (Galatians 5:22-23). Then, the book of 1 Corinthians is *filled* with instructions on how to use the gifts of the Spirit in the Church. *Not once* are we told the gifts have expired. Not once are we told tongues were to only be used by the Apostles on the Day of Pentecost. Not once are we told we shouldn't receive or give prophecy. We are told *not to despise prophecy*, but to *make room* for it. The instructions given are that there should be order, decency, and accountability to other people with the same gift. In other words, we shouldn't go crazy in our flesh, but be subjected to the Lord and in honor toward one another *as we operate* in the gifts of the Holy Spirit:

I Corinthians 14:39-40[102]
39 Therefore, brethren, desire earnestly to prophesy, and do not forbid to speak with tongues. 40 Let all things be done decently and in order.

WHY ARE TONGUES A SIGN OF HOLY SPIRIT BAPTISM?

Many might ask, "What's with this speaking in tongues thing?" In our natural thinking, it does seem like a strange manifestation for the Holy Spirit to cause to happen in and through us. Let me attempt to explain the two avenues of the use of tongues that I see in the New Testament.

First, the gift of tongues can be a *known language* that is spoken to someone from another language and culture. This was the gift given to the disciples of Jesus waiting in the Upper Room on the Day of Pentecost and this is what launched the Gospel of Jesus Christ to other nations just like Jesus said would happen. Those who had traveled from all over the world to celebrate the Day of Pentecost heard the good news of Jesus in his or her own language. There was no doubt something powerful was happening and the tongue was used as a sign from God that the message was true. Consider, if you heard a message in your own language from someone you didn't know from a different land who didn't originally know your language, would you maybe consider the message worth listening to?

CHAPTER 11

Second, the gift of tongues is a way to pray and commune with God that is beyond our known language, what has come to be known as a "heavenly prayer language." This also occurred in several places in the narrative of the early church as well.

> *Acts 19:1-7* [101] *(emphasis added)*
> *1 And it happened, while Apollos was at Corinth, that Paul, having passed through the upper regions, came to Ephesus. And finding some disciples 2 he said to them, "Did you receive the Holy Spirit when you believed?" So they said to him, "We have not so much as heard whether there is a Holy Spirit." 3 And he said to them, "Into what then were you baptized?" So they said, "Into John's baptism." 4 Then Paul said, "John indeed baptized with a baptism of repentance, saying to the people that they should believe on Him who would come after him, that is, on Christ Jesus." 5 When they heard this, they were baptized in the name of the Lord Jesus. 6 And when Paul had laid hands on them, the Holy Spirit came upon them, and **they spoke with tongues and prophesied.** Now the men were about twelve in all."*

...the gift of tongues is a way to pray and commune with God that is beyond our known language... a "heavenly prayer language"...

Here are a couple of thoughts to consider:

- Paul ministered to these disciples with an assumption that the infilling was an expectation as a Christian. His question as to whether they had received the Holy Spirit invited these believers into a greater experience in their relationship with God through their faith in Jesus Christ as Savior. Paul wanted these disciples to have this gift just like any other believer.

- When these twelve men heard there was more, they were hungry for more. They allowed themselves to be baptized in Jesus' name and accepted prayer to receive the Holy Spirit. Their humility and hunger for more of God opened them up to receive the clothing of power from on high that Jesus Himself spoke of. If they were open to what God had for them in their day, I suggest that we should be open to it as well–especially in our day.

- If tongues are only for the purpose of speaking a known language to another person, why then would these twelve men start speaking in tongues in this instance? They were already communicating with someone who spoke the same language. If tongues are only for speaking to people of a different earthly language, why would they speak in tongues when only Paul was standing there with them? There would be no need for another language unless the language was for another purpose. This unknown language was for communicating with God from their spirit in prayer.

Their humility and hunger for more of God opened them up to receive the clothing of power from on high...

We can see the combination of the gift of tongues and the gift of prophecy in this moment. God uses these two gifts often as a confirmation of His message. Let's look at 1 Corinthians 14.

I Corinthians 14:1-25 [102]

1 Pursue love, and desire spiritual gifts, but especially that you may prophesy. 2 For he who speaks in a tongue does not speak to men but to God, for no one understands him; however, in the spirit he speaks mysteries. 3 But he who prophesies speaks edification and exhortation and comfort to men. 4 He who speaks in a tongue edifies himself, but he who prophesies edifies the church. 5 I wish you all spoke with tongues, but even more that you prophesied; for he who prophesies is greater than he who speaks with tongues, unless indeed he interprets, that the church may receive edification.

CHAPTER 11

6 But now, brethren, if I come to you speaking with tongues, what shall I profit you unless I speak to you either by revelation, by knowledge, by prophesying, or by teaching? 7 Even things without life, whether flute or harp, when they make a sound, unless they make a distinction in the sounds, how will it be known what is piped or played? 8 For if the trumpet makes an uncertain sound, who will prepare for battle? 9 So likewise you, unless you utter by the tongue words easy to understand, how will it be known what is spoken? For you will be speaking into the air. 10 There are, it may be, so many kinds of languages in the world, and none of them is without significance. 11 Therefore, if I do not know the meaning of the language, I shall be a foreigner to him who speaks, and he who speaks will be a foreigner to me. 12 Even so you, since you are zealous for spiritual gifts, let it be for the edification of the church that you seek to excel. 13 Therefore let him who speaks in a tongue pray that he may interpret. 14 For if I pray in a tongue, my spirit prays, but my understanding is unfruitful. 15 What is the conclusion then? I will pray with the spirit, and I will also pray with the understanding. I will sing with the spirit, and I will also sing with the understanding. 16 Otherwise, if you bless with the spirit, how will he who occupies the place of the uninformed say "Amen" at your giving of thanks, since he does not understand what you say? 17 For you indeed give thanks well, but the other is not edified. 18 I thank my God I speak with tongues more than you all; 19 yet in the church I would rather speak five words with my understanding, that I may teach others also, than ten thousand words in a tongue. 20 Brethren, do not be children in understanding; however, in malice be babes, but in understanding be mature. 21 In the law it is written: "With men of other tongues and other lips I will speak to this people; And yet, for all that, they will not hear Me," says the Lord. 22 Therefore tongues are for a sign, not to those who believe but to unbelievers; but prophesying is not for unbelievers but for those who believe. 23 Therefore if the whole church comes together in one place, and all speak with tongues, and there come in those who are uninformed or unbelievers, will they not say that you are out of your mind? 24 But if all prophesy, and an unbeliever or an uninformed person comes in, he is convinced by all, he is convicted by all. 25 And thus the secrets of his heart are revealed; and so, falling down on his face, he will worship God and report that God is truly among you.

FOUNDATION STONES

The Bible you hold in your hand is filled with instructions on *how* to operate in the gifts of the Spirit. The Bible is not merely a window into how someone *else* served God. Yes, we need models to follow. But this window of God's Word we have received is to give us motivation to seek God for ourselves and see Him move through us in the *same way in our day*! The world we live in needs Jesus! Jesus moves as His people are filled with His Spirit. The Holy Spirit infilling is our *fuel* for moving the Gospel of Jesus Christ forward. Tongues are a sign. Prophecy is a sign. The manifestation of the Gifts of the Spirit through His baptism is a sign to the world that the message we proclaim is true!

There are many places throughout the book of Acts where speaking in tongues is the standard used to confirm Spirit baptism. Good hermeneutics (the discipline of interpreting scripture[103]) teaches us that if there is a pattern established in the Bible over and over, that experience can be expected. We see tongues associated with the Baptism in the Holy Spirit in three distinct places in the book of Acts alone:

- The Day of Pentecost: Acts 2
- The family of Cornelius: Acts 10
- The disciples in Ephesus: Acts 19

The manifestation of tongues is an expected outcome of the infilling of the Holy Spirit, enough so that Paul explained to us thoroughly in 1 Corinthians 14 *how* to use tongues decently and in order and for what purpose. He explained tongues even to the point that He says he wishes *all people* spoke in tongues. This speaks to the possibility that many will resist it. Many will scoff at it. Many will misunderstand it. And unfortunately, many will abuse it.

[Paul] says he wishes all people spoke in tongues...
Many will scoff at it. Many will misunderstand it.
And unfortunately, many will abuse it.

CHAPTER 11

Remember, everything must be done decently and in order. God is not chaotic. Sometimes God allows us to be uncomfortable, but He does not partner with fleshly agendas in using the gifts. His presence will withdraw quickly when people are trying to manifest gifts without submission to God or to the leadership authority that He has established in the Church. In fact, I believe the fleshly agenda of the gifts and the abuse of them by unsubmitted people is the main reason entire streams of Christianity have rejected the Baptism of the Holy Spirit and in some cases have become vehement in preaching against it. It's not because it's not a true doctrine, but because it's been abused by humans and the tainting of Satan to bring confusion and division to the Church and world. Consider God's desired outcome of the Baptism: edification. God wants the gifts to *build up* the Church. If they don't, the gift is not from God. And unfortunately, wrongful use of the gifts of the Spirit has closed many people off from experiencing what Jesus Himself describes as a gift from the Father.

Be open to the infilling Baptism of the Holy Spirit, and learn to be honorable in the use of His gifts! Through the power of the Spirit of God, the Gospel will powerfully move into the dark expanse around us, glorifying Jesus and inviting to salvation those who are lost. I'd like to encourage you to spend some time today, and in the days ahead, to *wait* on God and *ask* for the gift of the Holy Spirit Baptism if you have not received it yet. Be open to what God wants to do in and through you. Allow Him to clothe you with power from on high so you can be His witnesses in Jerusalem, Judea, Samaria, and the ends of the earth (Acts 1:8)!

REFLECTION QUESTIONS

1. What is the infilling of the Holy Spirit for? What do you think of the differentiation of being filled with the Holy Spirit at salvation and being given the gift of the Holy Spirit through the Baptism in the Holy Spirit?

_____
_____
_____
_____
_____
_____

2. The Holy Spirit often does not operate inside our neat little boxes of how we think things should go. Just like the story above where the Holy Spirit descended at the youth camp in the Philippines, try to think of a time when the Holy Spirit worked in such a way in your life. How did you know it was the Holy Spirit moving, rather than emotional hype?

_____
_____
_____
_____
_____
_____

3. We've learned that speaking in tongues is evidence that the Holy Spirit has infilled us. What are some other ways that we can know the Holy Spirit resides in us? (Galatians 5)

_____
_____
_____
_____
_____
_____

CHAPTER 12
FORGIVENESS

Set Free by Freeing Others

One of the most common areas of bondage we will ever encounter in our lives is the area of unforgiveness. When another person harms us in some way, we have a choice to make. We can either harbor the hurt and let it define us, or we choose to forgive so we can move past the offense. Every human being has hurt someone else, and every human being has *been hurt* by someone else. There are obviously varying measures and weights of the offenses committed. A small white lie is much easier to overlook than a heinous abuse of some kind, so the argument against forgiveness many times sounds something like this: "Forgiving that person will let them off the hook! I *can't* forgive them because they're not repentant and what they did to me was so terrible!"

One of the most common areas of bondage we will ever
encounter in our lives is the area of unforgiveness...
We can either harbor the hurt and let it define us,
or we choose to forgive so we can move past the offense.

FOUNDATION STONES

What we must realize is that justice cannot be left to us. Justice must be left to God. We are not righteous judges, and Jesus taught that we will be judged by the same measure we use. When hurt and offense cause deep wounds, we won't distribute justice very well.

Matthew 7:1-2 [2]
1 "Judge not, that you be not judged. 2 For with what judgment you judge, you will be judged; and with the measure you use, it will be measured back to you.

God does not condone offenses, and there are, rightfully, judicial consequences to some things people do to others on earth. Abuses and crimes need to be prosecuted. But, as countless victims who have overcome offenses will tell us, the only way to true spiritual and emotional freedom is by learning how to forgive like Jesus forgave us. Their freedom wasn't in seeing the offender incarcerated. It was found in learning to forgive and release offense. So, in this chapter, please understand that forgiveness is not excusing accountability from offenders. Remember, we each have been guilty of sin ourselves. What this chapter is all about is learning how to overcome the spiritual bondage that enters our hearts when we refuse to forgive. We do this by surrendering to God's way of forgiving trespasses against us *by faith*.

Let's explore Jesus' most famous message and see what He has to say about the need for forgiveness in our lives.

Matthew 6:9-15 [104]
9 In this manner, therefore, pray:
Our Father in heaven, Hallowed be Your name.
10 Your kingdom come. Your will be done On earth as it is in heaven.
11 Give us this day our daily bread.
12 And forgive us our debts, As we forgive our debtors.
13 And do not lead us into temptation, But deliver us from the evil one.
For Yours is the kingdom and the power and the glory forever. Amen.
14 "For if you forgive men their trespasses, your heavenly Father will also forgive you. 15 But if you do not forgive men their trespasses, neither will your Father forgive your trespasses.

CHAPTER 12

Looking at this, the Lord's Prayer, we see some sobering things:

- Worship is the first thing we do when we step before the Lord to pray.

- Jesus emphasizes God's Kingdom being established on earth as it is in heaven, through *us*, for His glory!

- We must receive from God daily what we need from His Word.

- We must forgive those who are in debt to us (people who have offended us in some way).

- We must route around temptations and sins so we can stay pure.

However, there's something Jesus says at the end of His instruction on how to pray that carries so much importance and weight that we can't miss it! Yet, it's not often included in teachings on the Lord's prayer on how to pray and interact with God. Jesus is so serious about this area of forgiveness that he actually applies the full weight of eternity to it so we don't miss how vital and important it is to God the Father.

Matthew 6:14-15 [104] *(emphasis added)*
14 "For if you forgive men their trespasses, your heavenly Father will also forgive you. 15 But if you do not forgive men their trespasses, neither will your Father forgive your trespasses.

Forgive: *to grant relief from payment of* [105]

The true sense of the word "forgive" is found in the selfless act of Christ giving His life for us upon the cross to cancel *our* debt of sin. We all know we don't deserve a pardon, and we certainly have not earned it. If you're like me, I'm overwhelmed and so thankful that Jesus was willing to wash away my sin from my record in heaven. Forgiveness is just that–it's unearned and undeserved. This is at the core of the meaning of forgiveness. We are granted a "pass" for wrongdoing, though we are *absolutely guilty.*

Jesus is telling us in His instruction on how to interact with God in prayer that we are to do the same thing Jesus did to establish a clean relationship and communication with God. Jesus is teaching us that because we *have been forgiven*, we *must* also forgive others who have sinned against us. It's not an option. Look again at what Jesus said after the Lord's Prayer:

Matthew 6:14-15 [104]
14 "For if you forgive men their trespasses, your heavenly Father will also forgive you. 15 But if you do not forgive men their trespasses, neither will your Father forgive your trespasses.

As a genuine, authentic Christian, you can't miss this! Our Bible is clear, "If you do not forgive men their trespasses, neither will your Father forgive your trespasses" (vs. 15).

Our Bible is clear, "If you do not forgive men their trespasses, neither will your Father forgive your trespasses"

FORGIVENESS IS A SALVATION ISSUE

Let's think through this together. Sin cannot enter heaven (Hebrews 12:14). The only way your sins are washed away is *if* you have been forgiven by God (1 John 1:9). So, if you *haven't* been forgiven by God, you can't enter heaven. And here in Matthew 5:15, Jesus just taught that if we don't forgive *others, we cannot be forgiven by God*. That should hit us between the eyes. That should impact our hearts with an urgency like we've never felt before to release forgiveness to those who have hurt us—even if it's difficult and takes a great deal of courage and faith. All of us have dealt with, or *are* dealing with, an earthly relationship where we've been hurt, lied to or abused. Maybe we've been judged and marred by the sin nature of someone else and it's left its mark on our hearts.

CHAPTER 12

Many people say things like "I will never trust again", or "I'll never forgive that person". Trust and forgiveness are two very different things. I would say you can forgive someone, but it doesn't mean you have to blindly trust them. It is possible to establish healthy boundaries with someone and still walk in forgiveness.

Or maybe you've even said, "I hate that person and I hope they get the judgment they deserve". While it sounds empowering for us to say these things like this, Jesus is teaching us in Matthew 5 that by its very nature, this is unforgiveness. If we are not willing to forgive, we *cannot be forgiven*. Without forgiveness, we are not eligible for eternal life in heaven. **Scripturally, forgiveness *is* a salvation issue.** What is salvation? Because of our faith in Christ, salvation is our deliverance from sin and death and eternal separation from God.

If we don't have salvation in Christ, we don't get to go to heaven. We actually go to hell at death–eternally separated from God. We *need* God's forgiveness to be in heaven with Him eternally. We need *His* salvation. We can't be saved without God's forgiveness. And according to Jesus, we don't receive forgiveness from the Father if we are unwilling to forgive others.

I John 4:20 [106]
20 If someone says, "I love God," and hates his brother, he is a liar; for he who does not love his brother whom he has seen, how can he love God whom he has not seen?

We need His salvation.
We can't be saved without God's forgiveness...according to Jesus,
we don't receive forgiveness from the Father
if we are unwilling to forgive others.

FOUNDATION STONES

Matthew 18:21-35 [89]

21 Then Peter came to Him and said, "Lord, how often shall my brother sin against me, and I forgive him? Up to seven times?" 22 Jesus said to him, "I do not say to you, up to seven times, but up to seventy times seven. 23 Therefore the kingdom of heaven is like a certain king who wanted to settle accounts with his servants. 24 And when he had begun to settle accounts, one was brought to him who owed him ten thousand talents. 25 But as he was not able to pay, his master commanded that he be sold, with his wife and children and all that he had, and that payment be made. 26 The servant therefore fell down before him, saying, 'Master, have patience with me, and I will pay you all.' 27 Then the master of that servant was moved with compassion, released him, and forgave him the debt.

28 "But that servant went out and found one of his fellow servants who owed him a hundred denarii; and he laid hands on him and took him by the throat, saying, 'Pay me what you owe!' 29 So his fellow servant fell down at his feet and begged him, saying, 'Have patience with me, and I will pay you all.' 30 And he would not, but went and threw him into prison till he should pay the debt. 31 So when his fellow servants saw what had been done, they were very grieved, and came and told their master all that had been done. 32 Then his master, after he had called him, said to him, 'You wicked servant! I forgave you all that debt because you begged me. 33 Should you not also have had compassion on your fellow servant, just as I had pity on you?' 34 And his master was angry, and delivered him to the torturers until he should pay all that was due to him. 35 "So My heavenly Father also will do to you if each of you, from his heart, does not forgive his brother his trespasses."

How relevant is this story to us today? We've been forgiven for *so* much it pales in comparison to most things other people have done *to* us. Why would we withhold forgiveness from someone else when God didn't withhold forgiveness from us? The master forgave a massive debt, but the heart of the servant was hardened toward his fellow servant and he became judge and jury over him as to whether or not he deserved his forgiveness. He wanted justice but didn't want to extend the same mercy that the master was willing to give him. Why would we expect to retain the King's kindness if we withhold that same kindness from someone else?

CHAPTER 12

Understandably, sometimes things are done *to* us that are so heinous that they can scar us for life. Some may have walked through an abusive relationship, an evil violation, a hatred, or betrayal. The list is endless. What do we do with that? We bring it before the Lord *every day*, asking Him for the grace to forgive the people who truly *don't* deserve it. Only by submitting it to God can we see a breakthrough in our ability to forgive. Just because they don't deserve it doesn't mean we have a right to withhold it, because Jesus didn't withhold forgiveness from us. So what does this mean? It truly means we forgive by *faith*–just like we receive our salvation.

WHAT IF I'VE ALREADY TRIED TO FORGIVE AND IT KEEPS COMING BACK UP?

I've experienced, like many others have, an offense creeping back into my heart after I've extended forgiveness. What do we do with that? Did we truly forgive or are we stuck in a loop? I have determined to keep forgiving no matter how hard it is. Forgive again. Then forgive some more! We forgive by faith every time we feel the unforgiveness creep back in. We must go before the Lord again and again to extend forgiveness until the bondage loses its grip on our hearts. We truly can't afford to harbor unforgiveness in our hearts–it costs us too much.

During one season of life in my early adulthood, I encountered an injustice that was done to my family and me that hurt like a knife in the heart. Despite attempts at reconciliation, there was no forward movement with the individuals involved. A huge gulf of separation and misunderstanding grew and, even though I did all I knew to do to repair the damage, the emotional carnage was severe. I would wake up every morning and sit with the Lord and ask for help to forgive. Then I would forgive by faith. Then I would go about my day. Some days it seemed like there was a great victory. Other days the hurt seemed to hover over my head like a dark cloud. Especially difficult was my weekly chore of mowing the lawn. At the time, my wife and I were renting a cute little house that had a giant lawn, which meant my push mower and I would spend about three hours a week together. I loved being outside in the sunshine and working on the yard, but I found that as the mowing progressed I would get lost in my thoughts and in the drone of the lawn mower.

During those times, I would start to reflect on the hurts and injustices that were done to my family and me and would start to stew over it all over again. By the time I was done mowing the lawn, I had had mock conversations in my mind, justified my hurt, and harbored anger and unforgiveness all over again! It was a toxic loop of hurt that was like a noose around my spiritual neck. So, each time I would have to go back to Jesus and, *by faith*, forgive again. It took quite some time, but I recognized my heart was healing when I started to notice I could mow the lawn without being angry when I was finished.

Think of this. Many times the person you're angry with doesn't even know how bad you're feeling about the whole thing. This can only mean one thing. And it's one thing that God knows very well: **forgiveness is for *you*.** Forgiveness is for *your* freedom in Christ. It's for *your salvation* in Him. Remember what Jesus taught us. If we don't forgive, we cannot *be* forgiven. Oh, how we need *His* forgiveness! What freedom and peace come in knowing that our hearts are clean before Christ and we have let someone else's trespass against us go so it no longer anchors us down in bondage.

Matthew 10:7-8 [67] *(emphasis added)*
7 And as you go, preach, saying, 'The kingdom of heaven is at hand.' 8 Heal the sick, cleanse the lepers, raise the dead, cast out demons. ***Freely you have received, freely give.***

FORGIVENESS IS BOTH INSTANT AND PROGRESSIVE

Forgiveness happens now, but it also happens over time. Let's look at what this means. We forgive the moment we recognize the need to. Even if the person is not present in person, (though an in-person conversation is very beneficial) we immediately confess our forgiveness. This keeps our hearts soft and our motives pure as we process through the offense. We must forgive *by faith*. Even if we don't feel it and even if we don't sense any change. Just forgive in obedience to God's Word! Then walk that forgiveness out through free will on a daily basis. This is the *fruit* of forgiveness, which is outlined in Paul's instructions to the church in Ephesus:

CHAPTER 12

Ephesians 4:32 [94]
32 And be kind to one another, tenderhearted, forgiving one another, even as God in Christ forgave you.

Exercise kindness. Be tender with one another. Forgive one another. We keep our attitudes in check as we process through the hurt by actively surrendering our right to personal justice. Forgiveness doesn't mean we always forget immediately. It doesn't mean it doesn't hurt. It means we are allowing God to take the reins of the healing and we're willing to continue to treat the other person with respect, kindness, and tenderness just like Jesus did for us when we were forgiven by Him! If we don't have contact, or *can't* have contact with the person for whatever reason (incarceration, court order, death, geographic distance), we still daily lay their offense before the Lord and leave the side of justice to Him and His Word. Every life will give an account. We must trust that God is a much better Judge than we are!

NOT FORGIVING OTHERS IS SELF-DESTRUCTIVE

By not forgiving others, we are operating in self-destructive behavior. It's like shoveling all the garbage into a garbage liner and putting it back under the sink of our kitchen, then being surprised that it starts to stink over time. I've heard it said that unforgiveness is like drinking poison and hoping it kills the other person. Unforgiveness is like rampaging through our garden with a shovel trying to crush the gophers to eradicate the varmints, only to discover we also destroyed our crop. Unforgiveness is like leaving the door unlocked to our soul and wondering how bitterness, hatred, anger, and the demonic strategies of depression, anxiety, and division get inside our hearts. Unforgiveness is like locking our front door at night, but realizing when we wake up that our garage door is wide open!

Unforgiveness is like drinking poison and hoping it kills the other person.

We are the doorkeeper to our *own* souls. We must recognize that God has given us the key to the lock to keep Satan out of our lives. Unforgiveness is like a neon *"open"* sign that attracts the enemy of our souls to infiltrate and make a base camp of destruction in our lives. Far too many Christians justify anger, hatred, and resentment toward other people who have created hurt in their lives. Many times, people will concede to reclusion, withhold trust, develop a critical and cynical heart toward anyone else who resembles someone who hurt them, and in many cases develop physical and mental sickness because of the unforgiveness. Many will develop hatred toward another person, all the while confessing Christ as Lord and Christianity as their standard. There is a discontinuity in this entire description. We will hate someone and *still claim to love God!*

1 John 4:20 [106]

20 If someone says, "I love God," and hates his brother, he is a liar; for he who does not love his brother whom he has seen, how can he love God whom he has not seen?

Many will develop hatred toward another person, all the while confessing Christ as Lord and Christianity as their standard.

We have to get to the point where we can see that withholding the gift of forgiveness from our brother or sister is our way of retaining our sense of power and self-righteousness. This is literally us saying, "I have the *right* to withhold mercy from this person because of how badly they hurt me. I am so right about it, that I will punish them by making sure they don't ever get forgiveness from me." That's our way of exerting power over the person who hurt us and protecting ourselves from future hurt. It's distrust in God's instruction of forgiveness. We sometimes determine that we can't, or won't, forgive the person and give them the satisfaction of getting away with what they did to us. This is hatred.

Hatred: *intense dislike or ill will* [107]

CHAPTER 12

Meanwhile, as we withhold forgiveness from others, we say we are grateful that Jesus has forgiven us. We didn't deserve God's forgiveness. We didn't earn that forgiveness. Why do we think the person who hurt us must deserve and earn forgiveness from us? This can be our way of exerting our own self-imposed justice on those who hurt us, and this withholding of forgiveness is more damaging to our own souls than we can ever realize.

> *1 John 2:9-11* [108]
> *9 He who says he is in the light, and hates his brother, is in darkness until now. 10 He who loves his brother abides in the light, and there is no cause for stumbling in him. 11 But he who hates his brother is in darkness and walks in darkness, and does not know where he is going, because the darkness has blinded his eyes.*

Unforgiveness can blind us. If we refuse to forgive, we are in darkness. We think we know where we're going, but we don't because the darkness of hatred and unforgiveness has blinded us. How do we take the blindness off? How do we see the light again?

Forgive.

Forgive by faith. Forgive continually. Forgive with God's help. We can't afford *not* to forgive because heaven is at stake. Our salvation is at stake. What did Jesus say?

> *Matthew 6:14-15* [104] *(**emphasis added**)*
> *14 "For if you forgive men their trespasses, your heavenly Father will also forgive you. 15 But if you do not forgive men their trespasses, **neither will your Father forgive your trespasses.***

Forgive by faith. Forgive continually. Forgive with God's help...

BEING FORGIVEN PAVES THE WAY TO THE GOSPEL

Colossians 3:12-17[109] (emphasis added)
12 Therefore, as the elect of God, holy and beloved, put on tender mercies, kindness, humility, meekness, longsuffering; 13 bearing with one another, and forgiving one another, if anyone has a complaint against another; **even as Christ forgave you, so you also must do.** *14 But above all these things put on love, which is the bond of perfection. 15 And let the peace of God rule in your hearts, to which also you were called in one body; and be thankful. 16 Let the word of Christ dwell in you richly in all wisdom, teaching and admonishing one another in psalms and hymns and spiritual songs, singing with grace in your hearts to the Lord. 17 And whatever you do in word or deed, do all in the name of the Lord Jesus, giving thanks to God the Father through Him.*

Many times, I learned that they never knew the weight of the hurt they had caused me in the first place... This does not always happen, but it does many times. By a simple gesture of forgiveness and repentance, a relationship is restored and the goodness of God is demonstrated.

It seems most people understand they are imperfect and they have made mistakes. Many times, when I've forgiven someone for something I was harboring against them, I learned that they never knew the weight of the hurt they had caused me in the first place. Most of the time, they grieve and apologize in return. This does not always happen, but it does many times. By a simple gesture of forgiveness and repentance, a relationship is restored and the goodness of God is demonstrated. This *cleans the conscience and opens the heart and spirit back up to being used by God.* You step back into the light of Christ!

What this also does is add credibility to the message of Jesus. If we are people who can forgive and give people the love they don't deserve, the world will understand Jesus a little bit better. We are the elect of God. We're on display to a hurting world! We are to live 'other-worldly' in such a way that shows the non-believer how they can find eternal life as well! If we're stumbling around in darkness just like the world is, no wonder people don't want to listen to our message of God's forgiveness. But when we practice forgiveness–when we are free and clean like Jesus wants us to be– and when we're in quality relationships with our brothers and sisters, the world will see Jesus in us! We'll shine like the stars in heaven:

1 John 1:7[110]
7 But if we walk in the light as He is in the light, we have fellowship with one another, and the blood of Jesus Christ His Son cleanses us from all sin.

Philippians 2:14-15[111]
14 Do all things without complaining and disputing, 15 that you may become blameless and harmless, children of God without fault in the midst of a crooked and perverse generation, among whom you shine as lights in the world...

When we practice forgiveness...the world will see Jesus in us!

FORGIVING REFLECTS YOUR CHRIST-LIKE CHARACTER AND CHANGES YOUR FUTURE

If there ever was a character in the Bible that underwent injustice and unfair treatment, it was Joseph from the book of Genesis. Joseph was the favorite son of his father and his eleven brothers became so jealous of him that they kidnapped him, sold him into slavery, and then concocted an untrue story of his death to lie to their father about their scheme to cover up their true actions. Joseph spent a large portion of his youth as a slave and prisoner, falsely accused of rape, and misunderstood. His family back home forgot about him. He was alone with his thoughts and didn't know if he'd ever be a free man again.

Let's put ourselves in his shoes. What would we have thought about our evil brothers if we were Joseph? What would we have thought about the plan of God? After years in bondage, slavery, and imprisonment, would we have come up with a thing or two to say to our brothers? Would we have developed a hatred toward them and maybe even nursed a few sinister fantasies about what we would do to them if we had the chance?

For years, Joseph sat as a captive in his own thoughts, deciding what his character and response would be. Maybe Joseph had his days of hatred and resentment because as a human, it's likely he had some emotions to work through. But the Bible describes a man of character even in prison. He decided often to not harbor hatred toward his brothers. The reason this is true is we get to clearly see in scripture that when he had the chance to exact his revenge on his brothers, it wasn't even in his heart to do so. Through a series of unique events, Joseph became second in command of Egypt. Because of him, the nation prospered, had enough food to feed the multitudes during a famine, and became the source of food even for his Hebrew family who traveled to Egypt to buy supplies.

His brothers didn't recognize him, but he knew who they were. He treated them with kindness. He provided for their needs. And when they realized who he was, they wept and bowed at his feet in repentance. Joseph didn't punish them when he had full authority to do so. He had mercy on them when they had been merciless to him.

Even after the brother's father passed away, the brothers were expecting the wrath of Joseph to fall. They anticipated that the mercy of their powerful brother would be exhausted and now they would be executed. But even in his power, Joseph humbled himself and demonstrated that he had an eternal viewpoint of his plight–not a temporal one.

Consider, this is one of the problems we face with unforgiveness. We look at the here and now. We look at the temporary and earthly realm for our retribution. What if we looked out a little farther and began to see what God could be up to in the situation? It's time to ask God for the bigger picture. Joseph understood God's bigger picture:

CHAPTER 12

Genesis 50:15-21[112] *(emphasis added)*

*15 When Joseph's brothers saw that their father was dead, they said, "Perhaps Joseph will hate us, and may actually repay us for all the evil which we did to him." 16 So they sent messengers to Joseph, saying, "Before your father died he commanded, saying, 17 'Thus you shall say to Joseph: "I beg you, please forgive the trespass of your brothers and their sin; for they did evil to you." ' Now, please, forgive the trespass of the servants of the God of your father." And Joseph wept when they spoke to him. 18 Then his brothers also went and fell down before his face, and they said, "Behold, we are your servants." 19 Joseph said to them, "Do not be afraid, for am I in the place of God? 20 But as for you, you meant evil against me; but **God meant it for good, in order to bring it about as it is this day, to save many people alive.** 21 Now therefore, do not be afraid; I will provide for you and your little ones." And he comforted them and spoke kindly to them.*

Proverbs 25:21-22[12]

21 If your enemy is hungry, give him bread to eat;
And if he is thirsty, give him water to drink;
22 For so you will heap coals of fire on his head,
And the Lord will reward you.

Often, when there's someone we have been hurt by in our lives, it's easy to see them as our enemy. Let's take this scripture to heart and bless those who have hurt us. Let's love them endlessly. Let's watch God turn their hearts around as undeserved love flows their way. We never know what larger picture God may be working on. This is the same thing Jesus did for us! We didn't deserve His forgiveness, but He extended it the moment we asked. The offending person doesn't deserve our forgiveness, but we also didn't deserve forgiveness when *we* were the offenders. Let's be determined to forgive them immediately.

We never know what larger picture God may be working on...

Let's realize we also may need forgiveness someday and we'd want the same mercy extended to us. Let's treat others the way we want to be treated! Does this mean there are no boundaries? Does this mean we allow ourselves to be abused? No, of course not. We need to prayerfully set up quality fences to ensure that we and our families are safe from harm and not put ourselves in a position to get abused again. But, truth be told, most of us run out of forgiveness a long time before we're ever close to being abused. Let's make it our aim to forgive to the point of pain and beyond. Let's ask the Holy Spirit to show us how to establish godly boundaries so we're not a doormat, but extend our capacity to forgive as Joseph did. Joseph had every right to disown his brothers and even have them tortured and executed–if we're looking at it through the lens of human justice. But, God demonstrated great patience and a far-reaching vision in Joseph's life to know that he was being used to save a nation, a people, and the lineage of the Messiah.

Let's remember:

Romans 5:7-9 [113]
7 For scarcely for a righteous man will one die; yet perhaps for a good man someone would even dare to die. 8 But God demonstrates His own love toward us, in that while we were still sinners, Christ died for us. 9 Much more then, having now been justified by His blood, we shall be saved from wrath through Him.

Christ cannot forgive you if you won't forgive others. Let's make it our aim today, before the sun goes down, to extend forgiveness to anyone we have unforgiveness against. Forgiveness is a salvation issue. It's a spiritual health issue. This is an imperative Foundation Stone in our walk with God. With God, nothing is impossible (Luke 1:37)!

REFLECTION QUESTIONS

1. Is there any unforgiveness in your heart that you need to take care of? Take some time to pray and ask the Lord about the incident(s) and how He sees it.

_____
_____
_____
_____
_____

2. Now, take some time to forgive this person (or persons) *by faith*. Feelings do not always follow suit with the decision we have made to forgive. Feelings lie. But that does not mean God is not working and moving in your life.

_____
_____
_____
_____
_____
_____

3. Sometimes, the hardest person to forgive is ourselves. Are there things you have done that Satan has been able to hold over your head? Release those things to Jesus and allow Him to extend his beautiful gift of grace and forgiveness over you.

_____
_____
_____
_____
_____
_____
_____
_____

CHAPTER 13
PRAYER & INTERCESSION

Communing With God

We have a way of elevating other humans to places of prominence. Their fame, fortune, or power causes us to think of certain people in an exalted way. Most of us will never meet a world-famous, powerful person. Chances are good we'll never personally meet the president of the United States, or our favorite music artists or actors. If we ever do get the chance to interact with someone like that, we can get tongue-twisted or say silly things because we're enamored by the position they hold and the high esteem we have for them. I've been intimidated to talk to certain people I admire or who hold positions I see as above my own. It's funny how it hits me that they're human after all when I meet someone like that.

Does it ever strike you how amazing it is that we can actually talk to God? I'm talking about the God who has no beginning and no end...He's the one who spins the earth at just the right speed to keep us firmly planted with gravity...

But let me ask you a question. Does it ever strike you how amazing it is that we can actually talk to God? I'm not talking about the leader of the free world or the world-famous music artist we admire who is adored by millions of fans. I'm talking about the God who has no beginning and no end. The God who, when He had the desire, spoke the universe, galaxies, and stars into existence. He brought everything out of nothing. He spoke the depths of the seas and the heights of the mountains into existence and hung the earth on its axis in perfect rhythm with the sun to give us our seasons. He placed the earth just far enough away from the sun to keep it from scorching in its heat, but not so far away that we freeze in the depths of outer space. He's the one who spins the earth at just the right speed to keep us firmly planted with gravity, but not so fast that we either compress under our own weight or fly off the surface of the earth in violent chaos. He's the God that created the one-of-a-kind fingerprints on our hands and put a smile on the face of our beautiful little toddler that is unique to her alone. He's the one that allows the oxygen molecules to tenderly transfer life into our bloodstream and the One who causes the colors of the rainbow to hover overhead during a spring rain. Nothing at all is impossible with Him. He is beyond the universe. He is amazing! He is above all! He is King Eternal and Majestic. He is amazingly holy, beautifully pure, and infinitely powerful. And He has given each of us individual access to a relationship with Him that includes a conversation with Him in a simple process called "prayer". Prayer is the discipline of holding a conversation with God because of His amazing invitation into a relationship with Him.

Prayer:
1: to make a request in a humble manner
2: to address God or a god with adoration, confession, supplication, or thanksgiving [114]

Prayer is not just thinking positive thoughts or contemplative quiet, though it includes both of these things. Prayer is actually holding a dialogue with God and letting Him hold a dialogue with us. Prayer is listening for His "still small voice" and obeying what He says. God's voice will always line up with His Word which is why daily Bible reading is a part of prayer. Our reading and growing in God's Word is the way we learn to recognize when He is speaking into our spirit. **If something we feel or hear in our minds contradicts the Word of God, it is not God speaking.**

CHAPTER 13

Prayer is not a way to strong-arm God into doing what we want Him to do, but meeting with Him, sharing our heart, and allowing Him to steer us in the direction of His heart and will. Prayer is not our attempt to change God's mind. Prayer is the tool God uses to change us into *His* likeness!

To be sure, any interaction we have with God can be defined as prayer. I'd go as far as to say singing in worship is prayer. These are moments where we're talking to God, sharing our hearts, and listening for His.

There are a few different biblical applications of prayer that can help us better understand the interactions we have with God. These different kinds of prayer can be outlined from Jesus' teaching in the Sermon on the Mount when He taught us the Lord's Prayer:

Matthew 6:9-13 [104]
9 'Our Father in heaven, hallowed be your name,
10 your kingdom come, your will be done, on earth as it is in heaven.
11 Give us today our daily bread.
12 And forgive us our debts, as we also have forgiven our debtors.
13 And lead us not into temptation, but deliver us from the evil one.'

I notice at least five types of prayer in Jesus' illustration of how to pray.

- **Prayer as Worship** - "Hollowed be your name..." (Vs.9)

- **Conversational Prayer for Relationship** - "Our Father..." (Vs. 9)

- **Prayer of Supplication** - "Your Kingdom Come and will be done...Give us this day our Daily Bread" (Vs. 10-11)

- **Prayer of Repentance and Forgiveness** - "forgive me as I forgive others..." (Vs. 12)

- **Prayer of Intercession** - "lead us not into temptation, but deliver us from the evil one..." (Vs. 13)

I'd really like to focus on three of these topics for this chapter:

- **Conversation** - talking with God

- **Supplication** - asking for things from God

- **Intercession** - asking God to intervene in a situation or in the life of someone else

CONVERSATIONAL PRAYER: LEARNING HOW TO SEEK GOD

Matthew 6:5-8 [104]

5 And when you pray, do not be like the hypocrites, for they love to pray standing in the synagogues and on the street corners to be seen by others. Truly I tell you, they have received their reward in full. 6 But when you pray, go into your room, close the door, and pray to your Father, who is unseen. Then your Father, who sees what is done in secret, will reward you. 7 And when you pray, do not keep on babbling like pagans, for they think they will be heard because of their many words. 8 Do not be like them, for your Father knows what you need before you ask him.

One question seems to rise to the top as we're learning how to pray. Why pray when God already knows what you need?

Again, prayer is not something we do to strong-arm God into doing something we want. That's not the way prayer works. God already knows what we need. He is Sovereign, meaning He has the overarching view of our lives and what He is doing, while our viewpoint is limited. He is waiting for us to approach Him and surrender to what He is doing, even if we can't see it yet. He wants us to stay open and transparent about what is happening in our hearts. I believe according to scripture there are times when intercession moves God to action or to change an outcome, which we will explore in greater detail in just a moment. But we must recognize that many times God has a grander plan than what we can understand:

CHAPTER 13

Isaiah 55:9 [115]
9 As the heavens are higher than the earth,
so are my ways higher than your ways
and my thoughts than your thoughts.

Proverbs 3:5-6 [116]
5 Trust in the Lord with all your heart
and lean not on your own understanding;
6 in all your ways submit to him,
and he will make your paths straight.

If we trust God's Word and believe that His ways are higher than ours, we must realize that regardless of how good we are at thinking up great ideas and asking for our heart's desires, God ultimately has the best answers. Prayer allows us to sit with God and listen to His Word, and His instruction, and have Him shift our human way of thinking to His heavenly way of thinking. Prayer is when we subject and surrender our will, emotions, and desires to His perfect will and let Him steer us in His direction.

Psalm 37:3-7 [117]
3 Trust in the Lord and do good;
dwell in the land and enjoy safe pasture.
4 Take delight in the Lord, and he will give you the desires of your heart.
5 Commit your way to the Lord; trust in him and he will do this:
6 He will make your righteous reward shine like the dawn,
your vindication like the noonday sun.
7 Be still before the Lord and wait patiently for him;
do not fret when people succeed in their ways,
when they carry out their wicked schemes.

When we learn to "take delight in the Lord", Psalm 37 says it is *then* God will give us the desires of our heart. It's at that point our desires become aligned with His desires anyway.

PRAYER OF SUPPLICATION: PRESENTING OUR NEEDS TO GOD

After we have spent time acknowledging that God's ways are higher than ours and His name is great, now we can begin to ask God for the desires of our hearts. Many times these desires will realign as we worship and spend time acknowledging God's greatness. We'll find we pray differently than our flesh would normally pray once we've spent time surrendering. This is where we might start to ask for God's direction for a decision we need to make or to ask Him for a healing, a miracle, or a change in our situation. This is where we ask for clarity in His Word as we ask for our "Daily Bread", which is a direct reference to Jesus. We need our daily relationship with Christ, our Savior. (Jesus told us He was our Bread from heaven in John 6.) This is where we deal with issues in our hearts, things like unforgiveness or relational conflicts we've had with another person. This is where we ask God to help us live for Him and where we release offenses.

Supplication: *to make a humble entreaty* [118]

Supplication is where we repent and receive God's atonement for our sins and trespasses. Truly, this is where we are asking for God to move in our individual lives, change us, provide for our needs, and move supernaturally in our situations.

Matthew 6:11-12 [104]
11 Give us this day our daily bread.
12 And forgive us our debts,
As we forgive our debtors.

[Supplication]...is where we deal with issues in our hearts,
things like unforgiveness or relational
conflicts we've had with another person.

CHAPTER 13

Supplication is about coming to God in humility. It's not praying out of selfish ambition or motives, but about genuinely seeking the heart of God to intervene in situations that impact people around us. Supplication is our heartfelt desire to see God move for the good of others just as much as for our own benefit.

INTERCESSORY PRAYER: FOR THE BENEFIT OF ANOTHER

Intercession in prayer is a beautiful ministry. This kind of prayer is a very selfless, others-centered way to walk in the love of God. This is because of the nature of what intercession is:

Intercession:
1: the act of interceding
2: prayer, petition, or entreaty in favor of another [119]

Intercession is the beautiful, selfless act of bringing the needs of another person before God in prayer. Literally, in intercession, you are standing in another person's place and petitioning God for an answer to *their* needs on *their* behalf. You can intercede for a person, be it a family member, friend, or someone unknown that's on your heart. You can also intercede for situations that impact groups of people, or even intercede for nations and major Earth calamities. For instance, you can pray over geopolitical conflicts, disasters, or circumstances of human suffering. The point is, intercessory prayer is not necessarily for you, but it is intentional prayer for the distinct benefit of another person or group of people. We see this modeled for us in several biblical examples:

- Abraham interceded for Sodom and Gomorrah - Genesis 18

- Moses interceded for the Hebrew Nation - Exodus 33

- Elijah interceded for the nation of Israel to receive rain - 1 Kings 18

- Jesus interceded for His disciples, present and future before He went to the cross - John 15-17

Intercession accomplishes several things worth noting here:

- Intercession is a way of "casting my cares" on the Lord and spending time with God in selfless pursuit of Him and the love of others.

- Intercession is a way for me to partner in petitioning God with my brothers and sisters.

- Intercession is a way to deepen my love and servanthood toward those I'm praying for.

- Intercession is a way God can steer my heart to understand what He is doing around me.

- Intercession sometimes moves God to an action that may have otherwise turned out differently.

Genesis 19:29[120] *(emphasis added)*
*29 And it came to pass, when God destroyed the cities of the plain, that **God remembered Abraham,** and sent Lot out of the midst of the overthrow, when He overthrew the cities in which Lot had dwelt.*

Abraham interceded on behalf of Lot and his family. God remembered Abraham's request and rescued them during the destruction of Sodom and Gomorrah.

Prayer is always relational. One of the most powerful breakthroughs we can experience is understanding that God desires to hold conversations with us more than He wants our ritualistic droning. It's important to cultivate moments of prayer in our everyday lives. We could call this the daily approach! Notice in the following verses of scripture that prayer was happening daily and at various times throughout the day:

CHAPTER 13

Psalm 63:1 [121] *(emphasis added)*
1 O God, You are my God;
Early will I seek You;
My soul thirsts for You;
My flesh longs for You
In a dry and thirsty land
Where there is no water.

Isaiah 26:9 [122] *(emphasis added)*
*9 With my soul **I have desired You in the night**,*
*Yes, by my spirit within me **I will seek You early**;*
For when Your judgments are in the earth,
The inhabitants of the world will learn righteousness.

Isaiah 26:3 [122]
3 You will keep him in perfect peace,
Whose mind is stayed on You,
Because he trusts in You.

Psalm 42:1-2 [123]
1 As the deer pants for the water brooks,
So pants my soul for You, O God.
2 My soul thirsts for God, for the living God.
When shall I come and appear before God?

Prayer is always relational. One of the most powerful breakthroughs we can experience is understanding that God desires to hold conversations with us more than He wants our ritualistic droning.

FOUNDATION STONES

As we're growing in prayer, we can use the Lord's Prayer as a template, or guideline, to help us spend time with God. While we might not pray the Lord's Prayer word for word, we can follow its pattern to help us approach God. Let's take a look at this pattern one more time: we can start with worship, we can bring our requests, we can confess sin and forgive others, and we can intercede for others for their benefit!

Matthew 6:9-13 [104]
9 'Our Father in heaven,
hallowed be your name,
10 your kingdom come, your will be done,
on earth as it is in heaven.
11 Give us today our daily bread.
12 And forgive us our debts,
as we also have forgiven our debtors.
13 And lead us not into temptation,
but deliver us from the evil one.'

REFLECTION QUESTIONS

1. How amazing is it that we get to talk to God? Have you ever thought about prayer in this simple, yet profound way? Take a moment to thank the Lord today that you've been given this awesome privilege.

_____
_____
_____
_____
_____
_____

2. What has been a struggle or something that you have found difficult about prayer? It could be the way you perceive prayer or how you feel that you aren't heard, for example.

_____
_____
_____
_____
_____
_____

3. Ask the Holy Spirit how He wants to shift those struggles in your heart and mind today and ask Him to teach you how to pray. (Luke 11:1) Maybe it's that you are familiar with one type of prayer (like supplication) but you want to grow in another kind of prayer (like intercession).

_____
_____
_____
_____
_____
_____

CHAPTER 14
FASTING

A Holy Discipline

Fasting! Oh, what a strange and difficult part of our worship to God! But fasting is a Foundation Stone nonetheless. Let's extend our study on prayer to include understanding the biblical principles and reasons we might engage in a fast. Before we get started, please know that this teaching is intended to help you grow in the understanding of fasting. Please carefully consider your physical limitations before embarking on a fast of extended length and consult your physician if you have any concerns. This teaching is not intended to provide medical advice and I encourage you to use care in your worship of God in the act of fasting.

On regular occasions, the Hebrew people were instructed to fast, pray, and abstain...from other activities that would defile and distract them before they went before God in worship or before they went into battle.

WHAT IS FASTING?

Fasting (spiritual): *going without food for a period of time to focus on prayer.*
1: to abstain from food
2: to eat sparingly or abstain from some foods [124]

Some biblical fasts lasted a day while some were greatly extended, even lasting up to forty days. Jesus embarked on a forty-day fast. Moses embarked on a few forty-day fasts. Many times, fasting included consecration which is the abstinence of other appetites. On regular occasions, the Hebrew people were instructed to fast, pray, and abstain from sexual relations with their spouses or other activities that would defile and distract them before they went before God in worship or before they went into battle. Certain festivals the Hebrews celebrated meant they would remove the yeast from their bread, which was representative of removing sin from their lives. The point of this symbolic act was to re-route their appetites toward the things of God. They were to truly seek Him first! Fasting is an extension of our verbal prayer, often resulting in intense intercessory prayer over a specific situation.

I've personally experienced great intimacy with the Lord as a result of abstaining from things like media or certain forms of recreation. In our culture and time in history, these things are such a consuming, driving force that this abstinence gives us the opportunity to clear our mind and soul and allow the fresh breath of heaven to enter back into our soul! Truly, fasting food and abstaining from certain other things we crave brings to light what our soul is actually searching for, and reminds us to redirect that appetite onto God and the things that please His heart!

The point of this symbolic act was to re-route their appetites toward the things of God. They were to truly seek Him first!

CHAPTER 14

Certainly, a true, biblical fast is abstaining from food. But I believe that abstinence from other appetites is part of the consecration that can occur during a fast to truly set our hearts apart for His glory and seek Him first. I would even argue from my own experience, and the observation of others, that fasting without abstaining from certain other things like media or certain other activities is like leaving the door to the appetite open and wondering why it's hard to set it aside for a while. Fasting and consecration (or being set apart for God), go hand in hand.

It's vital to focus on the *motive*–the *why*–of fasting. I truly think this is the most important place to start in our understanding of fasting as worship and growth in our relationship with God.

It's vital to focus on the motive–the why–of fasting...

DON'T FAST TO IMPRESS OTHERS

Fasting is a precious act of worship. But it's really easy for its purpose to be hijacked. The way our motive for fasting is hijacked is when we make a big deal about it in front of others. Jesus was *adamant* that we should not make a public spectacle out of our fasting. There are several reasons *not* to fast. Should we feel any of these things rising in our hearts, this is *not* the time to fast, or it's the time to repent and get back to a time of fasting that avoids these pitfalls.

A major pitfall to fasting is when we fast to impress other believers with our religion. Jesus was adamant about constantly evaluating the purity of our motives:

> *Matthew 6:16-18*[104]
>
> *16 "Moreover, when you fast, do not be like the hypocrites, with a sad countenance. For they disfigure their faces that they may appear to men to be fasting. Assuredly, I say to you, they have their reward. 17 But you, when you fast, anoint your head and wash your face, 18 so that you do not appear to men to be fasting, but to your Father who is in the secret place; and your Father who sees in secret will reward you openly.*

Luke 18:9-14 [125]
9 Also He spoke this parable to some who trusted in themselves that they were righteous, and despised others: 10 "Two men went up to the temple to pray, one a Pharisee and the other a tax collector. 11 The Pharisee stood and prayed thus with himself, 'God, I thank You that I am not like other men—extortioners, unjust, adulterers, or even as this tax collector. 12 I fast twice a week; I give tithes of all that I possess.' 13 And the tax collector, standing afar off, would not so much as raise his eyes to heaven, but beat his breast, saying, 'God, be merciful to me a sinner!' 14 I tell you, this man went down to his house justified rather than the other; for everyone who exalts himself will be humbled, and he who humbles himself will be exalted."

Fasting should certainly be a rhythm in the life of a believer! But it should never be a badge to impress other believers with our piety. Our fasting doesn't make us better Christians than others. If that ever enters our mind, we must repent of that thought and re-align our fast when we have that motive worked out!

DON'T FAST TO TRY AND MANIPULATE GOD

Another reason *not* to fast is to attempt to twist God's arm into doing *our* will.

Isaiah 58:2-3 [126]
2 Yet they seek Me daily,
And delight to know My ways,
As a nation that did righteousness,
And did not forsake the ordinance of their God.
They ask of Me the ordinances of justice;
They take delight in approaching God.
3 'Why have we fasted,' they say, 'and You have not seen?
Why have we afflicted our souls,
and You take no notice?'
"In fact, in the day of your fast you find pleasure,
And exploit all your laborers.

CHAPTER 14

Sometimes we can get discouraged when we don't see a breakthrough with our prayer and fasting right away. But let me encourage you, our prayer and fasting is not a tool to strong-arm God into doing what *we* request. Fasting is to draw closer to God in relationship. Yes, we'll present requests, but we'll do so from the understanding that He is God, and He has the answer in mind He desires to give. Our fasting only sets us apart and adjusts *our* hearts as we approach God. Fasting is more for *our* alignment spiritually than for us to get something from God. It's an embodiment of "humble yourselves in the sight of the Lord and He will lift you up" (James 4:10)!

Fasting does come with some possible side effects that many people get distracted by. If we're on an extended fast, we will experience some physical changes. Our body will likely react by losing weight. But weight loss is *not* a reason to fast.

Sometimes we can get discouraged when we don't see a breakthrough with our prayer and fasting right away. But...our prayer and fasting is not a tool to strong-arm God into doing what we request.

DON'T FAST TO LOSE WEIGHT

The loss of weight tends to get people excited and it becomes a topic of conversation. Because of our cultural desire for a certain body type and the difficulty we have staying thin with our access to rich foods, fasting as a weight loss tool has distracted many from the pure motive of fasting. When we fast and start seeing some weight loss, it can become a topic of conversation. Many begin sharing how much weight they've lost, and what recipes are being used if they are on a partial fast. This distraction can *quickly* cloud the purpose of a fast. Be very careful not to turn a fast into a diet plan.

There was a time in my life when this could have quickly become a stumbling block for me. I dealt with being overweight as a child and into adulthood. I struggled with overeating and did not desire to exercise. I had fully surrendered to God and was experiencing powerful intimacy with Him and growth in my personal life and ministry. I felt led to go on an extended fast, and surprisingly, my weight came off and came off *quickly*! My breakthrough in my health journey came through a fast! I was on a partial fast, following the model of Daniel's fast in Daniel 1. I primarily drank water and ate only vegetables. My body responded quickly to this change. But I never intended my fast to be a time of weight loss. I had to learn how to quickly re-route conversations with other believers who noticed that my body was getting smaller. Later, there were other times I started a fast, and somewhere down deep in my motive was the desire to lose more weight. God quickly put His finger on that motive and wouldn't let it go until I stopped the fast because my intentions were tainted.

Remember, fasting is for drawing closer to the Lord in prayer. It's not for losing weight or trying out new recipes. It's not for impressing other religious people. And fasting is *not* for twisting God's arm into doing what you want Him to.

So if these are *not* reasons to fast, what are some reasons *to* fast?

FASTING TO WORSHIP GOD

In our First World experience in Western Culture, we tend to look for any way to alleviate discomfort and provide for the satisfaction of our fleshly desires. While it is expected that we *will* get hungry and need to eat regularly, the interruption of our comfort and physical satisfaction is a great reminder to make sure that God is worshiped *first*. Truly, there is no greater reminder to communicate with God than when our stomach rumbles and our blood sugar declines a little. Most other appetites can be suppressed and forgotten, but hunger is the one appetite that will nag at us until it is addressed. This is the signal we use to remind us to seek God. It is a powerful and aggressive reminder. It's the reminder God asks us to use from time to time to seek His Kingdom first!

CHAPTER 14

Matthew 6:33 [104]
33 But seek first the kingdom of God and His righteousness, and all these things shall be added to you.

Fasting reminds us of what God has done in our past. He's provided for us before so why do we worry that He might not provide again? Fasting is a reminder that He is our Source and *we* are not! Fasting is a reminder to focus on God by seeking Him first above all things, including our physical comfort and well-being. *Fasting is a signal of trust!*

FASTING AS REPENTANCE AND CONSECRATION

Many times, Biblical fasting was accompanied by repentance. This intentional turning from sin included abstaining from food during times of mourning for an error that had been made. It can be a marked symbol of our authentic apology for our rebellion against God. In fact, in history, people who were in this state of remorse would sometimes put ashes on their heads and wear sackcloth. Sackcloth was the clothing of repentance. This outerwear accompanied by fasting and ashes demonstrated a sincere desire to apologize to God and return to Him.

Joel 2:12-14 [95]
12 "Now, therefore," says the Lord,
"Turn to Me with all your heart,
With fasting, with weeping, and with mourning."
13 So rend your heart,
and not your garments;
Return to the Lord your God,
For He is gracious and merciful,
Slow to anger, and of great kindness;
And He relents from doing harm.
14 Who knows if He will turn and relent,
And leave a blessing behind Him—
A grain offering and a drink offering For the Lord your God?

Paul the Apostle persecuted the early Church before his conversion. When he encountered Jesus on the road to Damascus, his instinctual response was to abstain from eating as an act of humility and repentance. He was preparing to be set apart. Let's look at it:

Acts 9:9 [127]
9 And he was three days without sight, and neither ate nor drank.

We know after this time of fasting, Ananias arrived, prayed for Paul, and the scales fell from his eyes. Paul's sight returned, he received the baptism in the Holy Spirit, and was baptized in water. This set in motion the powerful ministry that included writing much of the New Testament we now hold in our hands! Fasting was included in Paul's calling!

We know after Jonah gave God's warning to the Ninevites, their response was fasting and repentance. Every human being *and* all the animals were required to fast and repent. An entire kingdom fasted before God and then God relented in carrying out His judgment.

We can see the result of the true, humble repentance of God's people when God responds to their prayers. David says this about returning to God after he sinned against Him:

Psalm 51:17 [46] *(emphasis added)*
17 The sacrifices of God are a broken spirit,
A broken and a contrite heart—
These, O God, **You will not despise.**

Peter preached this on the Day of Pentecost:

Acts 3:19 [60]
19 Repent therefore and be converted, that your sins may be blotted out, so that times of refreshing may come from the presence of the Lord...

CHAPTER 14

FASTING DISCIPLINES OUR FLESH

Disciplining ourselves to grow in Christ is another reason to fast!

Matthew 4:4 [128]
4 But He answered and said, "It is written, 'Man shall not live by bread alone, but by every word that proceeds from the mouth of God.'"

I've found it incredibly helpful to listen to my body during my times of fasting. By this, I mean, every time I feel my stomach growl–every time I feel like my blood sugar is getting low–I'm reminded that I need to be in God's Word or that I need to pray. This is using our physical appetite to remind us of our spiritual appetite. It's like priming the pump to our walk with Christ by using the physical reminders of our hunger. So let me be clear. During a fast, *we will be hungry*! We're *supposed* to be hungry. That's the point. Our physical hunger is to help remind us to be spiritually hungry. And when we're spiritually eating (reading our Bible, praying, and spending time with God in worship), we are actually being spiritually nourished and refreshed!

During a fast, we will be hungry!
We're supposed to be hungry. That's the point.
Our physical hunger is to help remind us to be spiritually hungry.

FASTING FOR GOD'S DIRECTION

With all the voices shouting at us, many of which are giving their input into what we *ought* to be doing, we need a way of hearing the voice of God. Fasting is a tool God gives us to press through every other voice to hear His voice alone. Fasting can have a way of helping us find God's direction for our lives.

Ezra 8:21-23 [129] *(emphasis added)*
*21 Then I proclaimed a fast there at the river of Ahava, that we might humble ourselves before our God, **to seek from Him the right way for us and our little ones and all our possessions.** 22 For I was ashamed to request of the king an escort of soldiers and horsemen to help us against the enemy on the road, because we had spoken to the king, saying, "The hand of our God is upon all those for good who seek Him, but His power and His wrath are against all those who forsake Him." 23 So we fasted and entreated our God for this, and He answered our prayer.*

Fasting is included from cover to cover in our Bible.

There are some very specific times when it's important for us to fast and pray.

- When we are preparing for major decisions

- When we are preparing for the unknown (battles or difficulties ahead)

- When we are interceding on behalf of others for their decisions or unknowns

When we see a pattern in God's Word, we can rest assured God is trying to show us something that we need to pay attention to. Fasting is included from cover to cover in our Bible. In the Sermon on the Mount, Jesus taught about the motive of fasting and included a word that insinuates Christians *should be fasting* from time to time in their relationship with God. "When you fast…" (Matthew 6:16). This is in the Sermon on the Mount, right next to Jesus' teaching on prayer when He said, "When you pray". This demonstrates fasting is something we *should* be doing. This is not an option. Jesus is giving us a key to His Kingdom and to growing in our relationship with Christ that we *must* pay attention to. He gives us an entire chapter that filters our motives for fasting and gives us direction to keep it pure.

There's a chapter in the book of Isaiah that distills the action of fasting down to its core motives and shows us the reason why God calls us to it. Let's open our hearts to these truths:

CHAPTER 14

Isaiah 58:1-14 [126]

1 "Cry aloud, spare not;
Lift up your voice like a trumpet;
Tell My people their transgression,
And the house of Jacob their sins.
2 Yet they seek Me daily,
And delight to know My ways,
As a nation that did righteousness,
And did not forsake the ordinance of their God.
They ask of Me the ordinances of justice;
They take delight in approaching God.
3 'Why have we fasted,' they say, 'and You have not seen?
Why have we afflicted our souls, and You take no notice?'
"In fact, in the day of your fast you find pleasure,
And exploit all your laborers.
4 Indeed you fast for strife and debate,
And to strike with the fist of wickedness.
You will not fast as you do this day,
To make your voice heard on high.
5 Is it a fast that I have chosen,
A day for a man to afflict his soul?
Is it to bow down his head like a bulrush,
And to spread out sackcloth and ashes?
Would you call this a fast,
And an acceptable day to the Lord?
6 "Is this not the fast that I have chosen:
To loose the bonds of wickedness,
To undo the heavy burdens,
To let the oppressed go free,
And that you break every yoke?
7 Is it not to share your bread with the hungry,
And that you bring to your house the poor who are cast out;
When you see the naked,
that you cover him,
And not hide yourself from your own flesh?

FOUNDATION STONES

8 Then your light shall break forth like the morning,
Your healing shall spring forth speedily,
And your righteousness shall go before you;
The glory of the Lord shall be your rear guard.
9 Then you shall call, and the Lord will answer;
You shall cry, and He will say, 'Here I am.'
"If you take away the yoke from your midst,
The pointing of the finger, and speaking wickedness,
10 If you extend your soul to the hungry
And satisfy the afflicted soul,
Then your light shall dawn in the darkness,
And your darkness shall be as the noonday.
11 The Lord will guide you continually,
And satisfy your soul in drought,
And strengthen your bones;
You shall be like a watered garden,
And like a spring of water,
whose waters do not fail.
12 Those from among you
Shall build the old waste places;
You shall raise up the foundations of many generations;
And you shall be called the Repairer of the Breach,
The Restorer of streets to Dwell In.
13 "If you turn away your foot from the Sabbath,
From doing your pleasure on My holy day,
And call the Sabbath a delight,
The holy day of the Lord honorable,
And shall honor Him,
not doing your own ways,
Nor finding your own pleasure,
Nor speaking your own words,
14 Then you shall delight yourself in the Lord;
And I will cause you to ride on the high hills of the earth,
And feed you with the heritage of Jacob your father.
The mouth of the Lord has spoken."

CHAPTER 14

The act of fasting is one of the most powerful and selfless practices of worship and prayer we can participate in. Whenever we fast, we should grow in our walk with Jesus and our love for others even while we decrease in pride, arrogance, and religiosity. Ask the Lord to show you when to start a fast and then fast with expectation and faith!

REFLECTION QUESTIONS

1. Have you ever engaged in a biblical fast by abstaining from food? How did that affect your focus and relationship with God? What are some things you learned, either about yourself, or about a particular situation you were interceding for?

___

2. Have there been times you have fasted when the motive was not correct? How were you able to change those motives and get back on the right track?

___

3. What does it look like to seek His Kingdom first?

CHAPTER 15
THE TRINITY

Three In One

There is a doctrine that is incredibly important and absolutely necessary to our understanding of God. It's the bedrock of our understanding of the relationship between Jesus, God the Father, and the Holy Spirit. Because we don't see the three parts of our own being separated into different entities, it remains difficult for us to mentally grasp and comprehend the reality of God's triune being, even while the Bible makes the truth of it incredibly clear. As I read through scriptures describing this concept, it seems to me as if God doesn't go to great length to define this concept–He simply speaks of it and causes the authors of the scriptures to speak of it–as if it is a common, understood concept with language that is to be taken at face value. My thoughts are that the picture of this doctrine is greatly understood by spiritually-minded people, of which many cultures throughout history have been. However, our modern mindset wrestles with it because of our fleshly and intellectual limitations. This is the doctrine of the Trinity. Father, Son, and Holy Spirit–the Triune Godhead. Those are some big thoughts and words, and honestly, a concept many of us have struggled with over the years!

...the Trinity...Father, Son, and Holy Spirit...

We hear about the Father, Son, and Holy Spirit during baptism. It is in these names that we are baptized when we make a public declaration of our faith in the waters of baptism according to the Great Commission (Matthew 28:19). It is in these names that many times we partake of Holy Communion.

IS HE THREE OR ONE?

When we hear people pray, sometimes we hear them address Jesus. Sometimes we hear them address Father God. Sometimes we hear them address the Holy Spirit. Why the variations in names, and are they praying to separate entities? No! When we address these different names, we are still talking to God Himself through the avenue of the different parts of His being. We have a triune God. God in Three Persons. What in the world does that mean?

Let's be clear. We are not talking about three separate gods. God has made it abundantly clear in scripture that He is *One*–He is the I AM (Exodus 3:14). He's the One that has existed eternally before time began and He will exist forevermore. He is the One True God!

Deuteronomy 6:4-5[130]

4 Hear, O Israel: The Lord our God, the Lord is one! 5 You shall love the Lord your God with all your heart, with all your soul, and with all your strength.

Isaiah 43:10-11[131]
10 "You are My witnesses," says the Lord,
"And My servant whom I have chosen,
That you may know and believe Me,
And understand that I am He.
Before Me there was no God formed,
Nor shall there be after Me.
11 I, even I, am the Lord,
And besides Me,
there is no savior.

CHAPTER 15

ONE GOD, THREE REPRESENTATIONS

What we *do* see in scripture is a very consistent representation of *how* God reveals Himself. In the same way we are individual people, we have a soul, a spirit, and a body, so God manifests Himself in three parts, Father, Son, and Holy Spirit. The interesting thing about the Bible is that God doesn't necessarily explain to us how the Trinity works. He simply speaks of these three parts of Himself as a matter of fact.

Nowhere in scripture can we find the word "Trinity" to describe this relationship. Trinity is a word theologians and scholars have coined over the years to describe the three parts of God revealed in scripture in a way we can understand. But let me assure you, these three parts of God are actively and consistently described in the Bible and leave no doubt that the Trinity–the Triune manifestation of God–is who God is!

In essence, the word "Trinity" is in harmony with the descriptions of God we see in scripture. It can be understood this way: there are three distinct parts making up our One God. [131] Let's look at a few of those places today as we study. The first place we see God describe Himself in a plural form is found in the first chapter of Genesis:

> *Genesis 1:26-27* [65] *(emphasis added)*
> *26 Then God said, "Let **Us** make man in **Our** image, according to **Our** likeness; let them have dominion over the fish of the sea, over the birds of the air, and over the cattle, over all the earth and over every creeping thing that creeps on the earth." 27 So God created man in **His own image**; in the image of God He created him; male and female He created them.*

We were not created in the image of angels. We were created in the image of God. Who is the "Us" God was referencing? It is God referencing the parts of His Being; Father, Son, and Holy Spirit. He refers to Himself as "Us" and then the scripture says "God created mankind in *His own image*". We were not created in the image of angels or the image of other created beings. We were created in *God's own image!*

I love the passage from Isaiah 43:10-11 where God makes clear there is no Savior besides Himself. If that is the case, we have to understand Who it is that has come to earth when we see Jesus performing the redemptive sacrificial work on the Cross of Calvary. When Jesus came, there was a very clear confirmation of Who He was. All three parts of our Triune God came together at the baptism of Jesus:

Matthew 3:16-17 [85]

16 When He had been baptized, Jesus came up immediately from the water; and behold, the heavens were opened to Him, and He saw the Spirit of God descending like a dove and alighting upon Him. 17 And suddenly a voice came from heaven, saying, "This is My beloved Son, in whom I am well pleased."

Scripture very clearly reveals that Jesus is the image of God on earth.

Colossians 1:15-20 [133]

15 He [Jesus] is the image of the invisible God, the firstborn over all creation. 16 For by Him all things were created that are in heaven and that are on earth, visible and invisible, whether thrones or dominions or principalities or powers. All things were created through Him and for Him. 17 And He is before all things, and in Him all things consist. 18 And He is the head of the body, the church, who is the beginning, the firstborn from the dead, that in all things He may have the preeminence. 19 For it pleased the Father that in Him all the fullness should dwell, 20 and by Him to reconcile all things to Himself, by Him, whether things on earth or things in heaven, having made peace through the blood of His cross.

When Jesus came, there was a very clear confirmation of Who He was. All three parts of our Triune God came together at the baptism of Jesus...

CHAPTER 15

Jesus is revealed as the Firstborn of all creation. This means He carries the preeminence. He is before all things. Because He is preeminent, went to the grave, and came out of the grave, He is now the Firstborn from among the dead. This means He defeated death! He is Firstborn from death, meaning more are to be delivered from death by faith in His resurrection.

When Jesus had risen from the dead (a supernatural confirmation of His Deity), this also confirmed His identity and He is now seated in Heaven at the right hand of the Father.

If scripture tells us all things were created by Christ, who then is Christ? God Himself said He is One and there is no other. This means that if all things were created by Christ (Colossians 1:16), *Christ must be God*. And His resurrection proves it! He came out of the grave. He defeated death! The ground shook in response to the Creator defeating the grave!

Look at this scripture highlighting the interplay between God the Father and God the Son:

John 1:1-5; 14[4] *(emphasis added)*
*1 In the beginning was **the Word, and the Word was with God, and the Word was God**. 2 He was in the beginning with God. 3 All things were made through Him, and without Him nothing was made that was made. 4 In Him was life, and the life was the light of men. 5 **And the light shines in the darkness, and the darkness did not comprehend it**.*

*14 And the **Word became flesh and dwelt among us**, and we beheld His glory, the glory as of the only begotten of the Father, full of grace and truth.*

...if all things were created by Christ, Christ must be God.
And His resurrection proves it!

Jesus continued to emphasize the inseparable nature He shared with His Heavenly Father and the Holy Spirit in His final instructions to His disciples.

Matthew 28:18-20 [1]
18 And Jesus came and spoke to them, saying, "All authority has been given to Me in heaven and on earth. 19 Go therefore and make disciples of all the nations, baptizing them in the name of the Father and of the Son and of the Holy Spirit, 20 teaching them to observe all things that I have commanded you; and lo, I am with you always, even to the end of the age." Amen.

When God, described as One of the three parts of the Trinity, speaks of Himself, He is always faithful to the role of whichever part of His Character is speaking. For instance, we must realize the Father is the Source. The Father is the one seated on the Eternal Throne and the One who provides the sustenance of everything that is in existence. Jesus the Son–God in the flesh–is begotten of God. Begotten here doesn't mean He had a beginning as if He didn't exist, then did exist in order to be born. What it means is that the Son comes *from* the Father. In the same way, Jesus' title of "Firstborn" distinguishes that Christ the Son came *from* the Father. Not that He had a beginning. Yes, He was born of a woman into the world as a baby. But He was in existence before time began, creating all that is, according to Colossians 1. He simply had His fleshly beginning the moment He came into the womb of Mary.

In the same way, the Holy Spirit is the Spirit of Jesus–sent from the Father. In other words, God the Father is the Head, He begat (sent) His earthly manifestation in the Son, Jesus, and then when Jesus ascended to heaven, the Father and Son sent the Spirit of Jesus into the world to in-dwell all who would believe in the Son.

The Holy Spirit is mentioned as the Spirit of Jesus several times in the New Testament. Here are some examples:

Philippians 1:19 [134] *(emphasis added)*
*19 For I know that this will turn out for my deliverance through your prayer and the supply of the **Spirit of Jesus Christ**...*

CHAPTER 15

Acts 16:7 [135] *(emphasis added)*

*7 When they came to the border of Mysia, they tried to enter Bithynia, but the **Spirit of Jesus** would not allow them to.*

John 14:15-20 [58] *(emphasis added)*

*15 "If you love Me, keep My commandments. 16 And I will pray the Father, and He will give you another Helper, that He may abide with you forever— 17 the Spirit of truth, whom the world cannot receive, because it neither sees Him nor knows Him; but you know Him, **for He dwells with you** and will be in you. **18 I will not leave you orphans; I will come to you.** 19 "A little while longer and the world will see Me no more, but you will see Me. Because I live, you will live also. 20 At that day you will know that I am in My Father, and you in Me, and I in you.*

2 Corinthians 13:14 [136]

14 The grace of the Lord Jesus Christ, and the love of God, and the communion of the Holy Spirit be with you all. Amen.

...the Son comes from the Father

...Jesus' title of "Firstborn" distinguishes that Christ the Son came from the Father. Not that He had a beginning.

...He was in existence before time began, creating all that is...

The picture of the Trinity is one the Bible makes no qualms about. Every time you see the three parts of God interacting, there is not much further explanation other than it's just the way it is. Truthfully, if we were to let ourselves dwell on it, we realize that we are also made up of three parts as a human being. Our flesh, the part of ourselves we can see, feel, and touch, is one part. But deeper than that is our mind or our soul, which is our thoughts, will, and emotions. We can't feel or touch these attributes in a physical way, but without them, we would not be alive. And then deeper yet, our eternal value is rooted in our spirit, which is the part of us that makes us unique, immortal, and precious. This is the part of us that will return to God at the end of our life on earth. We must realize that our flesh is not immortal. It won't last forever. We don't start our journey without the flesh. But we don't complete the journey *with* the flesh. While we live in this troubled world, the experiences we have will lead us to make decisions to receive the truth and power of God into our lives so that our eternity can be experienced with God in heaven. Jesus' time on earth was brief, just like our flesh experience on earth is brief compared to eternity. But the coming of the Kingdom of God is eternal. We were made in God's image! The experience we have, starting with our flesh, believing in our soul, and returning to God with our spirit, is a model of the way God exists.

Think about this: God has *always* existed. By His Spirit, He hovered over the waters of the deep before creation started, according to Genesis 1:2. So already we see God the Father and God the Holy Spirit. He referred to Himself in the plural when He described the image in which He was going to create mankind. "Let Us make man in Our image..." (Genesis 1:26).

God has always existed...

Throughout the Old Testament, God describes Himself as a Savior. He forecasts His coming, His suffering, and His Redemption, then even prophesied that He would fill His people with His Spirit. These three manifestations of God are consistently and unequivocally declared in scripture. It's because of this consistent confirmation of scripture that we understand we can describe God with this unique word: Trinity. God in three persons. Three distinct personalities and job assignments, but One Being. God Almighty. The I AM.

CHAPTER 15

Jesus Himself described His own identity with the Words "I AM" that Jehovah God, The Father, described Himself with in the Old Testament. The same verbiage God used at the burning bush, Jesus used two different times! When Jesus was confronted about His spiritual authority, He had this to say to the religious leaders of His day. This, by the way, was one of the reasons they wanted to crucify Him:

John 8:5[6] (emphasis added)
58 Jesus said to them, "Most assuredly, I say to you, before Abraham was,
I AM."

The second instance happened in the Garden of Gethsemane when He was being arrested. Jesus asked the men who had come to arrest him who they were looking for:

John 18:4-6[137] (emphasis added)
4 Jesus therefore, knowing all things that would come upon Him, went forward and said to them, "Whom are you seeking?" 5 They answered Him, "Jesus of Nazareth." Jesus said to them, "I am He." And Judas, who betrayed Him, also stood with them. 6 Now when He said to them, "I am He," they drew back and fell to the ground.

Considering the power of Jesus' identity, do you think Jesus was arrested against His will when by the simple words of His mouth, the entire temple guard fell to the ground?

The same words He spoke, "I Am He", are the words "I AM". This is the title God used to describe Himself at the burning bush. No wonder they fell to the ground! Considering the power of Jesus' identity, do you think Jesus was arrested against His will when by the simple words of His mouth, the entire temple guard fell to the ground? He was on a mission, headed to the cross for the forgiveness of mankind! And He would not be stopped (Hebrews 12:2)!

FOUNDATION STONES

In this examination of scripture, we recognize the Father, Son, and Holy Spirit as our triune God. Three in One! God in His three distinctions is in unity with Himself, bringing the fulfillment of His will and glory to the earth and ultimately in eternity in the New Heavens and New Earth! Think of it this way: the Father is the Begetter; the Son is the Begotten; and the Holy Spirit is the One proceeding from the Father and the Son to help us live for God. Therefore, because these three persons in the Godhead are in a state of unity, there is but *One Lord God Almighty*, and His name is One. *I Am*. The God of Abraham, Isaac, and Jacob.

God was in the beginning. He's been with us throughout time, and now through His Holy Spirit, He has never left us or forgotten about us! He now makes His home *in us*! We are the temple of the Holy Spirit (1 Corinthians 6:19-20). What a beautiful hope and confidence we now enjoy. We're not orphans. We're not alone. We're not abandoned, nor will we ever be, should we place our faith in Jesus Christ as our Savior and Lord!

Let's look at one more place where Jesus makes clear the relationship these three parts of God have with one another to make our One True God:

John 15:26-27 [138]
26 "But when the Helper comes, whom I shall send to you from the Father, the Spirit of truth who proceeds from the Father, He will testify of Me. 27 And you also will bear witness, because you have been with Me from the beginning.

May we truly enjoy the beauty of our relationship with our God–the Father, Son, and Holy Spirit! Let's embrace the beauty of the way God has chosen to reveal Himself to us. Let's acknowledge God the Father as our Source, that He is good, sovereign, and praiseworthy. Let's receive Jesus Christ as our Savior, the One who paid our price and lived a perfect life for us! And let's embrace the Holy Spirit, the One who fills us, guides us, comforts us, and empowers us with God's strength every moment of every day. Let's serve God with our whole heart and give Him thanks that He cared for us and loved us so much that He even wanted to interact with us in the first place through the Father, Son, and Holy Spirit!

REFLECTION QUESTIONS

1. After reading this chapter, try to put in your own words the different manifestations of how God reveals Himself through scripture. Take some time to go on a "treasure hunt" through the Word and find the places where God reveals Himself in these three different ways:

_____
_____
_____
_____

God the Father:
_____
_____

God the Son:
_____
_____

God the Holy Spirit:
_____
_____

2. Do you think there is a correlation between Father God, Jesus, and the Holy Spirit and three parts that make us up as His children: Mind, Body, and Spirit?

_____
_____
_____
_____
_____

CHAPTER 15: REFLECTION QUESTIONS

3. Jesus and the Holy Spirit were not only present in the "New Testament", but all throughout the "Old Testament"–from the very beginning (John 1). Does this concept challenge the way you have thought about God in the past? If so, how?

_____
_____
_____
_____
_____

CHAPTER 16
WORSHIP

The Fortress of His Presence

Psalms 27[139]
1 "The Lord is my light and my salvation;
Whom shall I fear?
The Lord is the strength of my life; Of whom shall I be afraid?
2 When the wicked came against me To eat up my flesh,
My enemies and foes, They stumbled and fell.
3 Though an army may encamp against me, My heart shall not fear;
Though war may rise against me, In this I will be confident.
4 One thing I have desired of the Lord, That will I seek:
That I may dwell in the house of the Lord
All the days of my life,
To behold the beauty of the Lord, And to inquire in His temple.
5 For in the time of trouble He shall hide me in His pavilion;
In the secret place of His tabernacle He shall hide me;
He shall set me high upon a rock.
6 And now my head shall be lifted up above my enemies all around me;
Therefore I will offer sacrifices of joy in His tabernacle; I will sing, yes,
I will sing praises to the Lord.

FOUNDATION STONES

7 Hear, O Lord, when I cry with my voice!
Have mercy also upon me, and answer me.
8 When You said, "Seek My face,"
My heart said to You, "Your face, Lord, I will seek."
9 Do not hide Your face from me; Do not turn Your servant away in anger;
You have been my help; Do not leave me nor forsake me,
O God of my salvation.
10 When my father and my mother forsake me,
Then the Lord will take care of me.
11 Teach me Your way, O Lord,
And lead me in a smooth path, because of my enemies.
12 Do not deliver me to the will of my adversaries;
For false witnesses have risen against me,
And such as breathe out violence.
13 I would have lost heart, unless I had believed
That I would see the goodness of the Lord In the land of the living.
14 Wait on the Lord;
Be of good courage,
And He shall strengthen your heart;
Wait, I say, on the Lord!"

Have you ever known someone who seems to walk in extreme peace and confidence in their life and relationship with God, no matter what is happening in the world around them? Someone who seems to enjoy a measure of favor that is noticeably different than most other people you've met? Have you been around someone who seems to hang on to joy and kindness and has heaven's perspective no matter what is going on in the world or their individual lives, even if they have a wild past or are currently going through a turbulent situation? Sure, they have their struggles, but it seems there is protection and peace over their lives that is noticeable from the outside. What is this covering? What is this invisible strength they live under?

[Worship is] a fortress they reside in called favor...

CHAPTER 16

It's a fortress they reside in called *favor*. It's a byproduct of relationship with God that is growing, vibrant, obedient, and submissive to Him. There is a favor that is available from God for His people, and through scripture, I want to explore how it can be found. First off, let's define what favor means:

Favor: *to feel or show approval or preference for* [140]

While God favors all people He created, there are blessings available to those who favor God. God tells us that He draws near when we draw near to Him. That's the kind of favor we need. The favor of His *nearness!*

James 4:8a [141]
8 Draw near to God and He will draw near to you...

1 Peter 2:9-10 [142]
9 But you are a chosen generation, a royal priesthood, a holy nation, His own special people, that you may proclaim the praises of Him who called you out of darkness into His marvelous light; 10 who once were not a people but are now the people of God, who had not obtained mercy but now have obtained mercy.

If you have *chosen* to receive the call of God for salvation, *He has chosen you!* We have been restored to our original created value and now live in royalty and in the favor of our Heavenly Father. We've been made holy and acceptable to God (Romans 12:1). We've given Him an invitation to reside close to us and as a result, His presence now surrounds us, providing His covering and protection over our lives (James 4:8).

Protect: *to cover or shield from exposure, injury, damage, or destruction* [143]

If you have chosen to receive the call of God for salvation,
He has chosen you!

It's important to realize that we live in a fallen world and there are times when things happen to us that are unfortunate. Accidents, ailments, strife, and relational difficulties are some of the things we are susceptible to while we live in a fallen world. However, we must realize that the current situation we live in is temporary. The state of the world around us is not our permanent circumstance. We can live spiritually victorious lives, even if we face difficult situations in the physical. This is the importance of our pursuit of God and the cultivation of a deep relationship with Him. While chaos ensues around us, we can be strong and stable, aiming every day for our ultimate reward: God Himself for the rest of eternity (Genesis 15:1)!

Our Heavenly Father protects and strengthens us. This is a theme we find repeated often in scripture. Look at how the psalmist describes God's presence:

Psalm 91:1-2 [41]
1 He who dwells in the secret place of the Most High
Shall abide under the shadow of the Almighty.
2 I will say of the Lord, "He is my refuge and my fortress;
My God, in Him I will trust."

Psalm 28:7 [144]
7 The Lord is my strength and my shield; My heart trusted in Him, and I am helped; Therefore my heart greatly rejoices, And with my song I will praise Him.

Psalm 32:7 [145]
7 You are my hiding place; You shall preserve me from trouble; You shall surround me with songs of deliverance. Selah

---

While chaos ensues around us, we can be strong and stable, aiming every day for our ultimate reward: God Himself...

CHAPTER 16

The word "shield" can be defined as a verb. This is an active description meaning that something is being protected from danger, risk, or unpleasant circumstances. It can also be defined as a noun. A shield is a protective covering that resists danger, risk, or unpleasant experiences. In ancient warfare, a warrior would carry a large shield to guard against arrows, spears, and daggers. Without his shield, a warrior was very vulnerable to attack and wouldn't survive a battle. And without our close relationship with God–our Shield–we are also very susceptible to the affront of our adversary.

So how do we take advantage of our Shield? How do we build our faith in Christ in such a way that our life remains hidden behind God's immense protection? How do we get under the protective favor of God and remain there for our lifetime?

I believe this favor and protection is the natural byproduct of a relationship that is intentionally cultivated with God every day. When we surrender to God every day by spending time with Him in worship and adoration, soaking in His Word, and holding a conversation with Him in prayer, our spirit, soul, and body are transformed into His likeness, and our life is hidden inside His presence!

Psalm 28:7 [144]
7 The Lord is my strength and my shield; My heart trusted in Him, and I am helped; Therefore my heart greatly rejoices, And with my song I will praise Him.

...favor and protection is the natural byproduct of a relationship...with God... When we surrender to God every day by spending time with Him in worship and adoration...our life is hidden inside His presence!

Often in the Bible, our relationship with God is compared to a marriage. In the early days of a budding romance, the couple may feel insecure with one another as they are growing in their relationship. Each person, exploring the newness of the relationship, has to test the trustworthiness of the other person. But as the relationship grows and matures, confidence in the commitment of the other person grows. A proposal is made and a wedding is held. In a healthy marriage, the relationship only grows in sacredness. Their promise is affirmed and strengthened, while confidence in their covenant solidifies. It's no different with God. We should be *ever more confident* in our relationship with God the longer we know Him. Confidence is our firm trust and certainty in the security of our relationship with God! This certainty reveals the favor of God in our lives. We are not moved by the external storms of life because we confidently lean on the God of our Salvation. We will not be moved!

Proverbs 14:26 [146] *(emphasis added)*
26 In the fear of the Lord there is **strong confidence***, And His children will have a* **place of refuge***.*

Psalm 27 is a perfect example of the confidence we can walk in with God. King David seemed to have unwavering assurance that God was dependable even in the midst of what he endured throughout his life. The way David opened this Psalm seems almost too good to be true for the average person:

Psalm 27:1-3 [139]
1 "The Lord is my light and my salvation;
Whom shall I fear?
The Lord is the strength of my life; Of whom shall I be afraid?
2 When the wicked came against me
To eat up my flesh,
My enemies and foes, They stumbled and fell.
3 Though an army may encamp against me,
My heart shall not fear;
Though war may rise against me, In this I will be confident.

CHAPTER 16

David is saying that he has no worries about life because He trusts God. He gives credit to the Lord for a supernatural favor he's experiencing. It's easy to lament that David's statements seem unreachable in many ways. David declares, "I won't be afraid." He boasts, "My enemies fell," and he declares, "I'm confident I'll win!"

If we are facing hardships today, it might be easy to say, "Yay for you, David. But, that's not my experience right now." However, what I want to illuminate is that the first three verses of Psalm 27 could make a great ending to this Psalm instead of a beginning. We have to realize David is describing the *result* of Psalm 27:4-14–the verses that follow his declaration! I believe David may have started with these verses to get us to ask the question, "How do I experience those kinds of results, too?" David might respond, "I'm glad you asked! Here's where my victory comes from!" He spends the rest of this beautiful psalm describing *how* we can have this same kind of confidence. Do you want to know how to combat fear, walk in victory, and experience God's favor? Let's look at the rest of Psalm 27 through this lens! There are principles available to us that David reveals in his own life so we can understand how to fortify *our* lives in God. Psalm 27 teaches us how to stay in God's Favor, the fortress of God's presence.

GOD'S SECRET MEETING PLACE

Psalm 27:4-6 [139]
4 One thing I have desired of the Lord, That will I seek:
That I may dwell in the house of the Lord
All the days of my life,
To behold the beauty of the Lord, And to inquire in His temple.
5 For in the time of trouble
He shall hide me in His pavilion;
In the secret place of His tabernacle He shall hide me;
He shall set me high upon a rock.
6 And now my head shall be lifted up above my enemies all around me;
Therefore I will offer sacrifices of joy in His tabernacle;
I will sing, yes, I will sing praises to the Lord.

The promise of God's favor and protection is *directly tied* to us remaining in His presence. We've got to intentionally come to Him, pursuing Him in complete surrender and approaching His holiness, *His way*. There is a place of meeting where we can encounter God every day. Our intentional pursuit of relationship with Him looks like us making Him our number one priority. God comes before anything else in the day. Having a place to meet with Him where you have set aside a location and a block of time where He is your central focus is very important. For me, I have a chair I sit in every morning and my Bible rests on the coffee table within easy reach. There is an expectancy that I have that I'll meet God there! There's also a place where I meet with God every week alongside my brothers and sisters in Christ. My church sanctuary is a holy place! The altar where I meet with God is transformative! These places are precious because I *intentionally* pursue God there. If we don't give God time and we don't give Him a place, we will struggle to find *Him*! It's a precious, secret, sacred place of encounter that each of us can have!

Psalm 91:1 [41]
1 He who dwells in the secret place of the Most High
Shall abide under the shadow of the Almighty.

As a son or daughter of God, we should have a single-minded pursuit of God. This opens the door to the favor of God. David said he had one thing in mind: to be with God, behold Him, and inquire of Him in *His* house. Nothing else was more important. For David, this mindset and focus was what the rest of his life flowed from:

Psalm 27:4 [139]
4 One thing I have desired of the Lord,
That will I seek:
That I may dwell in the house of the Lord
All the days of my life,
To behold the beauty of the Lord,
And to inquire in His temple.

CHAPTER 16

This pursuit of God is very intentional. We are to come to God. We play a significant role in the relationship we have with God. We can't just expect God to come to us. We are to build Him a house and then come to *Him*. We are to come on *His* terms. God loves it when we seek Him above all else. He never intended for us to seek Him only for the assurance of heaven and then live our lives on earth distracted with everything else. He saved us and called us into relationship with Him that will last for eternity. *That's* where His presence and favor come from!

In the Old Testament, God's house is synonymous with The Temple, the physical place of worship. In the New Testament, God's House is the Church or the gathering of the believers! We are also individually called the Temple of the Holy Spirit. The idea is this: we are to prioritize coming *to God*. Whether this is in our personal time with Him in our homes, in the church building, or in any gathering with His people. We are to come to *His* house. The whole point is that we are to make an effort to pursue God. The Bible makes clear that when we come to God, He will meet us there.

WE MUST BECOME FAMILIAR WITH GOD'S FACE

Psalm 27:7-10 [139] *(**emphasis added**)*
7 Hear, O Lord, when I cry with my voice!
Have mercy also upon me, and answer me.
8 When You said,
*"**Seek My face**,"*
My heart said to You,
*"**Your face, Lord, I will seek**."*
9 Do not hide Your face from me;
Do not turn Your servant away in anger;
You have been my help;
Do not leave me nor forsake me,
O God of my salvation.
10 When my father and my mother forsake me,
Then the Lord will take care of me.

We can't be familiar with the face of someone we don't know. I'm not just talking about facial features. I'm talking about the nuances of knowing someone. What causes them to smile? What causes them to frown? What causes them to laugh? What do they like and dislike? This is the kind of look a small child will give their mom and dad. The look where the child grabs their face and says, "Look at me!" We see this in David's words! "Don't hide Your face from me! I want to see You, God!" We must *behold* Him, which is to look to Him, admire Him, adore Him, and become aware of who He is, what He looks like, what He expects, how He moves and behaves, how He loves, and how He disciplines and chastises. We must behold His beauty! This isn't a fleeting glance. This is our *study* of the face of God!

LEARN HOW TO WORSHIP EVERYDAY

Scripturally and experientially, I have become convinced that there is a favor that pours out on people who make the praise of God their number one priority. Praise and worship of God–*beholding His face*–can literally become a shield that stands between you and the many unique circumstances of life. Spending time with God invites His presence, His protection, and His favor into our lives. When we spend time listening to God and worshiping Him for who He is, wisdom enters in, good choices are made, honor is established, and blessings follow. This does not mean we'll never experience hardships, sickness, or tragedy. What it does mean is that our hearts will not waver or be insecure because of the winds and waves of this world.

Psalm 22 is a prophetic picture of the suffering and redemptive work of Jesus on the cross. But it's also a picture of the principle of worship and relationship that happens between God and His people. The truth is this: when we worship, we are making space for God. His throne of authority and glory can reside in our midst when we glorify Him and behold His face! In essence, when we worship, God pulls up a seat:

Psalm 22:3 [33]
3 But You are holy,
Enthroned in the praises of Israel.

CHAPTER 16

I believe this happens because worshiping God takes the focus off of us and our circumstances and elevates our gaze to God in Heaven. Our change in perspective causes a different outlook on our circumstances and reminds us that we are seated with Christ in Heavenly places (Ephesians 1:20), creating confidence and peace in every storm. Worshiping God literally makes the place we reside a holy sanctuary where God's presence is welcome to dwell and provide covering. This is why it's so important that we carefully vet the things we permit into our home—entertainment, conversations, activities, and even people. We want our *entire life* to be His sanctuary. We want Him to be welcome with us at all times!

When we know God's face, we know His *look*. We have conviction! His direction becomes easy to discern. He can direct us with a look from His eye and not the hammer of judgment!

In Psalm 27, we are instructed to become a student of God's Word:

Psalm 27:11-12 [139]
*11 Teach me Your way, O Lord, And lead me in a smooth path,
because of my enemies.
12 Do not deliver me to the will of my adversaries;
For false witnesses have risen against me, And such as breathe out violence.*

---

*...worshiping God takes the focus off of us and our
circumstances and elevates our gaze to God in Heaven.
Our change in perspective causes a different outlook
on our circumstances and reminds us that
we are seated with Christ in Heavenly places...*

As we learn to pursue God's presence in worship and relationship, we should grow in a passionate pursuit of truth. We have to acknowledge that truth is paramount. Truth needs to be elevated above our experience and our preferences. God is right, and we are blessed to know His righteousness. Within God's righteousness resides His favor. Our knowledge of the truth then produces wisdom, which smooths our path and routes us around much of life's turbulence and the adversaries we might come into contact with. Wisdom from God's Word is much like the radar that looks into the distant weather for an aircraft. If we can forecast the turbulence, we can route around it! Wisdom will also help us climb to a higher altitude if we do happen to hit some rough air.

GOD IS CONCERNED ABOUT YOUR SPIRIT FIRST

Psalm 27:13-14 [139]
13 I would have lost heart, unless I had believed
That I would see the goodness of the Lord
In the land of the living.
14 Wait on the Lord;
Be of good courage,
And He shall strengthen your heart;
Wait, I say, on the Lord!"

It's important to acknowledge that we will have trouble on earth. Sometimes death, violence, sickness, and hardship comes, even while we're pursuing God. We must remain confident and not lose heart. We must stay in His presence and stay in His Word. We must decide to stay in His sanctuary. We've got to stay in the fortress of His presence so we can see the goodness of the Lord in the midst of it all (Psalm 27:13). We must wait on God to restore our courage and strengthen our hearts. Eternity awaits, regardless of the outcome of our earthly circumstances, so we must keep our eyes focused on Him.

Our time with God should create *hope* and *optimism*. We can't truly spend time with God and then, in turn, become more despairing. We can't *truly* spend time in the fortress of God's Presence and become depressed. It simply doesn't work that way.

CHAPTER 16

1 Peter 5:6-7 [147] (emphasis added)
*6 Therefore humble yourselves under the mighty hand of God, that He may exalt you in due time, 7 **casting all your care upon Him, for He cares for you.***

Our confidence in life comes from our relationship with God and nowhere else!

Psalm 27:14 [139]
14 Wait on the Lord;
Be of good courage,
And He shall strengthen your heart;
Wait, I say, on the Lord!

How can we be confident even in difficulties?

-Become familiar with His secret place
-Become familiar with His face
-Become a student of His Word

These things build a fortress that provides safety, protection, confidence, and victory in the midst of every battle and shaking in life because we are *held by God*! This is how we cultivate a true worshiping heart! This is more than worship songs. This is a lifestyle of surrender, love, and intentional pursuit of God! When we draw near to Him, *He draws near to us* (James 4:8)!

REFLECTION QUESTIONS

1. Where is your "sweet spot", the place where you connect with God? Maybe it's a certain chair where you keep your Bible and journal and you spend time with the Lord every morning. Maybe it's standing in front of the sink while you're doing dishes. God can meet with us anywhere. Where is that place for you?

_____
_____
_____
_____
_____

2. Have you had an experience in your life where you were walking through something really hard, and you just began to worship the Lord, like Paul and Silas when they were in prison (Acts 16)? How did it change the atmosphere or attitude in your heart?

_____
_____
_____
_____

3. Time spent with Jesus is never wasted. He never forgets those times, even if we do, and they all make up our personal history with Jesus, a foundation for relationship. Take some time today to remember some of those times in worship and prayer that stand out to you, perhaps a defining moment. (This does not mean they have to be overwhelmingly "loud". These moments can be simple, but no less powerful, in what God was speaking to you or showing you in that season.)

_____
_____
_____

CHAPTER 17
THE RAPTURE

Jesus' Return for His Bride

One principle that helps me immensely in my everyday life and walk with Jesus is this: I need to begin with the end in mind. Where am I going? Why am I going there? What must be true to make sure I get there?

Our walk with God is the same way. We have a destination. This world is not our home. We live here for a moment, but we're aiming at an eternity where we will live forever. So all the things that happen here are small compared to the immensity of eternity. And yet, our eternal destination is *determined* by the things we believe *here* on earth. As a Christian, how do we "begin with the end in mind"? I believe we must understand where we're headed. We're headed to a face-to-face encounter with the Holy God. We're headed to eternity with God because of our faith in Jesus Christ. And we're headed there because of God's great plan.

I need to begin with the end in mind...
Where am I going? Why am I going there?

God's great plan is shown in Scripture to have a culmination—a crescendo of God's activity on earth and in the lives of His people. The Bible describes a moment in the future when Christ appears again and takes His people home to heaven. This is called The Rapture of the Church. It's the moment that Jesus describes when He returns for His faithful people and "catches them away" to be with Him forever. Jesus, as well as many other writers of the scriptures, made it very clear He would be coming back. Every believer will have a personal encounter with God after this life on earth is over. However, the Bible clearly reveals that there will be a specific moment in time when Jesus will return for His Church.

Titus 2:11-14 [97] *(emphasis added)*
11 For the grace of God that brings salvation has appeared to all men, 12 teaching us that, denying ungodliness and worldly lusts, we should live soberly, righteously, and godly in the present age, **13 looking for the blessed hope and glorious appearing of our great God and Savior Jesus Christ,** *14 who gave Himself for us, that He might redeem us from every lawless deed and purify for Himself His own special people, zealous for good works.*

The Bible describes a moment in the future when Christ appears again and takes His people home to heaven.

JESUS IS THE GROOM, WE ARE THE BRIDE

One of the representations God uses in scripture to describe His covenant relationship with us is found in that of a marriage between a husband and wife. Marriage was created by God to give us a picture of the relationship we should have with Him. He's comparing our earthly marriages to our relationship with Him. Earthly marriage is the illustration He chose to reveal His greater masterpiece! He shows this to us in the book of Ephesians when Paul is giving us instructions on how to conduct our earthly marriage relationships:

CHAPTER 17

Ephesians 5:28-32[148] *(emphasis added)*
*28 So husbands ought to love their own wives as their own bodies; he who loves his wife loves himself. 29 For no one ever hated his own flesh, but nourishes and cherishes it, just as the Lord does the church. 30 For we are members of His body, of His flesh and of His bones. 31 "For this reason a man shall leave his father and mother and be joined to his wife, and the two shall become one flesh." 32 **This is a great mystery, but I speak concerning Christ and the church.***

God even allows an entire book in the Bible to be dedicated to the imagery of God and His people being a Groom and a Bride. In the book of Hosea, He instructs his prophet (named Hosea) to marry a prostitute. An entire story unfolds, showing how Hosea's wife stepped out on their marriage in adulterous living, constantly running away and being bought back by her husband. This prophetic book, in which Hosea represents God and his wife represents Israel, is a picture of how God felt when Israel stepped out on their covenant with Him time and again, going after other gods and living in total contrast to how He had called them.

This prophetic book, in which Hosea represents God and his wife represents Israel, is a picture of how God felt when Israel stepped out on their covenant with Him time and again, going after other gods and living in total contrast to how He had called them.

In the New Testament, Jesus Himself uses the imagery of a groom and a bride in many places, including His parable of the ten virgins:

FOUNDATION STONES

Matthew 25:1-13[149]

1 "Then the kingdom of heaven shall be likened to ten virgins who took their lamps and went out to meet the bridegroom. 2 Now five of them were wise, and five were foolish. 3 Those who were foolish took their lamps and took no oil with them, 4 but the wise took oil in their vessels with their lamps. 5 But while the bridegroom was delayed, they all slumbered and slept. 6 "And at midnight a cry was heard: 'Behold, the bridegroom is coming; go out to meet him!' 7 Then all those virgins arose and trimmed their lamps. 8 And the foolish said to the wise, 'Give us some of your oil, for our lamps are going out.' 9 But the wise answered, saying, 'No, lest there should not be enough for us and you; but go rather to those who sell, and buy for yourselves.' 10 And while they went to buy, the bridegroom came, and those who were ready went in with him to the wedding; and the door was shut. 11 "Afterward the other virgins came also, saying, 'Lord, Lord, open to us!' 12 But he answered and said, 'Assuredly, I say to you, I do not know you.' 13 "Watch therefore, for you know neither the day nor the hour in which the Son of Man is coming."

While telling this story, Jesus is speaking to a crowd that would understand the traditions and imagery of a Galilean wedding very well. Jesus lived in the area of the Sea of Galilee, basing much of his activity around the city of Capernaum. The people in this particular area had some very interesting and unique traditions for the establishment of a marriage between a young couple. *(This information is based on the study and film called "Before the Wrath" by Brent Miller*[150]*):*

- The groom's father was always very involved in the choosing of the bride. He would help His son in the selection and bride price negotiations with the bride's family.

- Once a price was negotiated and agreed upon with the bride's family, the groom and bride would be hidden away from each other until the wedding day. The groom was to go and build an addition onto the house of the father. The bride would gather her family and her female attendees to prepare for the moment the groom would come calling–a moment in the future that was unknown.

CHAPTER 17

- The groom built onto the house until the father deemed it was ready for the bride. The groom didn't even know when the father would be satisfied.

- The bride and her attendees were to be prepared–ready to advance to the wedding at any moment.

- As soon as the groom's father was satisfied that the new home was ready, he would declare to his son, "Go get your bride". The groom would race to the bride's house with his own attendants. This could be any time of the day or night. His urgency was the result of high anticipation and celebration! The whole town would hear the procession of the groom and his attendees and would come out for the imminent celebration that would commence.

- The groom and bride may have not seen each other for a very long time. The anticipation was intense!

- The bride and her attendants were to keep their oil lamps trimmed and full in case their procession took place at night.

- When the groom and his attendants arrived and announced it was time to proceed with the wedding, the bride was brought out from her chamber and lifted into a carriage that would be transported by the groom's attendants. The bride's feet would not be allowed to touch the ground until she arrived at the wedding venue.

- When the bride and groom were brought together, the wedding ceremony would be a giant, city-wide celebration of the consummation of this highly anticipated marriage. There would be a wedding supper and a party that lasted seven days, which celebrated the beauty, holiness, and anticipation of a magnificent and pure union between a man and woman.

The bride and her attendants were to keep their oil lamps trimmed and full in case their procession took place at night.

This traditional Galilean marriage ceremony would have been understood very well by the people who listened to Jesus teach about the union between God and His people. What a beautiful understanding of God's heartbeat for us as His sons and daughters! What an amazing thing that God would choose to encode His heavenly intentions in a wedding ceremony practiced by a very specific group of people in a very specific part of the world where God chose to send His only begotten Son. All the imagery adds up. And we are waiting right now for the return of the eternal Groom. We're waiting for the moment when our Heavenly Father is satisfied with the mansion Jesus is building and declares to Him, "Son, go get Your Bride."

Mark 13:32 [151]

32 But of that day and hour no one knows, not even the angels in heaven, nor the Son, but only the Father.

HE IS PREPARING A PLACE FOR US

John 14:1-6 [58] *(emphasis added)*
1 "Let not your heart be troubled; you believe in God, believe also in Me. 2 In My Father's house are many mansions; if it were not so, I would have told you. ***I go to prepare a place for you. 3 And if I go and prepare a place for you, I will come again and receive you to Myself; that where I am, there you may be also.*** *4 And where I go you know, and the way you know." 5 Thomas said to Him, "Lord, we do not know where You are going, and how can we know the way?" 6 Jesus said to him, "I am the way, the truth, and the life. No one comes to the Father except through Me."*

Mankind is so incredibly special to God. He has proposed marriage to us and we have the option to accept His invitation to the wedding! We can be His Bride and forever dwell with Him in the place He is preparing for us to reside for eternity. Jesus is carefully, patiently, and skillfully preparing a place for His Bride. He doesn't want any to perish, but all to come to repentance so we can all go to be with Him for eternity (2 Peter 3:9)! It's amazing that Jesus would love us and anticipate our arrival so much that He has been preparing a place for us since He ascended into Heaven two millennia ago!

CHAPTER 17

HE'S COMING BACK

John 14:3 [58]
3 And if I go and prepare a place for you, I will come again and receive you to Myself; that where I am, there you may be also.

The belief in the rapture, or catching away of the Church, Christ's Bride, is not something that has been made up by theologians to explain some lofty doctrinal idea they're trying to flush out of scripture. This is a foundational belief system we hold to be true because Jesus Himself told us it would happen! We have to understand that the word "rapture" is not found in the Bible. This is a word used to describe the "catching away" that is talked about over and over in scripture. We will be "caught up" in the air.

1 Thessalonians 4:17 [152] *(emphasis added)*
*17 Then we who are alive and remain shall be **caught up** together with them in the clouds to meet the Lord in the air. And thus we shall always be with the Lord.*

Matthew 24:40-41 [153]
40 Then two men will be in the field: one will be taken and the other left.
41 Two women will be grinding at the mill: one will be taken and the other left.

Over and over, scripture tells us there is an event coming that will cause those who truly believe in Jesus to be caught up at a specific moment in time to meet Jesus–a moment where the marriage we've been waiting for will be complete.

We need to make sure we don't confuse the "Rapture" with the "Second Coming". The Rapture is what is described in 1 Thessalonians 4–a shout from the archangel and the trumpet call of God will cause us to ascend to Jesus and meet Him in the air. The Second Coming is what is described throughout the Bible, especially in places like Zechariah and Revelation, where the actual physical foot of Jesus Christ will touch down on the Mount of Olives. He will wage war against Satan and will win supremacy over all the earth for a 1,000-year millennial reign.

In this chapter we are studying "The Rapture" where Jesus returns for His Bride, the Church! These are the ones who have put their faith in Jesus as Savior because of His finished, covenant work on the cross. We accepted His wedding proposal by believing in Him as our Lord and Savior, and we are waiting in anticipation for His announcement that it's time for the wedding! This is the moment we are "caught up" and taken to the wedding–the Marriage Supper of the Lamb (Revelation 19:9)! The rapture is the announcement that it's time for the wedding!

We have to know that we won't be given the exact date when He will call for us, just like neither the bride nor the groom knew the exact moment the father would make the call in the Galilean wedding. But we are assured in scripture Jesus is coming and He wants us to make sure that we are ready for Him when He gets here!

After His resurrection, Jesus was about to ascend to heaven to prepare a place for us. All the disciples were standing with Him, preparing to watch Him leave, when Jesus said this:

> *Acts 1:7-11 [99] (emphasis added)*
> *7 And He said to them, "It is not for you to know times or seasons which the Father has put in His own authority. 8 But you shall receive power when the Holy Spirit has come upon you; and you shall be witnesses to Me in Jerusalem, and in all Judea and Samaria, and to the end of the earth." 9 Now when He had spoken these things, while they watched, He was taken up, and a cloud received Him out of their sight. 10 And while they looked steadfastly toward heaven as He went up, behold, two men stood by them in white apparel, 11 who also said, "Men of Galilee, why do you stand gazing up into heaven? This same Jesus, who was taken up from you into heaven, **will so come in like manner as you saw Him go into heaven.**"*

We have to know that we won't be given the exact date when He will call for us...But we are assured in scripture Jesus is coming...

CHAPTER 17

CHRIST'S RETURN IS IMMINENT

The return of Christ–first with the Rapture of the Church and then with His descent back to earth for the ultimate final victory in His Second Coming–is *imminent*! The Rapture and Second Coming *will* happen. According to scripture, the "catching away" could happen at any moment. Paul the Apostle told the Thessalonian church:

1 Thessalonians 4:13-18[152] *(emphasis added)*
13 But I do not want you to be ignorant, brethren, concerning those who have fallen asleep, lest you sorrow as others who have no hope. 14 For if we believe that Jesus died and rose again, even so God will bring with Him those who sleep in Jesus.

*15 For this we say to you by the word of the Lord, that we who are alive and remain until the coming of the Lord will by no means precede those who are asleep. 16 **For the Lord Himself will descend from heaven with a shout, with the voice of an archangel, and with the trumpet of God. And the dead in Christ will rise first. 17 Then we who are alive and remain shall be caught up together with them in the clouds to meet the Lord in the air.** And thus we shall always be with the Lord. 18 Therefore comfort one another with these words.*

The return of Christ–first with the Rapture of the Church...is imminent!

The Rapture and Second Coming will happen...
[and] the "catching away" could happen at any moment.

1 Thessalonians 5:1-11[154]
1 But concerning the times and the seasons, brethren, you have no need that I should write to you. 2 For you yourselves know perfectly that the day of the Lord so comes as a thief in the night. 3 For when they say, "Peace and safety!" then sudden destruction comes upon them, as labor pains upon a pregnant woman. And they shall not escape. 4 But you, brethren, are not in darkness, so that this Day should overtake you as a thief. 5 You are all sons of light and sons of the day. We are not of the night nor of darkness. 6 Therefore let us not sleep, as others do, but let us watch and be sober. 7 For those who sleep, sleep at night, and those who get drunk are drunk at night. 8 But let us who are of the day be sober, putting on the breastplate of faith and love, and as a helmet the hope of salvation. 9 For God did not appoint us to wrath, but to obtain salvation through our Lord Jesus Christ, 10 who died for us, that whether we wake or sleep, we should live together with Him. 11 Therefore comfort each other and edify one another, just as you also are doing.

1 Corinthians 15:51-52 [155] *(emphasis added)*
51 Behold, I tell you a mystery: We shall not all sleep, but we shall all be changed— 52 in a moment, in the twinkling of an eye, at the last trumpet. **For the trumpet will sound, and the dead will be raised incorruptible, and we shall be changed.**

Those who are raptured...[are] those who [accept] Christ's wedding proposal.

Those who are raptured will be those who have accepted Christ's wedding proposal. The wedding proposal is the covenant promise of God's eternal love for His people and His faithfulness to their eternal security. It is found on the cross where Jesus shed His blood and died for His Bride to wash her and cleanse her from the sin that had separated her from God. His resurrection is the confirmation of His Authority and the assurance of His return. If we believe in our hearts and confess with our mouths our faith in Christ Jesus, we shall be saved. We are then the Bride of Christ and can ascend to be with Jesus when the trumpet call sounds, whether we died on earth or are caught up alive to meet Him in the air.

CHAPTER 17

ARE YOU READY?

Matthew 24:36-44 [153] *(emphasis added)*
*36 "But of that day and hour no one knows, not even the angels of heaven, but My Father only. 37 But as the days of Noah were, so also will the coming of the Son of Man be. 38 For as in the days before the flood, they were eating and drinking, marrying and giving in marriage, until the day that Noah entered the ark, 39 and did not know until the flood came and took them all away, so also will the coming of the Son of Man be. 40 Then two men will be in the field: one will be taken and the other left. 41 Two women will be grinding at the mill: one will be taken and the other left. **42 Watch therefore, for you do not know what hour your Lord is coming.** 43 But know this, that if the master of the house had known what hour the thief would come, he would have watched and not allowed his house to be broken into. 44 Therefore you also be ready, for the Son of Man is coming at an hour you do not expect.*

James 5:7-8 [156] *(emphasis added)*
*7 Therefore be patient, brethren, until the coming of the Lord. See how the farmer waits for the precious fruit of the earth, waiting patiently for it until it receives the early and latter rain. **8 You also be patient. Establish your hearts, for the coming of the Lord is at hand.***

Luke 21:28 [157]
28 Now when these things begin to happen, look up and lift up your heads, because your redemption draws near.

It can be easy to put off the urgency of watching for the Lord's return, perhaps thinking that since Jesus hasn't returned yet, He won't return during our lifetime. This may or may not be true. We need to live our lifetime on earth for Christ while also knowing *today could be the day* of His return. Make sure to keep your eyes on Jesus, always looking up, because He is coming back soon!

REFLECTION QUESTIONS

1.What are some concepts about the rapture that you were taught before that maybe don't align with scripture? Maybe you are new to this whole idea of the rapture. It's a word that's tossed around sometimes, but may have lost its meaning. Take a moment to write down some things that jumped out at you during today's study, and maybe some things that you would like to study in greater detail:

_____
_____
_____
_____
_____
_____
_____
_____
_____
_____

2. What do you think it means to "keep your lamp trimmed" like the parable of the ten virgins? What does that mean for you specifically? Is there anything that might need to change in your life to make sure you are living totally committed to God?

_____
_____
_____
_____
_____
_____
_____
_____

REFLECTION QUESTIONS: CHAPTER 17

3. Fear is a huge ploy of the enemy to keep us bound and hidden when we should be free and full of faith to share with others. If there is or has been any fear attached to this subject for you, take some time to write down the things that have had a foothold of fear for you and ask the Lord what He thinks about them and how He thinks about you. What is the lie you may be believing about the rapture and the end times, and what is God's truth?

CHAPTER 18
BIBLICAL GIVING

Displaying God's Generosity

God, by the very nature of His character, is a generous giver. If we've received the amazing salvation He provides, we cannot deny He is extravagant and is willing to do whatever it takes to make sure His sons and daughters have a way back to Him for eternity.

John 3:16[158] (emphasis added)
*16 For God so loved the world that He **gave** His only begotten Son, that whoever believes in Him should not perish but have everlasting life.*

Humanity was made in the image and likeness of God, which is way more than a reference to His appearance. We were created in His character as well, representing Him to the world around us.

Genesis 1:27 [65] (emphasis added)
*27 So God created man **in His own image**; in the image of God He created him; male and female He created them.*

As a son or daughter who is made in the image of God, we are created to resemble Him in character and action. God wants us to grow to the "measure of the stature of the fullness of Christ" (Ephesians 4:13). This will certainly include generosity because God is generous. He gave His only begotten Son for our benefit.

Generous: *liberal in giving*[159]

Throughout scripture, we see the instruction of God to give. We're to give to the poor, we're to give to one another, and we are instructed to give to God off the top of our income to make sure our hearts remain focused heavenward and we're not reliant on our own means and our own ability to provide for ourselves. This also ensures we are not ensnared by the world's systems to the detriment of our faith, trust, and dependence on our Heavenly Father.

Unfortunately in the Church, the area of money has become highly contentious and controversial, and as a result, very infrequently will there be a solid Biblical teaching on giving for fear of offenses, misunderstandings, and grumblings. As a result of this lack of solid and balanced teaching, there are toxic and untrue belief systems that are wrapped around the area of giving. There are also extreme and misguided teachings that lead to bondage and difficulties in the areas of money management and generosity in people's personal lives. Because the truth about biblical finances tends to be hidden, the mission of the Church as a whole–the expansion of the Gospel of Jesus Christ–is restricted because too few people are giving to support the work of God's Kingdom. One study suggests that only about 21% of attendees give a faithful tithe to their local church, though that number may be lower.[160]

Throughout scripture, we see the instruction of God to give.
This...ensures we are not ensnared by the world's systems
to the detriment of our faith, trust, and dependence on our Heavenly Father.

CHAPTER 18

What this suggests is that for every ten people, only two of them are supporting the work and benefits that all ten of them are receiving. The financial care of a pastor, the facilitation of Christian growth, youth and kids ministries, corporate worship times, weddings, funerals, benevolence, special events, missions work, and even keeping the lights and heat on, are provided by two out of ten people in any given church service! This means that the other eight of the ten attend and enjoy the benefits the Church provides without contributing financially at all.

Yet, there remains a cultural perception outside the church, (and many times by the 80% who do not give) that the Church has lots of money and should help everyone who asks at whatever amount requested, no questions asked. In many people's minds, the Church should do everything it does for free. Examples would include pastoral counseling services, weddings and receptions, funerals, baby showers, rent and utility assistance, food services, youth and children's ministry, and many other things. Yet these services often have *significant* overhead. Somehow there is a disconnect in the understanding of where the money that the Church has actually comes from. For whatever reason, the *minority* of people attending church (21%) are providing for the many (79%). And the many often don't seem to notice.

Yet, there remains a cultural perception...that the Church has lots of money and should help everyone...no questions asked.
In many people's minds, the Church should do everything...for free.

Take into consideration that many of the largest donations in the church come from older adults and we can see that the Church in our day and age is headed down a path of starvation as we move into the next generation. As those in the older generation begin their transition to heaven, the Church will be left in the hands of a generation who have a cynicism toward giving. What will happen to the Church if the giving percentage continues to go down as it has for many years now? It should concern us deeply to think that the Church will lose its footing and influence simply because God's people have stopped giving to keep it well-funded, alive, and relevant into the coming ages.

Many reasons are likely present for the lack of contribution to the local Church by its constituents. Certainly, past abuses by unscriptural or misunderstood teaching on giving have played a role. But the larger concern is the fact that most people who love God are often living lifestyles outside of their means and have debt payments that eat up their financial margin. Taking care of God's house is left to someone else because any extra money they have is usually spent on themselves first. I would suggest that God's portion doesn't come from our 'extra'. Scripturally, God's portion comes first.

As we're building our Christian foundation, I would be remiss to neglect the area of giving, specifically in the area of being a good steward of God's resources, and giving a tithe to the house of God we are a part of.

Before we dive into the powerful depth of understanding God's heart in the area of giving, it might be helpful to see the extremes and abuses of scriptural personal finances for what they are. The first extreme is what can be labeled the "Prosperity Gospel". This belief system, in a nutshell, is that God wants us to be completely rich financially as a direct result of how much money we give to someone's ministry. This can become toxic because it elevates our works above grace and labels those who are not prosperous as having less faith than the wealthy. This is unscriptural and untrue. The second extreme is the elevation of someone's spirituality because of extreme poverty. In this view, the poorer we are, the more holy we are because the possession of any kind of finances or property is seen as a compromise to our holiness. *Both of these extremes are an abuse of the truth God clearly lines out in scripture.* What we need is a balanced view of God's Word in the area of giving.

We live in one of the most prosperous countries and one of the most prosperous eras the world has ever seen. As a result, we have access to almost anything we could possibly want or need in an instant. Easy debt, student loans, large mortgages, high-interest credit cards, aggressive marketing, and our human propensity to "keep up with the Joneses" have put shackles around our figurative wrists and have made it difficult for us to do anything with our finances except merely pay our monthly personal responsibilities and debt payments. And yet, we can't escape the instruction of God's Word to give to our local church–not just random gifts, though that's important, too–but regularly and at a specified percentage. *First.*

CHAPTER 18

WHAT IS A TITHE?

If you've been in the Church very long, you may have heard this interesting, but seemingly archaic, word: *tithe*. But what is a tithe?

A tithe is a tenth, or ten percent. In the Old Testament, this included agricultural increase: grain or sheep or other agrarian commodities. It represents ten percent of the income one receives as a result of their work in order to survive.

Leviticus 27:30 [161]
30 And all the tithe of the land, whether of the seed of the land or of the fruit of the tree, is the Lord's. It is holy to the Lord.

In modern times, because of our monetary system, even agricultural gain is measured in dollars. So we can look at our paycheck or the profit of a business, and we give God a tenth of that increase, ten percent.

...there seems to be a contention in the heart of many believers about the necessity of giving a tithe at all. Is tithing biblical for modern Christians since we're no longer under the Old Covenant law?

However, there seems to be a contention in the heart of many believers about the necessity of giving a tithe at all. Is tithing biblical for modern Christians since we're no longer under the Old Covenant law? While we don't find a percentage allocated to "giving" in the New Testament, *giving* at its core is very much anticipated as a *normal* and *expected* part of a Christian's everyday life. Paul has much to say on the subject:

2 Corinthians 9:6-15 [162] *(emphasis added)*
*6 But this I say: He who sows sparingly will also reap sparingly, and he who sows bountifully will also reap bountifully. 7 **So let each one give as he purposes in his heart**, not grudgingly or of necessity; for God loves a cheerful giver. 8 And God is able to make all grace abound toward you, that you, always having all sufficiency in all things, may have an abundance for every good work. 9 As it is written:*

> *"He has dispersed abroad,*
> *He has given to the poor;*
> *His righteousness endures forever."*

10 Now may He who supplies seed to the sower, and bread for food, supply and multiply the seed you have sown and increase the fruits of your righteousness, 11 while you are enriched in everything for all liberality, which causes thanksgiving through us to God. 12 For the administration of this service not only supplies the needs of the saints, but also is abounding through many thanksgivings to God, 13 while, through the proof of this ministry, they glorify God for the obedience of your confession to the gospel of Christ, and for your liberal sharing with them and all men, 14 and by their prayer for you, who long for you because of the exceeding grace of God in you. 15 Thanks be to God for His indescribable gift!

New Covenant Giving can use the principle of the tithe as our starting point of generosity. I believe that the entire Bible is the counsel of God's word. We don't see giving going away in the New Testament, so we can align with the principle of the tithe as the *baseline* for the giving we see in the New Testament.

We need to question our motives. Why would we *not* want to give a tithe to God? Why would we say we want to be more like Jesus and then try to be *less* generous? The Bible is full of examples of the tenth being where we start. But now that we're under the New Covenant of grace, freely receiving from God what we have never deserved, I believe the New Testament makes the case that we should look to being *more* generous as New Covenant Christians, not less!

CHAPTER 18

First, we must establish that giving at any level is very Biblical.

Deuteronomy 16:16-17 [163] (emphasis added)
16 Three times a year all your males shall appear before the Lord your God in the place which He chooses: at the Feast of Unleavened Bread, at the Feast of Weeks, and at the Feast of Tabernacles; and **they shall not appear before the Lord empty-handed.** *17 Every man shall give as he is able, according to the blessing of the Lord your God which He has given you.*

Throughout the Bible, we see that God anticipates that His people will be open-handed for a number of reasons. He always reveals the reason as being that we give from our heart first. Giving or not giving is out of the overflow of our hearts. If we give, we do it because we love to give. If we hold back, it's because something in our heart hangs on so tight that we can't separate from something we think belongs to us. Understand that we are simply stewards of what God has given us to manage. We don't actually own *any* of it. To remain closed-fisted reveals that something in our heart thinks we own something we don't. All we possess has been given by God. We merely manage something He has blessed us with. When He asks for it, He anticipates we will give it. If we won't give, we start practicing self-centeredness, revealing we don't trust God to provide again. God wants to bless us. However, He does not want us to be mastered by the idol that money can become in our lives. *He wants to be our Lord.* He doesn't want money to rule over us. So He asks us to be givers, and sometimes asks for extra, to keep our hearts centered on Him.

With that said, we look to the next question many have about giving a tithe. God instructs us to give our tithe to our 'storehouse' (Malachi 3). This means that God instructs us to give ten percent of our increase to our home church–the place where we fellowship with other believers and where we worship God. We're to take care of the priests (pastors/shepherds) who take care of us. The tithe is not supposed to go to our favorite ministries somewhere other than our local church. Those gifts are offerings. The tithe is to go to our local fellowship to take care of the priesthood who tends *that* fellowship, to help the poor close to where we live, and to maintain the place of worship where we come together. But this begs the question:

DOES GOD NEED MY MONEY?

First, remember, it's not *our* money. We're stewards of something God has given to us! So, does God or even the Church, really need our money?

Psalm 24:1 [56]
1 The earth is the Lord's, and all its fullness,
The world and those who dwell therein.

Psalm 50:10 [164]
10 For every beast of the forest is Mine,
And the cattle on a thousand hills.

No, God doesn't need your money. Certainly, the church can put your money to good use. Yes, the church needs to build its budget on the fellowship's contribution. But your tithe is not first given for the church's benefit. Your tithe is given for a much more powerful, albeit surprising, reason. Giving is for you, not God! God doesn't *need* your money. Remember, God is All-Sufficient. God simply wants us to learn how to be generous for our own sake. He wants you to be like Him, and *He is a Giver!*

John 3:16 [158] *(emphasis added)*
*16 For God so loved the world that He **gave** His only begotten Son, that whoever believes in Him should not perish but have everlasting life.*

God doesn't need your money.
God simply wants us to learn how to be generous for our own sake.
He wants you to be like Him, and He is a Giver!

CHAPTER 18

HOW SHOULD THE TITHE BE USED?

Once our tithe is given to our local fellowship, it has been entrusted to God. Now it's in the stewardship of the governing body of the Church to make sure it's used scripturally. As a giver, we obviously want to ensure our local church tends the finances wisely, but we also must realize we gave the finances to God. This trust helps us take our hands away from controlling it as "ours" after we've given it . At this point, the ones who make an account to God for its use are those who have been entrusted to do it by God and the confidence of the people. What is the tithe used for once it's given to the Church?

First and foremost, the tithe is to take care of the priesthood. This is the first place the Bible instructs the use of the tithe. Tithe is meant to take care of the priests (our modern-day pastors who serve full-time in the church). Why? Because God did not allow the priests (the Levites) to have their own land and income. They didn't have another source of finances to provide for their needs. He wanted the rest of the nation of Israel to take care of the ones who tended to the worship of God in the temple and took care of the spiritual health of the people.

First and foremost, the tithe is to take care of the priesthood.

Deuteronomy 18:1-5 [165]

1 The priests, the Levites—all the tribe of Levi—shall have no part nor inheritance with Israel; they shall eat the offerings of the Lord made by fire, and His portion. 2 Therefore they shall have no inheritance among their brethren; the Lord is their inheritance, as He said to them.

3 "And this shall be the priest's due from the people, from those who offer a sacrifice, whether it is bull or sheep: they shall give to the priest the shoulder, the cheeks, and the stomach. 4 The first fruits of your grain and your new wine and your oil, and the first of the fleece of your sheep, you shall give him. 5 For the Lord your God has chosen him out of all your tribes to stand to minister in the name of the Lord, him and his sons forever.

Today, most churches in America (including the one I attend) are governed by a Board of Directors who oversee the stewardship of the finances. The salary of the paid staff is set by the Board of Directors who also oversee any decisions for changes or raises to that salary. *The pastors' remuneration is not theirs to decide.* Those elected to steward the income decide as a team how much of the finances given are to be used to sustain the pastoral ministry. This ensures that the pastors cannot adjust their own income based on the ebb and flow of weekly giving.

Some might wonder why the care of the priesthood is above the care of the poor. The reason the pastoral ministry is the first priority when it comes to the use of the tithe is to make sure the Church continues to operate for generations to come. Without leadership, the Church will flounder. The pastor and pastoral team need to be sustained so that everything else can continue to operate and the torch of the Good News of Jesus Christ can continue to the next generation.

After the priority of taking care of the priesthood, the next place the tithe is used from the storehouse is to help the widow, the orphan, and the poor.

> *Deuteronomy 26:11-15* [166] *(emphasis added)*
> *11 So you shall rejoice in every good thing which the Lord your God has given to you and your house, you and the Levite and the stranger who is among you. 12 "When you have finished laying aside all the tithe of your increase in the third year—the year of tithing—**and have given it to the Levite, the stranger, the fatherless, and the widow, so that they may eat within your gates and be filled**, 13 then you shall say before the Lord your God: 'I have removed the holy tithe from my house, and also have **given them to the Levite, the stranger, the fatherless, and the widow**, according to all Your commandments which You have commanded me; I have not transgressed Your commandments, nor have I forgotten them. 14 I have not eaten any of it when in mourning, nor have I removed any of it for an unclean use, nor given any of it for the dead. I have obeyed the voice of the Lord my God, and have done according to all that You have commanded me. 15 Look down from Your holy habitation, from heaven, and bless Your people Israel and the land which You have given us, just as You swore to our fathers, "a land flowing with milk and honey."'*

CHAPTER 18

The tithes, and even offerings, were then used to help take care of the physical temple (or worship center, or church building) itself.

> *Exodus 25:1-9* [167] *(emphasis added)*
> *1 Then the Lord spoke to Moses, saying: 2 "Speak to the children of Israel, that they bring Me an offering. From everyone who gives it willingly with his heart you shall take My offering. 3 And this is the offering which you shall take from them: gold, silver, and bronze; 4 blue, purple, and scarlet thread, fine linen, and goats' hair; 5 ram skins dyed red, badger skins, and acacia wood; 6 oil for the light, and spices for the anointing oil and for the sweet incense; 7 onyx stones, and stones to be set in the ephod and in the breastplate.* **8 And let them make Me a sanctuary, that I may dwell among them.** *9 According to all that I show you, that is, the pattern of the tabernacle and the pattern of all its furnishings, just so you shall make it.*

Remember, giving the tithe is our baseline. Giving ten percent to our local church as our obedience to God is the expected starting point of our generosity.

> *Leviticus 27:30* [161] *(emphasis added)*
> *30 And all the tithe of the land, whether of the seed of the land or of the fruit of the tree,* **is the Lord's. It is holy to the Lord.**

Tithe: HEBREW - מַעֲשֵׂר ma-aser (mah-as-ayr): *the tenth part (payment of the tenth)* [168]

Remember, giving the tithe is our baseline.
Giving ten percent to our local church as our obedience
to God is the expected starting point of our generosity.

To be clear, giving a tithe in the Bible would look like this: if someone owns ten sheep, God got the best one as a sacrifice and the shepherd would keep the other nine to build their flock. Today, if we earn ten dollars, God gets one dollar first and we get to keep nine dollars. If we earn one hundred thousand dollars yearly, God is given the first ten thousand while we get ninety thousand to live on. Instead of viewing our income as our money from which we give to God, we need to realize that God owns all of it from the start. We wouldn't even have our income if it weren't for the skills, time, and blessing God has provided for us to begin with. This means He gives us ninety percent of what we earn and only asks us for one-tenth of our income as an act of worship. The tithe already belongs to God! He simply asks us to release it to Him. Remember Leviticus 27:30. "The Tithe is the Lord's. It's holy to the Lord."

We can see where the Bible teaches that the tithe is God's by what God tells the prophet Malachi in chapter 3. If we use the tenth for ourselves, we are stealing from God.

Malachi 3:8-12 [169]
8 "Will a man rob God? Yet you have robbed Me!
But you say, 'In what way have we robbed You?' In tithes and offerings.
9 You are cursed with a curse, For you have robbed Me,
Even this whole nation.
10 Bring all the tithes into the storehouse,
That there may be food in My house,
And try Me now in this," Says the Lord of hosts,
"If I will not open for you the windows of heaven
And pour out for you such blessing
That there will not be room enough to receive it.
11 "And I will rebuke the devourer for your sakes,
So that he will not destroy the fruit of your ground,
Nor shall the vine fail to bear fruit for you in the field,"
Says the Lord of hosts;
12 "And all nations will call you blessed,
For you will be a delightful land," Says the Lord of hosts.

CHAPTER 18

In many countries of the world, we are expected to pay taxes on our income. Invariably, this question comes up, "Should I give God a tithe from my gross income (pre-tax), or net income (after tax)?" Ultimately, the principle is to give! Though Biblical arguments could possibly be made for either amount, ultimately, why do we try to wiggle out of being generous? I want to be *more* like Jesus, not less. Jesus is generous and doesn't look for ways to be less generous. Jesus gave His all, so it is a good exercise to look toward giving beyond the baseline! If we're willing to give the bigger number, we train ourselves to be open-handed like God is, rather than keep back more for ourselves. The point is this: we should give what our heart compels us to give. We should just give! We should become bigger givers throughout our lives! Let's stretch our giving so we become a better giver all the time until we go home to heaven to be with Jesus!

Why do we try to wiggle out of being generous?
I want to be more like Jesus, not less...
Jesus gave His all, so it is a good exercise to look
toward giving beyond the baseline!
The point is this: we should give what our heart compels us to give.

WHAT IS A TITHE VS. AN OFFERING?

While a tithe is giving ten percent from the top of our income, an offering comes from our abundance and extra. It is additional giving from a heart that is moved to meet a need or worship God in extravagance. Offerings are a decision from our heart to give extra.

Leviticus 27:28[161]
28 'Nevertheless no devoted offering that a man may devote to the Lord of all that he has, both man and beast, or the field of his possession, shall be sold or redeemed; every devoted offering is most holy to the Lord.

Offerings are something extra we want to give. Offerings are something we *want* to devote to the Lord as a gift over and above the tithe which was already His at the beginning. Offerings come from the ninety percent God has allowed us to keep after the tithe.

Offering: HEBREW - מִנְחָה minha - *gift, tribute, offering, present, oblation [a thing presented or offered to God], sacrifice, donation* [170]

2 Corinthians 9:7 [162] *(emphasis added)*
*7 So let each one give **as he purposes in his heart**, not grudgingly or of necessity; for **God loves a cheerful giver**.*

WHAT IF I CAN'T AFFORD TO TITHE?

If we can't afford to tithe, we are very likely spending God's tenth on ourselves. In some extreme circumstances, this might not be the case, but considering the statistics of the modern American citizen, the case could be made that reducing our debt and living within our means would break some margin free so we can obey God.

Consider these staggering statistics, current at the time of this writing:

- The average payment for a new car is $726 per month and the average payment for a used car is over $500 per month. Consider that some families own two financed cars![171]

- America's median mortgage payment is $1,768. This means half of the payments are more than this.[172]

- Many American consumers are paying over $400 per month in credit card payments.[173]

If we can't afford to tithe, [we're] likely spending God's tenth on ourselves.

CHAPTER 18

Add to these "normal" bills our groceries, utilities, vacations, eating out and luxury coffee drinks, pretty soon we realize that we're often spending God's portion. What if we tithed first, instead of waiting to see what is left over? When we make a budget, this is simply an itemized list of our expenses in prioritized order. The reason God is not honored with His portion is that we don't put God on the top of the list! Don't eat up the tithe. Make sure God's portion is the top line item on your budget.

Tithes and offerings are a vital Foundation Stone for a few reasons. First, God is generous and He uses the tithe in our life to make us more like Him! Second, He uses our tithe to take care of our local storehouse and leaders so the Good News of Jesus Christ moves in our neighborhoods! Third, God uses our tithes and offerings to take care of those who are in need. Fourth, He uses our tithes to make sure our church facilities stay in good working order. And fifth, our gifts should be used to fund the advancement of the Gospel around the world by supporting missionaries and works of the Kingdom in the farther reaches we have access to.

If there is truly no wiggle room in your budget to give your tithe and you legitimately are having to choose between feeding your family and tithing, of course, feed your family even as you try to give *something*. But if you can't give because your lifestyle and luxuries make it impossible to give, it might be time to sell some things to make sure God is the top line item of your budget! Remember, it's not just those in the 21% that should be responsible to keep our God-given mission going. We all need to be taking part in advancing the Good News, taking care of our Church, our pastors, the poor, the building, and the works of the Kingdom around the world until we see Jesus face to face! Become more like Jesus! Give and see what God can do with your obedience and the trusting act of worship that is the tithe!

REFLECTION QUESTIONS

1. After reading this chapter, do you believe your financial priorities are in order?

2. If yes, great! If not, ask the Lord to show you how to get your priorities in the right order. Take some time to write down what He is speaking to you below:

3. If you are ready to go to the next level of generosity, pray this today: "Lord, I am so thankful that You gave *everything* so I could be reunited with Father God in complete and whole relationship. I want to give all, just as you did. Help me to lay down my selfishness in favor of seeing Your kingdom and Your will being done–on earth as it is in heaven! I give you my life, my family, and my finances. In Jesus name, Amen."

CHAPTER 19
CRUCIFIED WITH CHRIST
"I No Longer Live"

Christianity has always had a polarizing effect on the world. From the establishment of the redemptive work of Jesus on the Cross until today, the surrender of a life to the service of Christ has always been controversial. And while it is understandable there may be a time when individuals will 'explore' faith in Christ, there will always come a moment when our stand will be challenged. Do we serve God or don't we? Is our life His, or our own? Would we trade this world for Him, or would we rather not?

...The surrender of a life to the service of Christ has always been controversial... [while] there may be time[s] when individuals will 'explore' faith in Christ, there will always come a moment when our stand will be challenged.

FOUNDATION STONES

For eons, many believers in Jesus have made the ultimate sacrifice of surrendering their lives unto death instead of renouncing Christ. As Christians who live on this earth, we are called to surrender our lives for our love of God. Which is easier, to die one time as a martyr for Christ, or to die for Christ every day by laying down our lives in surrender and obedience, living wholeheartedly for Him alone?

Let's allow God's Word to challenge us:

Galatians 2:15-19 [174]
15 We who are Jews by nature, and not sinners of the Gentiles, 16 knowing that a man is not justified by the works of the law but by faith in Jesus Christ, even we have believed in Christ Jesus, that we might be justified by faith in Christ and not by the works of the law; for by the works of the law no flesh shall be justified. 17 But if, while we seek to be justified by Christ, we ourselves also are found sinners, is Christ therefore a minister of sin? Certainly not! 18 For if I build again those things which I destroyed, I make myself a transgressor. 19 For I through the law died to the law that I might live to God."

Consider, the law of God points to Jesus. The moral law, the festivals and ceremonies, and the guidelines from the Old Covenant all point to the life, death, burial, and resurrection of Christ. The law painted the picture of salvation that Jesus performed in His death. Salvation is found in no other name than that of Jesus. We can't be saved by following the law. We are saved by believing in the Law-Maker by faith. This happens by believing in the fulfillment of the law of God that Jesus accomplished in His sacrifice on the cross. What Paul is saying in Galatians 2 is that unless we receive Jesus, all our efforts to obey the law are pointless. We are no closer to God by observing the law in perfection than if we didn't follow it. The *only way* to the Father is through faith in Jesus (John 14:6). Jesus is the Bridge. That's why we must surrender our lives to Him and live in faith for Jesus. Paul continues his discourse in the next verse:

Galatians 2:20 [174]
20 I have been crucified with Christ; it is no longer I who live, but Christ lives in me; and the life which I now live in the flesh I live by faith in the Son of God, who loved me and gave Himself for me.

CHAPTER 19

If Jesus has been crucified and His work is complete, what does this verse mean? Why do we need to be crucified with Christ? Is this a literal crucifixion, or does it mean something different? What can it look like to be crucified with Christ and then live unto God? Let's dissect this verse and understand its weight and significance in our daily lives.

"I NO LONGER LIVE"

Galatians 2:20a [174]
20a I have been crucified with Christ; it is no longer I who live...

In order to understand this verse, we've got to revisit the understanding of what crucifixion was in Jesus' day.

Crucifixion: *the execution of a person by nailing or binding them to a cross. This was a criminal's death* [175]

Hebrews 7:27 makes clear that the crucifixion of Christ was God's redemptive work "once for all".

Hebrews 7:27b [176] *(emphasis added)*
*27b...this He did (crucifixion) **once for all** when He offered up Himself.*

Salvation is found in no other name than that of Jesus.
We can't be saved by following the law.
We are saved by believing in the Law-Maker by faith.

Since what Jesus did on the cross is a complete work, we don't need to be physically crucified to fulfill any requirements for God. Paul is giving us a word picture–a metaphor–so we can understand the heart behind our submission to God. This word picture can be understood to mean:

- God before self

- The Gospel before comfort

- Service before self-service

- Surrender of our will and obedience to God's will

- A willingness to lay down our life every day to be a believer in Jesus

Paul came from a Jewish, very zealous and very religious, background. The law of God was incredibly sacred and no detail was to be missed for fear of God's judgment. When Paul encountered Jesus Christ on the road to Damascus (Acts 9) and had the revelation that faith in Jesus' redemption was the gate to God and not the works of the law, he realized that self-righteousness had to go. He learned we can't get to heaven by our own effort. Jesus wouldn't have confronted Paul on the Road to Damascus if the requirement had been abiding by the letter of the law. Paul was good at that. What he was missing was a relationship with Jesus Christ and the righteousness that comes through faith. Jesus told Paul he had been "kicking against the goads" (Acts 9:5). In other words, Paul was resisting the main thing being offered by God which was a belief in Jesus Christ and surrender of the personal will.

Paul had a revelation that day: the only way to eternal life was through Jesus Christ and not through his personal works. This became the message he preached and the life he lived. Followers of Jesus knew salvation by faith in Christ alone to be true and sound doctrine, but when they started to slip into works, law, and duty again, it rubbed Paul the wrong way and he aggressively corrected the error. He had been forever transformed. Look at how he teaches the Church about this powerful understanding by using a confrontation he had with the apostle Peter as an example:

CHAPTER 19

Galatians 2:11-20 [174]

11 Now when Peter had come to Antioch, I withstood him to his face, because he was to be blamed; 12 for before certain men came from James, he would eat with the Gentiles; but when they came, he withdrew and separated himself, fearing those who were of the circumcision. 13 And the rest of the Jews also played the hypocrite with him, so that even Barnabas was carried away with their hypocrisy. 14 But when I saw that they were not straightforward about the truth of the gospel, I said to Peter before them all, "If you, being a Jew, live in the manner of Gentiles and not as the Jews, why do you compel Gentiles to live as Jews? 15 We who are Jews by nature, and not sinners of the Gentiles, 16 knowing that a man is not justified by the works of the law but by faith in Jesus Christ, even we have believed in Christ Jesus, that we might be justified by faith in Christ and not by the works of the law; for by the works of the law no flesh shall be justified. 17 "But if, while we seek to be justified by Christ, we ourselves also are found sinners, is Christ therefore a minister of sin? Certainly not! 18 For if I build again those things which I destroyed, I make myself a transgressor. 19 For I through the law died to the law that I might live to God. 20 I have been crucified with Christ; it is no longer I who live, but Christ lives in me; and the life which I now live in the flesh I live by faith in the Son of God, who loved me and gave Himself for me.

Paul was wrestling against a religious system of rules, regulations, duty, and appearances. He recognized it because he had been trapped by it himself.

Salvation doesn't come by works of the law. If it did, it would have already worked. Salvation comes through accepting the Lordship of Jesus and His work of redemption in His death, burial, and resurrection. This salvation does not come from self-imposed righteousness. It doesn't come through a list of successes that outweighs our list of failures. Salvation *only comes* through the gateway Jesus created. He built the bridge with His life. He unlocked the gate of heaven with His own blood payment. Only *One* is worthy to unlock the gate, and we're not it! We can walk through that gate now by accepting the direction Jesus made for us. This acceptance of faith removes every act of pretentious self-righteousness.

FOUNDATION STONES

Philippians 3:3-14 [177]

*3 For we are the circumcision (**true believers**), who worship God in the Spirit, rejoice in Christ Jesus, and have no confidence in the flesh, 4 though I also might have confidence in the flesh. If anyone else thinks he may have confidence in the flesh, I more so: 5 circumcised the eighth day, of the stock of Israel, of the tribe of Benjamin, a Hebrew of the Hebrews; concerning the law, a Pharisee; 6 concerning zeal, persecuting the church; concerning the righteousness which is in the law, blameless. 7 But what things were gain to me, these I have counted loss for Christ. 8 Yet indeed I also count all things loss for the excellence of the knowledge of Christ Jesus my Lord, for whom I have suffered the loss of all things, and count them as rubbish, that I may gain Christ 9 and be found in Him, not having my own righteousness, which is from the law, but that which is through faith in Christ, the righteousness which is from God by faith; 10 that I may know Him and the power of His resurrection, and the fellowship of His sufferings, being conformed to His death, 11 if, by any means, I may attain to the resurrection from the dead. 12 Not that I have already attained, or am already perfected; but I press on, that I may lay hold of that for which Christ Jesus has also laid hold of me. 13 Brethren, I do not count myself to have apprehended; but one thing I do, forgetting those things which are behind and reaching forward to those things which are ahead, 14 I press toward the goal for the prize of the upward call of God in Christ Jesus.*

If we are fully surrendered to Jesus, self-righteousness is defeated and self-centered living has to go! Life tends to funnel us into living for ourselves. We will focus on our own desires, aspirations, and ego-boosting efforts. Our careers, our money, and our promotion must take a secondary position compared to our surrender to God! Paul is teaching the Galatians that true living is the living that is done for the benefit of other people in the name of Jesus.

Matthew 25:40 [149]

40 And the King will answer and say to them, 'Assuredly, I say to you, in as much as you did it to one of the least of these My brethren, you did it to Me.'

CHAPTER 19

CHRIST LIVES IN ME

Galatians 2:20b [174]
20b...it is no longer I who live, but Christ lives in me...

When we are surrendered to Jesus, the power of the Holy Spirit can indwell us. This means we're not just talking about simply changing our behaviors. Changing our behavior is the result of Christ living in us. But this indwelling is a deeper transformation than just *"willing"* ourselves into behavior change. Outward transformation happens when *inward transformation* is realized because of the power of the Holy Spirit living in us! This is transformation from the indwelling, empowering, life-giving, sin-squashing, bondage-expelling, devil-defeating presence of the Holy Spirit in us!

Acts 1:8 [99]
8 But you shall receive power when the Holy Spirit has come upon you; and you shall be witnesses to Me in Jerusalem, and in all Judea and Samaria, and to the end of the earth."

According to Acts 1, this was the last sentence Jesus spoke while on Earth. In fact, He just finished telling His disciples not to worry about times and dates, but to be filled with the Spirit and be His witnesses in the world. Christ wanted to dwell *in us* with new life after our spiritual crucifixion, our surrender, to God!

Jesus anticipated that we would carry on His work with the power of the Spirit of God in us, which means the things Jesus did are the things we should want to do! Now that Christ lives in me and now that I'm filled with the Holy Spirit, I long to do the things Jesus did! What did Jesus do? How did Jesus live?

- Jesus loved
- Jesus met the needs of other people.
- Jesus healed the sick.
- Jesus preached the Kingdom of God.
- Jesus laid down His life every day.

John 14:12 [58]
12 Most assuredly, I say to you, he who believes in Me, the works that I do he will do also; and greater works than these he will do, because I go to My Father.

If we've been crucified with Christ, and therefore have Christ living in us, we live for Him now, doing the things He did! This happens, not because of our good deeds or our careful observance of every rule, but because our gratitude to God for what Jesus did makes us *live* like Jesus!

Galatians 2:20b [174] *(emphasis added)*
*20b ...the life which I now live in the flesh **I live by faith in the Son of God**, who loved me and gave Himself for me.*

If we've been crucified with Christ... we live for Him now, doing the things He did!

Jesus didn't tell us to follow Him with no benefit! Through faith, we are given victory even in this life with the promise of eternity with God in the next! We die to ourselves, are filled with His Spirit and now we live by faith in Jesus Christ because He first loved us. He doesn't ask us to do anything He didn't do Himself! We will live by faith in Christ in this life as we fully surrender to God. This means we're not checking off a list of religious 'do's and don'ts'. We're living by *faith*! We received Jesus by faith, and now we are going to live by faith! Paul is declaring to us that we can have this experience while we "live in the flesh". In this life, we live by faith in the Son of God!

We must live by faith in this life because we are confident that what we have received from God is because He loves us and gave His life for us. We haven't made too many mistakes or walked too far away from God as to be disqualified from His forgiveness and calling. His blessings are for everyone who believes and lives their lives in surrender to Him. Letting the life of Christ resonate in us bolsters our confidence that it's because He loves us that we have received anything at all!

CHAPTER 19

*Romans 10:9-13[20] (**emphasis added**)*
*9 ... if you confess with your mouth the Lord Jesus and believe in your heart that God has raised Him from the dead, you will be saved. 10 For with the heart one believes unto righteousness, and with the mouth confession is made unto salvation. 11 For the Scripture says, **"Whoever believes on Him will not be put to shame."** 12 For there is no distinction between Jew and Greek, for the same Lord over all is rich to all who call upon Him. 13 For "whoever calls on the name of the Lord shall be saved."*

We can't belittle the act of Christ giving His life on the cross by declaring that we're the one exception to His saving power and grace. We also can't carry our own agendas and still be surrendered to Him. If we're a believer but we're having a hard time moving past initial salvation and into bold, surrendered living, we must courageously lay our lives back down, being crucified with Christ so it's not us living, but Christ *in* us! If we are reluctant to believe that the life of Christ resides in us through faith, we must take a leap of faith today. We must trust that the same power that filled Paul and Peter and other surrendered people around us is also available to us!

REFLECTION QUESTIONS

1. What does it look like for you personally to be submitted to God, just as Jesus laid down His life for the Church?

2. Is there any place in your heart where there is still selfishness, compromise, or things that need to be submitted to God?

3. If yes, then take a moment to pray and ask the Lord to give you the wisdom and strength to lay those things down and fully submit to Him.

CHAPTER 20
THE GREAT COMMISSION

If Not You, Then Who?

We've talked a lot about what Christ Jesus has done for us—His redemption, forgiveness, covenant, and transformation in our lives and motives. But what I get so excited about is knowing that God is restoring us so that we can be in full operation again, back to our original working order. This is so we become who God created us to be, and do what He's called us to do.

In my hometown, we have an annual classic car show called The Klamath Kruise. Cars from decades past are displayed in the town's largest park and crowds of thousands come out to walk the rows, remember the past, and admire the giant engines, shiny paint, and freshly renewed upholstery of cars that are older than many of the owners. Awards are given, stories are told, and then the day culminates with a nostalgic cruise of Main Street in Downtown Klamath Falls. As the sun sets, glistening classics roar by to the sound of oldies music and the glee of adoring fans.

---

*[It's] exciting...knowing that God is restoring us...
back to our original working order.*

It goes without saying that most of those old cars have gone through days of neglect and many spent years forgotten in a garage, junkyard, or someone's back field. Rust and corrosion had eaten many of them beyond recognition. Some probably even had weeds growing up through dead engines and holes in the floorboards. The only way any of these cars can fully function today is because someone had the vision to first see what they were created to be, and then to see what they could be again! Years of careful restoration, tinkering, painting, and buffing have turned them into masterpieces far exceeding their original design.

Just like those old cars, we also incur dents, bruises, and all kinds of malfunctions that need to be repaired. But God isn't interested in just having you back to factory specifications. He wants to see you restored better than new! He wants you to be His "showpiece"!

As in the example of the old cars, we have been given a mission. Their mission was to cruise highways in style. Our mission is to be co-heirs with Christ and to live victoriously as God's sons and daughters! The road ahead of God's people will require extra horsepower and features to make the trip. That horsepower and those features are only installed by the Master with the intention to use us for a great purpose. We've been restored, and then we've been given a mission. God has given us a calling to something greater than ourselves!

Calling: *a strong inner impulse toward a particular course of action especially when accompanied by conviction of divine influence* [178]

Our mission is to be co-heirs with Christ and to live victoriously as God's sons and daughters!

The road ahead of God's people will require extra horsepower... with the intention to use us for a great purpose.

CHAPTER 20

It is God's aim and ambition to reach every person with His Good News. God restored us so we could be the vehicle through which He accomplishes His mission. God's mission is for the world to know His Good News of salvation. Because we are in partnership with God from the standpoint of our sonship and relationship with God, His mission now becomes a cooperation. Thus the "co" is in front of the "mission". The "mission" is God's assignment. The "co" is us accomplishing the mission *with* God and every other believer in Christ.

It's amazing that we get to partner with God in His Divine focus and that we don't have to declare the Gospel all by ourselves! That's why it's important to serve God with a family of believers who are also passionate about the "co-mission". The process of living out God's instructions is empowering and effective when we share the Gospel together with the Holy Spirit's leading and the cooperation of other believers around us!

Each Gospel account, (Matthew, Mark, Luke, and John) has a version of what is called "The Great Commission". What is the Commission and how do we walk it out?

It's amazing that we get to partner with God in His Divine focus...
That's why it's important to serve God with a family of believers
who are also passionate about the "co-mission".

Matthew 28:16-20 [1]

16 "Then the eleven disciples went away into Galilee, to the mountain which Jesus had appointed for them. 17 When they saw Him, they worshiped Him; but some doubted. 18 And Jesus came and spoke to them, saying, "All authority has been given to Me in heaven and on earth. 19 Go therefore and make disciples of all the nations, baptizing them in the name of the Father and of the Son and of the Holy Spirit, 20 teaching them to observe all things that I have commanded you; and lo, I am with you always, even to the end of the age." Amen."

Mark 16:12-20 [179]

12 "After that, He appeared in another form to two of them as they walked and went into the country. 13 And they went and told it to the rest, but they did not believe them either. 14 Later He appeared to the eleven as they sat at the table; and He rebuked their unbelief and hardness of heart, because they did not believe those who had seen Him after He had risen. 15 And He said to them, "Go into all the world and preach the gospel to every creature. 16 He who believes and is baptized will be saved; but he who does not believe will be condemned. 17 And these signs will follow those who believe: In My name they will cast out demons; they will speak with new tongues; 18 they will take up serpents; and if they drink anything deadly, it will by no means hurt them; they will lay hands on the sick, and they will recover." 19 So then, after the Lord had spoken to them, He was received up into heaven, and sat down at the right hand of God. 20 And they went out and preached everywhere, the Lord working with them and confirming the word through the accompanying signs. Amen."

Luke 24:46-49 [98]

46 "Then He said to them, "Thus it is written, and thus it was necessary for the Christ to suffer and to rise from the dead the third day, 47 and that repentance and remission of sins should be preached in His name to all nations, beginning at Jerusalem. 48 And you are witnesses of these things. 49 Behold, I send the Promise of My Father upon you; but tarry in the city of Jerusalem until you are endued with power from on high.""

John 20:21 [180]

21 So Jesus said to them again, "Peace to you! As the Father has sent Me, I also send you."

The process of living out God's instructions is empowering and effective when we share the Gospel together...

CHAPTER 20

WHY ARE WE PART OF GOD'S MISSION?

Knowing that God is all-powerful and He can do anything He wants, why do we even have a part to play in His mission at all? Why would He even want to involve us in His plan? Simply put, God created us in His image, and He is forming His character in us. The same gift we received from God is available to anyone and He wants our compassion to overflow to others so we resemble God even as we extend His invitation to those around us. Each one of us most likely believes in God as a result of someone sharing Jesus with us!

Christ is choosing to make His appeal to the world *through* us!

2 Corinthians 5:20[91]
20 Now then, we are ambassadors for Christ, as though God were pleading through us: we implore you on Christ's behalf, be reconciled to God.

Jesus ascended into heaven, filled us with the Holy Spirit, and now we are endued with power from on high. Because the Holy Spirit lives in us, He prompts us to share the same message with other people that we received ourselves in order to be saved. The same Spirit that raised Christ from the dead lives in us now (Romans 8:11). By God's will, we are the mouthpieces for His message! This is the Great Commission!

The same Spirit that raised Christ from the dead lives in us now...

I've often thought about the fact that God could just boom from heaven the truth of the mystery of salvation so that everyone would be transformed. But He has chosen to bring His message through broken people who have been in the process of restoration, repair, and deliverance in order to support, with evidence, the power of the Gospel. When non-believing people see the transformation and authentic faith of a believer, they will be brought to a decision because they are literally seeing the narrative played out before their eyes in the life of someone tangible and touchable.

Are we living our lives in such a way that God can tell His story of redemption through us? Though in process, and yet to be perfected, are we all right with God using our life as an illustrated message to how He can save and deliver people? Are we willing to allow God to use our mouths and our stories to tell unbelievers the truth of a God who loves them and wants to transform them? That's the "co" part of the mission! God *loves* to tell His message through broken vessels. We are like fragile clay pots holding the world's greatest treasure.

> *2 Corinthians 4:5-15* [181] *(emphasis added)*
> *5 For we do not preach ourselves, but Christ Jesus the Lord, and ourselves your bondservants for Jesus' sake. 6 For it is the God who commanded light to shine out of darkness, who has shone in our hearts to give the light of the knowledge of the glory of God in the face of Jesus Christ.* **7 But we have this treasure in earthen vessels, that the excellence of the power may be of God and not of us.** *8 We are hard-pressed on every side, yet not crushed; we are perplexed, but not in despair; 9 persecuted, but not forsaken; struck down, but not destroyed—10 always carrying about in the body the dying of the Lord Jesus, that the life of Jesus also may be manifested in our body. 11 For we who live are always delivered to death for Jesus' sake, that the life of Jesus also may be manifested in our mortal flesh. 12 So then death is working in us, but life in you. 13 And since we have the same spirit of faith, according to what is written, "I believed and therefore I spoke," we also believe and therefore speak, 14 knowing that He who raised up the Lord Jesus will also raise us up with Jesus, and will present us with you. 15 For all things are for your sakes, that grace, having spread through the many, may cause thanksgiving to abound to the glory of God.*

The all-surpassing power of the Gospel belongs to God! He will get the glory for the story when we are faithful to share it! No person on earth is qualified to share this story and that's *exactly* why God loves to tell it to the world through us!

No person on earth is qualified to share this story and that's exactly why God loves to tell it to the world through us!

CHAPTER 20

WE GET TO CO-LABOR WITH CHRIST!

We're not just slaves. We're not just subjects in God's Kingdom. We're not just mindless drones with no personality or unique distinguishing parts of our lives to contribute. We're God's *sons and daughters!* He wants His story told through us because we are a part of His family now.

Matthew 9:35-38 [182]
35 Then Jesus went about all the cities and villages, teaching in their synagogues, preaching the gospel of the kingdom, and healing every sickness and every disease among the people. 36 But when He saw the multitudes, He was moved with compassion for them, because they were weary and scattered, like sheep having no shepherd. 37 Then He said to His disciples, "The harvest truly is plentiful, but the laborers are few. 38 Therefore pray the Lord of the harvest to send out laborers into His harvest."

The great need we see in the world truly is God's harvest, but we are the laborers in His field. What an amazing thing it is to be trusted with the greatest truth the world has ever known. We're the heralds! We're the messengers! We're the mouthpiece! It's time now to proclaim it with all our hearts and lives!

EMPOWERED FOR THE MISSION

It's easy to feel powerless and small when it comes to carrying the world's greatest message. But there is such encouragement from God's Word for us as simple "jars of clay". We don't have to do it on our own! If we surrender to Him, God will fill us with the power of the Holy Spirit to share the Good News of Jesus Christ with our lives and our own personal stories. The Holy Spirit empowers us to share God's salvation message with the people around us.

Acts 1:8 [99]
8 "But you shall receive power when the Holy Spirit has come upon you; and you shall be witnesses to Me in Jerusalem, and in all Judea and Samaria, and to the end of the earth."

You might be thinking, "I'm not a preacher. How can I share the message?" Well, there's good news for you. Jesus instructed us to not fret about what to say and how to say it!

Luke 12:11-12 [183]
11 "Now when they bring you to the synagogues and magistrates and authorities, do not worry about how or what you should answer, or what you should say. 12 For the Holy Spirit will teach you in that very hour what you ought to say."

I believe God wants us to be full with the Word and His presence every day and have our tool belts filled with God's truth. Then the Holy Spirit can call on those tools when someone is in front of us so we can share the Good News with them! Let's be good stewards of the Gospel by preparing our hearts for action and expecting an opportunity to share every day. Let's not fret about not having every word planned out when we feel cornered. God will fill our mouths with His truth when it is needed! Every word we speak will be exactly what is needed. Maybe it will be a lot of words. Maybe only a few. But it will be just right when we are surrendered to Him!

Let's be good stewards of the Gospel by preparing our hearts for action and expecting an opportunity to share every day.

OUR TESTIMONIES AND SURRENDERED LIVES

We can never underestimate the power of our testimonies. A personal testimony is the story of what God has done for us. The powerful thing about our personal story is that it is irrefutable. When I share how God has moved in my life and the life of my family, no one can convince me it didn't happen. God gets the glory, and the hearer has to contend with the truth of how God touched *me personally*.

CHAPTER 20

> *Revelation 12:10-11* [184] *(emphasis added)*
> *10 Then I heard a loud voice saying in heaven, "Now salvation, and strength, and the kingdom of our God, and the power of His Christ have come, for the accuser of our brethren, who accused them before our God day and night, has been cast down. 11 And they overcame him by the blood of the Lamb and **by the word of their testimony**, and they did not love their lives to the death."*

Often, someone's life is transformed by hearing someone else's story coupled with the truth of scripture. Many times I've watched people get victory over a bondage of unforgiveness, or an addiction to drugs, alcohol, or pornography, by hearing about someone else's struggle and victory in that area. Something in us is hard-wired to respond with faith when we hear that someone else has overcome a similar struggle. Our spirit begins to stand up in hope, risking the belief, "If it can happen for them, maybe it can happen for me!" Be willing to share your story, linking it directly to the Gospel, and watch God use it to bring transformation and salvation to another person!

HIDING GOD'S WORD IN OUR HEARTS

It's important to spend time with God every day by reading His Word. The more often we read, study, and converse with God, the more we will have stored up in our hearts to share with others when the opportunity arises.

> *Jeremiah 15:16* [185]
> *16 Your words were found, and I ate them, And Your word was to me the joy and rejoicing of my heart; For I am called by Your name, O Lord God of hosts.*

The more often we read, study, and converse with God, the more we will have stored up in our hearts to share with others when the opportunity arises.

Since we are still on this side of heaven, we are all called to the Great Commission. As humans, we tend to demean our own contributions. But each of us can do *something* to share the Good News with other people! What are some ways we can fulfill God's mission every day? The most powerful way we share the Gospel is to build relationships with people. Be willing to know people's names. Share your life with your neighbors. Get to know your regular grocery store clerk. Listen to the hearts of your co-workers. Get involved with the schools your kids go to. Building relationships creates credibility and authenticity which opens doors to people's hearts. It's amazing how investing our lives in people around us adds strength to the message our lives proclaim.

Practice sharing the Gospel. Maybe even practice in the mirror! Be ready to tell the story of God's love to people.

Get involved in service to other people! Realize that your life is not your own and you were created to reach people with hope. Be determined to not allow your life to be all about you. Be willing to share your life with anyone and everyone around you to build a bridge to them that the love of God can cross!

Ask God for a fresh infilling of His Holy Spirit so you're full, empowered, emboldened, and compassionate in each and every situation God opens to you.

Remember, the mission is great! It's a mission of cooperation with God. Let's be about The Great Commission!

REFLECTION QUESTIONS

1. Simply-put, the Great Commission is about sharing your faith with the people around you. Who is one person you know needs a relationship with God, but is not currently serving Him?

_____
_____
_____
_____
_____

2. With this one person in mind, is there anything that is holding you back from sharing your faith with them?

_____
_____
_____
_____
_____

3. What is one way you could start to do that, if you have not already? (Remember, the power of a testimony is huge! Don't overcomplicate it. Simply telling the story of what God has done in your life can give an opportunity to open a conversation.)

_____
_____
_____
_____
_____
_____
_____
_____

CLOSING REMARKS

You've only just begun! I'm hopeful that you have found your Christian foundation strengthened and your faith in God growing like never before. My aim in this study volume is that you've not only grown intellectually, but you've grown in your intimate relationship with Your Heavenly Father. Having a resilient and faithful walk with God will help you overcome a contrary world and will cause your joy to overflow because you know Jesus Christ personally! Continue to let your daily prayer be, "Jesus, help me know You. I want to be more like You!"

If *Foundation Stones* has been a blessing to you, please consider leaving an Amazon review, and purchase a few more copies to give away to others who would benefit. This will help *Foundation Stones* reach more people with the transformative power of the Gospel of Jesus Christ!

Consider starting a small group with family and friends once a week, using *Foundation Stones* as a tool of discipleship. Read the pages together, explore the scriptures, and talk about the truths. Watch God build the faith of your family and friends right before your eyes!

Did you know *Foundation Stones* is also a podcast? In fact, that's where this book started. If you've enjoyed these studies, many other studies are available in podcast form. Simply search "Foundation Stones by Refuge City Church" on any podcast platform to get started today.

Let's continue to build our faith in Jesus one Foundation Stone at a time...

Much love in Christ,

-Jim Weaver

RESOURCES

1. Matthew 28:16-20 (NKJV). (n.d.). Bible Gateway. https://www.biblegateway.com/passage/?search=Matthew%2028%3A16-20&version=NKJV

2. Matthew 7:1-2; 9-11; 13-14; 24-25 (NKJV). (n.d.). Bible Gateway. https://www.biblegateway.com/passage/?search=Matthew%207%3A1-2%3B%209-11%3B%2013-14%3B%2024-25&version=NKJV

3. Answer, B. (2021, July 3). How many Bibles are sold each year? The Bible Answer. https://thebibleanswer.org/bibles-sold-each-year/

4. John 1:1-5; 12a; 14; 29 (NKJV). (n.d.). Bible Gateway. https://www.biblegateway.com/passage/?search=John%201%3A1-5%2C%2014&version=NKJV

5. abide. (2024). In Merriam-Webster Dictionary. https://www.merriam-webster.com/dictionary/abide

6. John 8:10-11; 31-32; 58 (NKJV). (n.d.). Bible Gateway. https://www.biblegateway.com/passage/?search=John%208%3A31-32&version=NKJV

7. Psalm 119:1-16; 97-106 (NKJV). (n.d.). Bible Gateway. https://www.biblegateway.com/passage/?search=Psalm%20119%3A1-8&version=NKJV

8. Jeremiah 17:9-10 (NKJV). (n.d.). Bible Gateway. https://www.biblegateway.com/passage/?search=Jeremiah%2017%3A9-10&version=NKJV

9. Hebrews 4:12-13; 15-16 (NKJV). (n.d.). Bible Gateway. https://www.biblegateway.com/passage/?search=Hebrews%204%3A12-13&version=NKJV

10. meditate. (2024). In Merriam-Webster Dictionary. https://www.merriam-webster.com/dictionary/meditate

11. Psalm 1 (NIV). (n.d.). Bible Gateway. https://www.biblegateway.com/passage/?search=Psalm%201&version=NIV

12. Proverbs 25:2; 21-22 (NKJV). (n.d.). Bible Gateway. https://www.biblegateway.com/passage/?search=Proverbs%2025%3A2&version=NKJV

13. salvation. (2024). In Merriam-Webster Dictionary. https://www.merriam-webster.com/dictionary/salvation#:~:text=%3A%20preservation%20from%20destruction%20or%20failure,sal%2D%CB%88v%C4%81%2Dshn%C9%99l

14. sin. (2024). In Merriam-Webster Dictionary. https://www.merriam-webster.com/dictionary/sin

15. Exodus 20:3-17 (NKJV). (n.d.). Bible Gateway. https://www.biblegateway.com/passage/?search=Exodus%2020%3A3-17&version=NKJV

16. 1 Peter 1:15-17 (NIV). (n.d.). Bible Gateway. https://www.biblegateway.com/passage/?search=1%20Peter%201%3A15-17&version=NIV

17. Romans 1:18-20 (NKJV). (n.d.). Bible Gateway. https://www.biblegateway.com/passage/?search=Romans%201%3A18-20&version=NKJV

18. Romans 3:22-24 (NIV). (n.d.). Bible Gateway. https://www.biblegateway.com/passage/?search=Romans%203%3A22-24&version=NIV

19. Romans 6:23 (NIV). (n.d.). Bible Gateway. https://www.biblegateway.com/passage/?search=Romans%206%3A23&version=NIV

RESOURCES

20. *Romans 10:8-13; 17 (NKJV). (n.d.). Bible Gateway. https://www.biblegateway.com/passage/?search=Romans%2010%3A9-10&version=NKJV*

21. *Ephesians 2:8-9; 14-16 (NKJV). (n.d.). Bible Gateway. https://www.biblegateway.com/passage/?search=Ephesians%202%3A8-9&version=NKJV*

22. *Romans 8:3-4; 15-16 (NKJV). (n.d.). Bible Gateway. https://www.biblegateway.com/passage/?search=Romans%208%3A3-4&version=NKJV*

23. *Revelation 13:8 (NKJV). (n.d.). Bible Gateway. https://www.biblegateway.com/passage/?search=Revelation%2013%3A8&version=NKJV*

24. *Romans 10:9-10 (NIV). (n.d.). Bible Gateway. https://www.biblegateway.com/passage/?search=Romans%2010%3A9-10&version=NIV*

25. *John 3:16 (NIV). (n.d.). Bible Gateway. https://www.biblegateway.com/passage/?search=John%203%3A16&version=NIV*

26. *Isaiah 9:6-7 (NKJV). (n.d.). Bible Gateway. https://www.biblegateway.com/passage/?search=Isaiah%209%3A7a&version=NKJV*

27. *Lucey, C. (2020, October 21). What is the medical account of the crucifixion? Christianity.com. https://www.christianity.com/wiki/jesus-christ/medical-account-of-the-crucifixion.html*

28. *1 Corinthians 2:8 (NKJV). (n.d.). Bible Gateway. https://www.biblegateway.com/passage/?search=1%20Corinthians%202%3A8&version=NKJV*

29. *Romans 6:1-19; 23 (NKJV). (n.d.). Bible Gateway. https://www.biblegateway.com/passage/?search=Romans%206%3A23&version=NKJV*

*30. Leviticus 17:1; 11 (NKJV). (n.d.). Bible Gateway.
https://www.biblegateway.com/passage/?search=Leviticus%2017%3A1&version=NKJV*

*31. Hebrews 9:22 (NKJV). (n.d.). Bible Gateway.
https://www.biblegateway.com/passage/?search=Hebrews%209%3A22b&version=NKJV*

*32. Luke 22:2; 7-20; 24-27; 44 (NKJV). (n.d.). Bible Gateway.
https://www.biblegateway.com/passage/?search=Luke%2022%3A44&version=NKJV*

*33. Psalm 22: 3; 14-18 (NKJV). (n.d.). Bible Gateway.
https://www.biblegateway.com/passage/?search=Psalm%2022%3A14-18&version=NKJV*

*34. Deuteronomy 21:22-23 (NKJV). (n.d.). Bible Gateway.
https://www.biblegateway.com/passage/?search=Deuteronomy%2021%3A22-23&version=NKJV*

*35. Isaiah 53 (NKJV). (n.d.). Bible Gateway.
https://www.biblegateway.com/passage/?search=Isaiah%2053%3A5&version=NKJV*

36. 351 Old Testament Prophecies fulfilled in Jesus Christ | New Testament Christians.Com. (n.d.). https://www.newtestamentchristians.com/bible-study-resources/351-old-testament-prophecies-fulfilled-in-jesus-christ/

*37. Luke 9:23-24 (NKJV). (n.d.). Bible Gateway.
https://www.biblegateway.com/passage/?search=Luke%209%3A23-24&version=NKJV*

*38. Genesis 2:16-17 (NKJV). (n.d.). Bible Gateway.
https://www.biblegateway.com/passage/?search=Genesis%202%3A16-17&version=NKJV*

*39. Genesis 3:21 (NKJV). (n.d.). Bible Gateway.
https://www.biblegateway.com/passage/?search=Genesis%203%3A21&version=NKJV*

RESOURCES

40. Genesis 4:9-10 (NKJV). (n.d.). Bible Gateway. https://www.biblegateway.com/passage/?search=Genesis%204%3A9&version=NKJV

41. Psalm 91 (NKJV). (n.d.). Bible Gateway. https://www.biblegateway.com/passage/?search=Psalm%2091%3A1-16&version=NKJV

42. remission definition - Google Search. (n.d.). https://www.google.com/search?client=safari&rls=en&q=remission+definition&ie=UTF-8&oe=UTF-8

43. covenant. (2024). In Merriam-Webster Dictionary. https://www.merriam-webster.com/dictionary/covenant#:~:text=2-,a,breach%20of%20such%20a%20contract

44. testament. (2024). In Merriam-Webster Dictionary. https://www.merriam-webster.com/dictionary/testament

45. promise. (2024). In Merriam-Webster Dictionary. https://www.merriam-webster.com/dictionary/promise

46. Psalm 51:1-5; 10-13; 17(NKJV). (n.d.). Bible Gateway. https://www.biblegateway.com/passage/?search=Psalm%2051%3A5&version=NKJV

47. Genesis 22:1-2; 12-18 (NKJV). (n.d.). Bible Gateway. https://www.biblegateway.com/passage/?search=Genesis%2022%3A1-2&version=NKJV

48. Isaiah 61:2 (NKJV). (n.d.). Bible Gateway. https://www.biblegateway.com/passage/?search=Isaiah%2061%3A2&version=NKJV

49. Psalm 138:2 (NKJV). (n.d.). Bible Gateway. https://www.biblegateway.com/passage/?search=Psalm%20138%3A2&version=NKJV

50. Isaiah 11:10 (NKJV). (n.d.-b). Bible Gateway. https://www.biblegateway.com/passage/?search=Isaiah%2011%3A10&version=NKJV

51. *Ephesians 3:1-6 (NKJV). (n.d.). Bible Gateway.*
https://www.biblegateway.com/passage/?search=Ephesians%203%3A1-
6&version=NKJV

52. *2 Corinthians 1:21-22 (NKJV). (n.d.). Bible Gateway.*
https://www.biblegateway.com/passage/?search=2%20Corinthians%201%3A21-
22&version=NKJV

53. *repent. (2024). https://www.merriam-webster.com/dictionary/repenting*

54. *1 John 1:9 (NKJV). (n.d.). Bible Gateway.*
https://www.biblegateway.com/passage/?
search=1%20John%201%3A9&version=NKJV

55. *Hebrews 12:14 (NKJV). (n.d.). Bible Gateway.*
https://www.biblegateway.com/passage/?
search=Hebrews%2012%3A14&version=NKJV

56. *Psalm 24:1; 3-4 (NKJV). (n.d.). Bible Gateway.*
https://www.biblegateway.com/passage/?search=Psalm%2024%3A3-
4&version=NKJV

57. *Matthew 5:20 (NKJV). (n.d.). Bible Gateway.*
https://www.biblegateway.com/passage/?
search=Matthew%205%3A20&version=NKJV

58. *John 14:1-6; 12; 15-20 (NKJV). (n.d.). Bible Gateway.*
https://www.biblegateway.com/passage/?search=John%2014%3A6&version=NKJV

59. *Acts 2:1-21; 37-38 (NKJV). (n.d.). Bible Gateway.*
https://www.biblegateway.com/passage/?search=Acts%202%3A37-
38&version=NKJV

60. *Acts 3:19 (NKJV). (n.d.). Bible Gateway.*
https://www.biblegateway.com/passage/?search=Acts%203%3A19&version=NKJV

RESOURCES

61. *2 Chronicles 7:14 (NKJV). (n.d.). Bible Gateway. https://www.biblegateway.com/passage/?search=II%20Chronicles%207%3A14&version=NKJV*

62. *Hebrews 3:7-15 (NKJV). (n.d.). Bible Gateway. https://www.biblegateway.com/passage/?search=Hebrews%203%3A7-15&version=NKJV*

63. *confession. (2024). In Merriam-Webster Dictionary. https://www.merriam-webster.com/dictionary/confession#:~:text=%3A%20a%20written%20or%20oral%20acknowledgment,party%20accused%20of%20an%20offense*

64. *Hebrews 11:1-3 (NKJV). (n.d.). Bible Gateway. https://www.biblegateway.com/passage/?search=Hebrews%2011%3A1-3&version=NKJV*

65. *Genesis 1:2-3; 26-27 (NKJV). (n.d.). Bible Gateway. https://www.biblegateway.com/passage/?search=Genesis%201%3A3&version=NKJV*

66. *Luke 6:45 (NKJV). (n.d.). Bible Gateway. https://www.biblegateway.com/passage/?search=Luke%206%3A45&version=NKJV*

67. *Matthew 10:7-8; 32-33 (NKJV). (n.d.). Bible Gateway. https://www.biblegateway.com/passage/?search=Matthew%2010%3A32-33&version=NKJV*

68. *Romans 4:16-18 (NKJV). (n.d.). Bible Gateway. https://www.biblegateway.com/passage/?search=Romans%204%3A16-18&version=NKJV*

69. *Proverbs 18:21 (NKJV). (n.d.). Bible Gateway. https://www.biblegateway.com/passage/?search=Proverbs%2018%3A21&version=NKJV*

70. *James 3:3-11 (NKJV). (n.d.). Bible Gateway. https://www.biblegateway.com/passage/?search=James%203%3A5%2C%2010-11&version=NKJV*

71. Acts 11:26 (NKJV). (n.d.-b). Bible Gateway. https://www.biblegateway.com/passage/?search=Acts%2011%3A26b&version=NKJV

72. Strong's Greek: 5546. Χριστιανός (Christianos) -- a Christian. (n.d.). https://biblehub.com/greek/5546.htm

73. sanctify. (2024). In Merriam-Webster Dictionary. https://www.merriam-webster.com/dictionary/sanctify

74. sanctification. (n.d.). In Merriam-Webster Dictionary. https://www.merriam-webster.com/dictionary/sanctification

75. process. (2024). In Merriam-Webster Dictionary. https://www.merriam-webster.com/dictionary/process

76. become. (2024). In Merriam-Webster Dictionary. https://www.merriam-webster.com/dictionary/become

77. John 3:30 (NKJV). (n.d.). Bible Gateway. https://www.biblegateway.com/passage/?search=John%203%3A30&version=NKJV

78. Hebrews 10:12; 14 (NKJV). (n.d.). Bible Gateway. https://www.biblegateway.com/passage/?search=Hebrews%2010%3A14&version=NKJV

79. Hebrews 10:14 (NIV). (n.d.). Bible Gateway. https://www.biblegateway.com/passage/?search=Hebrews%2010%3A14&version=NIV

80. Matthew 22:34-40 (NKJV). (n.d.). Bible Gateway. https://www.biblegateway.com/passage/?search=Matthew%2022%3A34-40&version=NKJV

81. Isaiah 40:3 (NKJV). (n.d.). Bible Gateway. https://www.biblegateway.com/passage/?search=Isaiah%2040%3A3&version=NKJV

82. G907 - baptizō - Strong's Greek Lexicon (kjv). (n.d.). Blue Letter Bible. https://www.blueletterbible.org/lexicon/g907/kjv/tr/0-1/

RESOURCES

83. *2 Kings 5:9-14 (NKJV). (n.d.). Bible Gateway.* https://www.biblegateway.com/passage/?search=2%20Kings%205%3A9-14&version=NKJV

84. *Acts 22:12-16 (NKJV). (n.d.). Bible Gateway.* https://www.biblegateway.com/passage/?search=Acts%2022%3A16&version=NKJV

85. *Matthew 3:13; 16-17 (NKJV). (n.d.). Bible Gateway.* https://www.biblegateway.com/passage/?search=Matthew%203%3A13&version=NKJV

86. *Exodus 12:14 (ESV). (n.d.). Bible Gateway.* https://www.biblegateway.com/passage/?search=Exodus%2012%3A14&version=ESV

87. *Mark 15:25; 33-34; 37-38 (NKJV). (n.d.-b). Bible Gateway.* https://www.biblegateway.com/passage/?search=Mark%2015%3A25&version=NKJV

88. *1 Corinthians 11:23-32 (NKJV). (n.d.). Bible Gateway.* https://www.biblegateway.com/passage/?search=1%20Corinthians%2011%3A23-32&version=NKJV

89. *Matthew 18:20-35 (NKJV). (n.d.). Bible Gateway.* https://www.biblegateway.com/passage/search=Matthew%2018%3A20&version=NKJV

90. *1 Corinthians 11:18-22; 26-32 (ESV). (n.d.). Bible Gateway.* https://www.biblegateway.com/passage/?search=1%20Corinthians%2011%3A18-22&version=ESV

91. *2 Corinthians 5:14-15; 20 (NKJV). (n.d.). Bible Gateway.* https://www.biblegateway.com/passage/?search=2%20Corinthians%205%3A14-15&version=NKJV

92. *Romans 6:1-4 (ESV). (n.d.). Bible Gateway.* https://www.biblegateway.com/passage/?search=Romans%206%3A1-4&version=ESV

93. ordinance. (2024). In Merriam-Webster Dictionary. https://www.merriam-webster.com/dictionary/ordinance#:~:text=1,authoritative%20decree%20or%20direction%20%3A%20order

94. Ephesians 4:1-6; 13; 20-24; 32 (NKJV). (n.d.). Bible Gateway. https://www.biblegateway.com/passage/?search=Ephesians%204%3A1-6&version=NKJV

95. Joel 2:12-14; 28-30 (NKJV). (n.d.). Bible Gateway. https://www.biblegateway.com/passage/?search=Joel%202%3A28-30&version=NKJV

96. John 6:44 (NKJV). (n.d.). Bible Gateway. https://www.biblegateway.com/passage/?search=John%206%3A44&version=NKJV

97. Titus 2:11-15 (NKJV). (n.d.). Bible Gateway. https://www.biblegateway.com/passage/?search=Titus%202%3A11-15&version=NKJV

98. Luke 24:45-49 (NKJV). (n.d.). Bible Gateway. https://www.biblegateway.com/passage/?search=Luke%2024%3A45-49&version=NKJV

99. Acts 1:4-11 (NKJV). (n.d.-b). Bible Gateway. https://www.biblegateway.com/passage/?search=acts%201%3A4-8&version=NKJV

100. Ephesians 5:18 (NLT). (n.d.). Bible Gateway. https://www.biblegateway.com/passage/?search=Ephesians%205%3A18&version=NLT

101. Acts 19:1-7 (NKJV). (n.d.). Bible Gateway. https://www.biblegateway.com/passage/?search=acts%2019%3A1-7&version=NKJV

102. 1 Corinthians 14:1-25; 39-40 (NKJV). (n.d.). Bible Gateway. https://www.biblegateway.com/passage/?search=1%20Corinthians%2014%3A39-40&version=NKJV

RESOURCES

103. hermeneutic. (n.d.). In Merriam-Webster Dictionary. https://www.merriam-webster.com/dictionary/hermeneutic#:~:text=1,method%20or%20principle%20of%20interpretation

104. Matthew 6:5-18; 33 (NKJV). (n.d.). Bible Gateway. https://www.biblegateway.com/passage/?search=Matthew%206%3A9-15&version=NKJV

105. forgive. (2024). In Merriam-Webster Dictionary. https://www.merriam-webster.com/dictionary/forgive#:~:text=%3A%20to%20cease%20to%20feel%20resentment,see%20requital%20sense%201)%20for

106. 1 John 4:20 (NKJV). (n.d.). Bible Gateway. https://www.biblegateway.com/passage/?search=1%20John%204%3A20&version=NKJV

107. hatred. (2024). In Merriam-Webster Dictionary. https://www.merriam-webster.com/dictionary/hatred#:~:text=%3A%20ill%20will%20or%20resentment%20that,mutual%20%3A%20prejudiced%20hostility%20or%20animosity

108. 1 John 2:9-11 (NKJV). (n.d.). Bible Gateway. https://www.biblegateway.com/passage/?search=1%20John%202%3A9-11&version=NKJV

109. Colossians 3:12-17 (NKJV). (n.d.). Bible Gateway. https://www.biblegateway.com/passage/?search=Colossians%203%3A12-17&version=NKJV

110. 1 John 1:7; 9 (NKJV). (n.d.). Bible Gateway. https://www.biblegateway.com/passage/?search=1%20John%201%3A7&version=NKJV

111. Philippians 2:14-15 (NKJV). (n.d.). Bible Gateway. https://www.biblegateway.com/passage/?search=Philippians%202%3A14-15&version=NKJV

112. Genesis 50:15-21 (NKJV). (n.d.). Bible Gateway. https://www.biblegateway.com/passage/?search=Genesis%2050%3A15-21&version=NKJV

113. Romans 5:7-9 (NKJV). (n.d.). Bible Gateway. https://www.biblegateway.com/passage/?search=Romans%205%3A7-9&version=NKJV

114. pray. (2024). In Merriam-Webster Dictionary. https://www.merriam-webster.com/dictionary/pray#:~:text=intransitive%20verb-,1,%2C%20confession%2C%20supplication%2C%20or%20thanksgiving

115. Isaiah 55:9 (NKJV). (n.d.). Bible Gateway. https://www.biblegateway.com/passage/?search=Isaiah%2055%3A9&version=NKJV

116. Proverbs 3:5-6 (NKJV). (n.d.). Bible Gateway. https://www.biblegateway.com/passage/?search=Proverbs%203%3A5-6&version=NKJV

117. Psalm 37:3-7 (NKJV). (n.d.). Bible Gateway. https://www.biblegateway.com/passage/?search=Psalm%2037%3A3-7&version=NKJV

118. supplicate. (n.d.). https://www.merriam-webster.com/dictionary/supplication

119. intercession. (n.d.). In Merriam-Webster Dictionary. https://www.merriam-webster.com/dictionary/intercession#:~:text=%3A%20prayer%2C%20petition%2C%20or%20entreaty,intercessor

120. Genesis 19:29 (NKJV). (n.d.). Bible Gateway. https://www.biblegateway.com/passage/?search=Genesis%2019%3A29&version=NKJV

121. Psalm 63:1 (NKJV). (n.d.). Bible Gateway. https://www.biblegateway.com/passage/?search=Psalm%2063%3A1&version=NKJV

RESOURCES

122. *Isaiah 26:3; 9 (NKJV). (n.d.). Bible Gateway.*
https://www.biblegateway.com/passage/?search=Isaiah%2026%3A9&version=NKJV

123. *Psalm 42:1-2 (NKJV). (n.d.). Bible Gateway.*
https://www.biblegateway.com/passage/?search=Psalm%2042%3A1-2&version=NKJV

124. *fast. (2024). In Merriam-Webster Dictionary. https://www.merriam-webster.com/dictionary/fasting*

125. *Luke 18:9-14 (NKJV). (n.d.). Bible Gateway.*
https://www.biblegateway.com/passage/?search=Luke%2018%3A9-14&version=NKJV

126. *Isaiah 58 (NKJV). (n.d.). Bible Gateway.*
https://www.biblegateway.com/passage/?search=Isaiah%2058%3A2-3&version=NKJV

127. *Acts 9:9 (NKJV). (n.d.). Bible Gateway.*
https://www.biblegateway.com/passage/?search=Acts%209%3A9&version=NKJV - not actually cited, (Acts 9 and Acts 9:5 are in parenthesis, but not actually quoted?)

128. *Matthew 4:4 (NKJV). (n.d.). Bible Gateway.*
https://www.biblegateway.com/passage/?search=Matthew%204%3A4&version=NKJV

129. *Ezra 8:21-23 (NKJV). (n.d.). Bible Gateway.*
https://www.biblegateway.com/passage/?search=Ezra%208%3A21-23&version=NKJV

130. *Deuteronomy 6:4-5 (NKJV). (n.d.). Bible Gateway.*
https://www.biblegateway.com/passage/?search=Deuteronomy%206%3A4-5&version=NKJV

131. *Isaiah 43:10-11 (NKJV). (n.d.). Bible Gateway.*
https://www.biblegateway.com/passage/?search=Isaiah%2043%3A10-11&version=NKJV

132. *Trinity. (2024). In Merriam-Webster Dictionary.* https://www.merriam-webster.com/dictionary/Trinity#:~:text=1,closely%20related%20persons%20or%20things

133. *Colossians 1:15-20 (NKJV). (n.d.). Bible Gateway.* https://www.biblegateway.com/passage/?search=Colossians%201%3A15-20&version=NKJV

134. *Philippians 1:19 (NKJV). (n.d.). Bible Gateway.* https://www.biblegateway.com/passage/?search=Philippians%201%3A19&version=NKJV

135. *Acts 16:7 (NKJV). (n.d.). Bible Gateway.* https://www.biblegateway.com/passage/?search=Acts%206%3A7&version=NKJV

136. *2 Corinthians 13:14 (NKJV). (n.d.). Bible Gateway.* https://www.biblegateway.com/passage/?search=2%20Corinthians%2013%3A14&version=NKJV

137. *John 18:4-6 (NKJV). (n.d.). Bible Gateway.* https://www.biblegateway.com/passage/?search=John%2018%3A4-6&version=NKJV

138. *John 15:26-27 (NKJV). (n.d.). Bible Gateway.* https://www.biblegateway.com/passage/?search=John%2015%3A26-27&version=NKJV

139. *Psalm 27 (NKJV). (n.d.). Bible Gateway.* https://www.biblegateway.com/passage/?search=Psalm%2027%3A1-14&version=NKJV

140. *favor. (2024). In Merriam-Webster Dictionary.* https://www.merriam-webster.com/dictionary/favor#:~:text=of%202%20noun-,fa%C2%B7%E2%80%8Bvor%20%CB%88f%C4%81%2Dv%C9%99r,the%20favor%20of%20the%20king

141. James 4:8 (NKJV). (n.d.). Bible Gateway. https://www.biblegateway.com/passage/?search=James%204%3A8a&version=NKJV

142. 1 Peter 2:9-10 (NKJV). (n.d.). Bible Gateway. https://www.biblegateway.com/passage/?search=1%20Peter%202%3A9-10&version=NKJV

143. protect. (2024). In Merriam-Webster Dictionary. https://www.merriam-webster.com/dictionary/protect

144. Psalm 28:7 (NKJV). (n.d.). Bible Gateway. https://www.biblegateway.com/passage/?search=Psalm%2028%3A7&version=NKJV

145. Psalm 32:7 (NKJV). (n.d.). Bible Gateway. https://www.biblegateway.com/passage/?search=Psalm%2032%3A7&version=NKJV

146. Proverbs 14:26 (NKJV). (n.d.). Bible Gateway. https://www.biblegateway.com/passage/?search=Proverbs%2014%3A26&version=NKJV

147. 1 Peter 5:6-7 (NKJV). (n.d.). Bible Gateway. https://www.biblegateway.com/passage/?search=1%20Peter%205%3A6-7&version=NKJV

148. Ephesians 5:18; 28-32 (NKJV). (n.d.). Bible Gateway. https://www.biblegateway.com/passage/?search=Ephesians%205%3A18&version=NKJV

149. Matthew 25:1-13; 40 (NKJV). (n.d.). Bible Gateway. https://www.biblegateway.com/passage/?search=Matthew%2025%3A1-13&version=NKJV

150. Films, I. (n.d.). Before The Wrath (Official Movie). Before the Wrath. https://www.beforethewrath.com/

RESOURCES

151. Mark 13:32 (NKJV). (n.d.). Bible Gateway. https://www.biblegateway.com/passage/?search=Mark%2013%3A32&version=NKJV

152. 1 Thessalonians 4:13-18 (NKJV). (n.d.). Bible Gateway. https://www.biblegateway.com/passage/?search=1%20Thessalonians%204%3A17%20&version=NKJV

153. Matthew 24:36-44 (NKJV). (n.d.). Bible Gateway. https://www.biblegateway.com/passage/?search=Matthew%2024%3A40-41&version=NKJV

154. 1 Thessalonians 5:1-11 (NKJV). (n.d.). Bible Gateway. https://www.biblegateway.com/passage/?search=1%20Thessalonians%205%3A1-11&version=NKJV

155. 1 Corinthians 15:51-52 (NKJV). (n.d.). Bible Gateway. https://www.biblegateway.com/passage/?search=1%20Corinthians%2015%3A51-52&version=NKJV

156. James 5:7-8 (NKJV). (n.d.). Bible Gateway. https://www.biblegateway.com/passage/?search=James%205%3A7-8&version=NKJV

157. Luke 21:28 (NKJV). (n.d.). Bible Gateway. https://www.biblegateway.com/passage/?search=Luke%2021%3A28&version=NKJV

158. John 3:16 (NKJV). (n.d.). Bible Gateway. https://www.biblegateway.com/passage/?search=John%203%3A16&version=NKJV

159. generous. (2024). In Merriam-Webster Dictionary. https://www.merriam-webster.com/dictionary/generous#:~:text=a,by%20abundance%20or%20ample%20proportions

160. Dawes, Z., Jr. (2022, September 13). One in five U.S. Christians give at least 10% of income to church. Good Faith Media. https://goodfaithmedia.org/one-in-five-u-s-christians-give-at-least-10-of-income-to-church/

161. Leviticus 27:28; 30 (NKJV). (n.d.). Bible Gateway. https://www.biblegateway.com/passage/?search=Leviticus%2027%3A30&version=NKJV

162. 2 Corinthians 9:6-15 (NKJV). (n.d.). Bible Gateway. https://www.biblegateway.com/passage/?search=2%20Corinthians%209%3A6-15&version=NKJV

163. Deuteronomy 16:16-17 (NKJV). (n.d.). Bible Gateway. https://www.biblegateway.com/passage/?search=Deuteronomy%2016%3A16-17&version=NKJV

164. Psalm 50:10 (NKJV). (n.d.). Bible Gateway. https://www.biblegateway.com/passage/?search=Psalm%2050%3A10&version=NKJV

165. Deuteronomy 18:1-5 (NKJV). (n.d.). Bible Gateway. https://www.biblegateway.com/passage/?search=Deuteronomy%2018%3A1-5%20&version=NKJV

166. Deuteronomy 26:11-15 (NKJV). (n.d.). Bible Gateway. https://www.biblegateway.com/passage/?search=Deuteronomy%2026%3A11-15&version=NKJV

167. Exodus 25:1-9 (NKJV). (n.d.). Bible Gateway. https://www.biblegateway.com/passage/?search=Exodus%2025%3A1-9&version=NKJV

168. H4643 - ma'ăśēr - Strong's Hebrew Lexicon (kjv). (n.d.). Blue Letter Bible. https://www.blueletterbible.org/lexicon/h4643/kjv/wlc/0-1/

169. Malachi 3:8-12 (NKJV). (n.d.). Bible Gateway. https://www.biblegateway.com/passage/?search=Malachi%203%3A8-12&version=NKJV

RESOURCES

170. *H4503 - minḥâ - Strong's Hebrew Lexicon (kjv). (n.d.). Blue Letter Bible. https://www.blueletterbible.org/lexicon/h4503/kjv/wlc/0-1/*

171. *Davis, M. (2024, September 20). Average car payment and auto loan statistics: 2024. LendingTree. https://www.lendingtree.com/auto/debt-statistics/*

172. *Kilroy, A. (2024, October 17). Average mortgage payment by city and state. Quicken Loans. https://www.quickenloans.com/learn/average-mortgage-payment*

173. *Backman, M. (2023, March 12). Here's How Much the Average American Is Spending on Credit Card Debt Monthly. The Motley Fool. https://www.fool.com/the-ascent/credit-cards/articles/heres-how-much-the-average-american-is-spending-on-credit-card-debt-monthly*

174. *Galatians 2:11-20 (NKJV). (n.d.). Bible Gateway. https://www.biblegateway.com/passage/?search=Galatians%202%3A15-19&version=NKJV*

175. *crucify. (2024). https://www.merriam-webster.com/dictionary/crucifying*

176. *Hebrews 7:27 (NKJV). (n.d.). Bible Gateway. https://www.biblegateway.com/passage/?search=Hebrews%207%3A27b&version=NKJV*

177. *Philippians 3:3-14 (NKJV). (n.d.). Bible Gateway. https://www.biblegateway.com/passage/?search=Philippians%203%3A3-14&version=NKJV*

178. *calling. (2024). In Merriam-Webster Dictionary. https://www.merriam-webster.com/dictionary/calling*

179. *Mark 16:12-20 (NKJV). (n.d.). Bible Gateway. https://www.biblegateway.com/passage/?search=Mark%2016%3A12-20&version=NKJV*

180. *John 20:21 (NKJV). (n.d.). Bible Gateway.*
https://www.biblegateway.com/passage/?search=John%2020%3A21&version=NKJV

181. *2 Corinthians 4:5-15 (NKJV). (n.d.). Bible Gateway.*
https://www.biblegateway.com/passage/?search=2%20Corinthians%204%3A5-15&version=NKJV

182. *Matthew 9:35-38 (NKJV). (n.d.). Bible Gateway.*
https://www.biblegateway.com/passage/?search=Matthew%209%3A35-38&version=NKJV

183. *Luke 12:11-12 (NKJV). (n.d.). Bible Gateway.*
https://www.biblegateway.com/passage/?search=Luke%2012%3A11-12&version=NKJV

184. *Revelation 12:10-11 (NKJV). (n.d.). Bible Gateway.*
https://www.biblegateway.com/passage/?search=Revelation%2012%3A10-11%20&version=NKJV

185. *Jeremiah 15:16 (NKJV). (n.d.). Bible Gateway.*
https://www.biblegateway.com/passage/?search=Jeremiah%2015%3A16&version=NKJV

Made in the USA
Columbia, SC
19 March 2025